Reference Sources in English and American Literature

Reference Sources in English and American Literature

——•——

An Annotated Bibliography

ROBERT C. SCHWEIK
State University of New York

DIETER RIESNER
University of Trier

W · W · Norton & Company · Inc · New York

Copyright © 1977 by W.W. Norton & Company, Inc.
Printed in the United States of America.

Library of Congress Cataloging in Publication Data

Schweik, Robert C
    A student's bibliography of English and American literature.

    Includes indexes.
    1. English literature—Bibliography. 2. American literature—
Bibliography. I. Riesner, Dieter, joint author. II. Title.
        Z2011.S415 [PR83] 016.82 77-974
    ISBN 0 393 09104 X (Paper Edition)
    ISBN 0 393 04484 4 (Cloth Edition)
            All Rights Reserved
            First Edition

Originally published in Germany under the title *English and American Literature:
A Guide to Reference Materials,* copyright
© 1976 Erich Schmidt Verlag, Berlin

1 2 3 4 5 6 7 8 9 0

Contents

Preface

This book is designed to serve as a guide to reference materials for the study of English and American literature, and to important classes of supplementary works such as sources of information on biography and folklore. In general, we have not depended upon any single rigid principle of inclusion, but have sought in every case to consider what kinds of materials are available, and which of those would be most valuable to today's students and scholars. In the area of literary history, for example, we have provided entries for general histories of English and American literature, but cite only those period and genre histories which we feel have special value as reference works. And, in order to enable users to learn whether or not a reference work will be helpful for a particular purpose, we have provided descriptive annotations which summarize the nature, scope, and organization of all but a few of the sources we cite; in some cases we have also noted important criticisms of the limitations of major reference tools. For students, we have included a discussion of how to use reference works critically and a glossary of the chief terms used in our annotations.

In the process of compiling this book we have learned much about the necessity (and value) of compromise when faced with questions of what ought or ought not be included. Thus, except for Shakespeare, we have not listed works restricted to a single author, nor have we cited works on such relatively peripheral topics as dance and sport; but because of such decisions, we have been able to provide better coverage of other areas we do treat, such as descriptive bibliography and editing, and fuller listings of materials on topics of increasing interest to students of literature, such as cinema. In order to make our guide as up-to-date as possible, we have cited some works announced for publication but not yet published; in all such cases we have made clear that these were not available for our examination, and, of course, readers should be aware that their subsequent publication cannot be assured.

The organization of this guide and the form of its entries have been designed to meet practical needs rather than a rigidly consistent scheme. We have usually provided author entries, but when a work is best known by its title, we have given that first. In the arrangement of entries we have adopted these general rules: (1) materials relating to both English and American literature are listed under English and cross-referenced under American; (2) materials relating to both a literary period and a genre are listed under the period and cross-referenced under the genre; (3) among the genres, poetry is taken first, then drama, then fiction, and last prose nonfiction; and (4) primary materials are listed before secondary. If a work has been reprinted more than once, we indicate that fact by simply adding the term *Rptd.* to the entry; in the case of single reprintings, or of reprintings at a much later date than the original publication, we cite the place and date of the reprinting. Apart from these rules, we have tried in every case to adopt arrangements particularly suitable to the material at hand. Thus in some cases we have followed an historical arrangement; in others, an inverted chronology; and in still others, arrangements by level of generality or other organizational patterns according to the logic of the case. Of course no arrangement can be ideal for all purposes, but we hope that the analytic table of contents, the extensive system of cross-references, and the detailed subject index we have provided will enhance the usefulness and convenience of this guide.

In preparing this book we were fortunate to have the kind assistance of very many associates and colleagues; for special advice and encouragement we are particularly indebted to Professor Douglas Shepard of the State University of New York, Professor Helmut Gneuss of the University of Munich, Dr. E. Kahleyss of Erich Schmidt Verlag, and John W.N. Francis of W.W. Norton & Company, Inc.

Robert C. Schweik
State University of New York

Dieter Riesner
University of Trier

Using Reference Sources

A scholar preparing a study of modern American poetry needs to learn whether there were any textual differences between the Paris and the New York editions of Hart Crane's *The Bridge;* a graduate student preparing a thesis on British literary societies in the nineteenth century wishes to know where to obtain a photocopy of the Manchester Literary and Philosophical Society's *Memoirs and Proceedings;* an undergraduate writing a brief explicatory paper on Matthew Arnold's "Dover Beach" must consult some representative modern explications of the poem. The fact is that all serious students of literature are united not only in the bond of a common scholarly pursuit but also in a common dependence upon the tools of literary scholarship. More experienced scholars will methodically proceed to find what information they need with an enviable efficiency that is the result of long practice in using reference tools for literary research. There is no real substitute for that experience, but there are some suggestions which can make it easier to acquire and some useful cautions that can forewarn against pitfalls which you will certainly encounter along the way.

Analyzing the Problem

First of all, it is wise to cultivate the time-saving habit of looking at information problems analytically before going off in search of an answer—or, worse yet, before assuming that no answer can be found. This involves acquiring the knack of seeing how concrete details of a specific problem may relate to the more general classes of information that reference sources provide. For example, if you were writing about Carl Sandburg's poetry you might wish to compare his "Chicago" with some other poetic treatments of the same city. Are there other poems about Chicago? And where could a convenient list of citations to them be had? To find the answer you must first translate your question into something more general: you need to see that Chicago is the subject of Sandburg's poem and that what is required is a subject index to poetry. With this in mind, a check of the heading POETRY in the index to this guide will turn up references to such works as *Granger's Index to Poetry* (350) which include subject categories and contain precisely the kind of information you need.

Of course there are problems for which no amount of analysis will help, simply because no tool provides the needed information: thus, anyone seeking a convenient subject index to poetry published in British literary periodicals in the last six months is out of luck. But often the real difficulty will be almost the opposite—you will be faced with a number of sources, all of which can provide some sort of appropriate information, and the problem will be to discover which will supply the needed information most efficiently. For example, in preparing a brief explicatory paper on Arnold's "Dover Beach," you might at first reflect that Arnold is a Victorian poet and think (not unreasonably) of consulting bibliographies which cover Victorian poetry. The range of these is considerable: it includes such enormous compilations as the *New CBEL* (6), narrower works such as Faverty's *The Victorian Poets: A Guide to Research* (119), and general current bibliographies such as that appearing in *Victorian Studies* (116), which, in turn, would lead you to the very comprehensive *Bibliography of Matthew Arnold 1932–1970* by Vincent Tollers. Surely by consulting these and other similar sources it will be possible to find citations to nearly all of the recent explicatory comment written on "Dover Beach." Unfortunately, however, none of these sources provides that information in the most convenient form—as a list of references to representative explications of "Dover Beach." Hence, it would be a waste of time to begin sifting through these more general bibliographies without first considering whether some other sources might make the task easier. The problem, after all, can be translated into other terms than "Victorian poetry"; how about "explications"? What you need is really a list of explications of a particular poem, and a check of the heading EXPLICATIONS in the index of this guide will turn up sources which provide ready-made lists of references to explications—obviously a saving of time and effort.

If, then, for no other reason than the time saved, it is worth cultivating the habit of thinking analytically about sources when specific information is needed. Fortunately, there are some excellent works designed to provide practical assistance in developing this habit. Students wanting practice in analyzing specific information problems can work through the very helpful exercises provided in Richard Altick's *The Art of Literary Research* (642), a book which in this and many other ways is a mine of valuable guidance on scholarly technique; and there is James Thorpe's *Literary Scholarship: A Handbook for Advanced Students of English and American Literature* (641) which describes and illustrates procedures for methodically working through research projects. These and other sources listed on pp. 126–127 can profitably be exploited by anyone who wishes to benefit from the experience of seasoned scholars.

Avoiding Pitfalls

Of course only a thorough personal familiarity with reference tools themselves will enable a user to get the most out of them while avoiding the pitfalls which many of them contain. Here again, however, there are some suggestions and cautions which can be of help.

First, it pays in using a reference tool to be alert to its peculiarities of organization and indexing. There are few more frustrating experiences for a scholar than to have found the right source, to have held it in hand, and yet, somehow, to have failed to get the needed information from it. This can happen more easily than might at first be thought. Someone looking up an author bibliography in Robert E. Spiller's *Literary History of the United States* (248) might well take up the bibliography volume, turn directly to the name of the author wanted, and assume that he has found all that Spiller has to offer—though actually he might be consulting only the basic bibliography, originally published in 1948, while entirely overlooking two separately appended supplementary bibliographies which update it. Similarly, Halkett and Laing's nine-volume *Dictionary of Anonymous and Pseudonymous English Literature* (966) may on casual inspection appear to consist of a single alphabetical list of titles with identifications of their authors; in fact, volumes 8 and 9 provide additional separately alphabetized lists which must also be consulted; and, between these, in volume 7, there are indexes of authors, indexes of initials and pseudonyms, and, yes, still more titles supplementary to the main list. Few reference works are so awkwardly arranged as Robert Peddie's *Subject Index of Books Published Before 1880* (900), which has two separate alphabets for each of its four volumes; but practically any reference work can have its own organizational quirks, and it will always pay to be forewarned by consulting whatever information is given in the front matter of the work itself and, of course, the annotation provided in this guide. For example, our note on Greg's *A Bibliography of English Drama to the Restoration* (61) reveals that important introductory information is not always given in predictable places.

Another trap for the unwary lies in the unexpected differences between what the titles of some reference works proclaim and what, in fact, they are. There is nothing in the title of *Dissertation Abstracts International* (820) to warn the user that it is "international" only in a very limited sense; nor does even the full title of Besterman's *World Bibliography of Bibliographies* (670) make clear that it includes only bibliographies published separately, not those included as parts of books or serials. Similarly, there is nothing in the title of Arthur Coleman's *Epic and Romance Criticism* (357) to suggest that it includes citations to criticisms of such poems as Hopkins' "The Wreck of the Deutschland" and Ginsberg's "Howl"; nor would anyone using the first volume of Howard Hill's *Index to British Bibliography* (1) be likely to suspect that nearly half of the second volume, titled *Shakespearian Bibliography and Textual Criticism,* is, in fact, devoted not to Shakespeare but to supplementing the general materials provided in the first volume.

In still other cases it is possible to be misled because the scope of a reference work will have varied greatly over the course of time. Thus the annual bibliography published by the Modern Language Association of America (11) has undergone such vast changes in its coverage that the bibliography which appeared in 1953 is quite different in coverage and purpose from that published ten years later. Similarly, anyone using the *Catalogue général* of the Bibliothèque Nationale (1217) must be alert to the fact that the earliest volumes reflect only the holdings of the library in the late nineteenth century and have not been updated. Any serious scholar must, simply in self defense, accumulate in the course of his career a storehouse of information about the pecularities of the reference tools he uses; we have tried in this book to provide a handy guide to many of those peculiarities by way of helping to make the mastery of that information easier (and we hope more painless) to acquire.

Using Reference Materials Critically

But in the long run a thorough command of the field of literary reference tools can only come through a personal commitment to scholarly research, and it is here that all serious students of literature accept a common responsibility: that obligation scholars assume for the accuracy of what they write and the special duty they have to avoid the dissemination and perpetuation of error. In this pursuit there is one lesson all researchers must learn sooner or later, and the sooner the better: you can never discount the possibility of being led into error—serious error—by *any* reference work. For example, the imposing bulk and obvious authority of the Library of

Congress *National Union Catalog* (1203–1205) or the solid three-volume assurance of Walford's *Guide to Reference Material* (660) may seem to offer mute promise of reliability; and, for the most part, they are precisely what they seem—repositories of carefully prepared and scrupulously checked bibliographic fact. But not always. Unsuspecting scholars who consult the *National Union Catalog 1958–1962* (N.Y. 1963, vol. 45, p. 251) for information about Barbara Tuchman's book *The Zimmermann Telegram* may or may not learn the truth: if they consult the card for the New York edition, they will be informed that the title name belongs to Alfred Zimmermann (1859–1925); but the very next card, for the London edition, asserts that the name in question belongs to Arthur Zimmermann (1864–1940). And whoever checks Walford's *Guide* for information on histories of literary criticism will come across the following entry:

> Weller, R. *A History of Modern Criticism, 1350–1950.*
> London, Cape, 1955.– v. 1–.

He may hunt for this book for some time before he discovers that the name of its author is *Wellek,* and when he does he will find also that Wellek's *A History of Modern Criticism* begins not in the improbable year 1350 but in 1750.

Such examples can easily be multiplied. In the widely used annual bibliographies published by the Modern Humanities Research Association (10) and the Modern Language Association (11) one may find every conceivable kind of bibliographical error: inaccurate names, titles, volume numbers, page numbers, and dates; omissions and duplications; cross-references missing and cross-references to nonexistent items; citations of articles under headings that have no relation to their contents; and coverage at times so uneven that important journals may be overlooked for a year, then covered again with no note taken of the hiatus. Similarly, such important selective bibliographies as the *New CBEL* (6) can be quirky in their methods of organization, notoriously capricious in selectivity, and far from error-free. For years students using Richard Altick's *The Art of Literary Research* (642) were asked to provide corrections for a list of erroneous entries in the original *CBEL* (4); now, in the revised edition of his book, he has provided a similar list for the *New CBEL.* In each case, of course, his list is only a tiny sampling drawn from a vastly greater number of errors, many no doubt still waiting to be (perhaps painfully) discovered.

Yet, such works as Walford's *Guide,* the *National Union Catalog,* the MHRA and MLA annual bibliographies, and the *CBEL* and *New CBEL* are generally reliable; the amount of error in them, in proportion to their size and scope, is relatively small. In other kinds of reference works a scholar sometimes needs—early trade bibliographies, for example, which were often produced by the most slapdash of procedures, or some current biographical reference works which rely exclusively on data supplied by the biographees themselves—the potential for incompleteness, error, and sometimes downright deception goes up enormously. But the overriding fact is that a scholar cannot discount the possibility of error—serious error—in *any* of the reference tools he or she uses.

Hence, when scholarship is being pursued in earnest, and nothing less than the most scrupulous care will suffice, an awareness of the potential for error and incompleteness in all reference works will prompt users to take what steps they can to avoid being the victim of even presumably reliable sources. Consulting scholarly reviews is certainly one wise precaution to take. Before using even such well known sources as *Dissertation Abstracts International* (820) or the *Encyclopædia Britannica* (1139), it would be well to look at the reviews cited in our annotations, and for newly published reference works there are the critical surveys, reviews, and review citations which appear in current issues of such journals as *Literary Research Newsletter* (658) and *Reference Services Review* (667). The fact that a newly published reference work bears the imprint of a distinguished university press is no guarantee of its worth: *The Oxford Companion to Film* (786b), for example, is part of a widely respected Oxford University Press series; yet a reading of Mark Crispin Miller's detailed analysis of its limitations in the *New York Review of Books* (Sept. 16, 1976) would probably persuade many students of film to use some other source, such as the most recent edition of Halliwell's *The Filmgoer's Companion* (793).

Unfortunately, not even the most scrupulous of reviewers can touch upon every error or weakness in a reference work, and many sources, such as current bibliographies, are usually not reviewed at all. Nevertheless, there is a way to help protect yourself from being misled by the inevitable limitations in such works: by making use of overlapping sources. The deficiencies in one or more of them will thus be compensated for by the strengths of others, and the discovery of conflicting information in different sources, will, at least, signal that further inquiry is necessary.

This principle obviously applies in those cases where thoroughness is required. Even a casual comparison of a given year's listings for almost any major author in the annual MHRA and MLA bibliographies is likely to reveal striking omissions in each, and a further comparison of these with equivalent listings in more specialized period bibliographies will nearly always bring to light still other materials. What may be less obvious, however, is that a similar principle applies when selectivity rather than thoroughness is important. Many works cited in this guide are valuable precisely because they do not attempt exhaustiveness but instead list only a selection of the most important scholarship. Given the enormous amounts of material published annually in the fields of British and American literature, it would hardly be possible for scholars to keep abreast of major developments, even in the areas in which they specialize, without such tools. But indispensable as these tools are, in consulting any one of them the user is left to the mercy of the compiler's fallible and sometimes biased judgment in selection and annotation. The annual *Year's Work in English Studies* (15), for example, provides an invaluable guide to important scholarship published on English and American literature; but even apart from questions of judgment involved in the selection and annotation of any individual work, it has tended to scant non-British scholarship. Anyone studying, say, the literature of the Victorian period would be likely to get a much more balanced view of what was important in Victorian scholarship published in any one year if he were also to consult the annual selective reviews published in *Victorian Poetry* (120) and in *Studies in English Literature* (108). Consulting more than one of several overlapping selective works can be of value for two reasons: both because whatever duplication there is in them can help to focus attention on scholarship of commonly accepted importance, and because differences in coverage can signal degrees of bias, oversight, or both. But whether the goal is exhaustiveness or selectivity, reference tools should be used critically and comparatively. For the critical user, a flawed source can be far better than none at all; for the unwary, it can be a cause of error and an enormous waste of time.

Our injunction to use reference works critically applies, of course, to this book as well. And we should emphasize, finally, that neither this nor any other guide to reference tools can substitute for close personal and critical inspection of the reference works themselves. At best this book will provide a helpful map to the world of literary reference sources; its ultimate goal is to help you acquire an immediate personal familiarity with that enormously varied and complex world itself. Our hope is that it will help to shorten the time-consuming process of acquiring the necessary basic experience in using the tools of literary scholarship and in this way enable you to get on to the more important and interesting business of using those tools for creative purposes in literary study.

Glossary

This is a glossary of the chief terms and abbreviations used to describe the arrangement and contents of the bibliographies, indexes, and other reference works included in this book. For definitions of the technical terms used in bookmaking, publishing, and the book trade, see Geoffrey Glaister's *A Glossary of the Book* (630), Victor Strauss' *The Printing Industry* (631), and Jean Peters' *The Bookman's Glossary* (920). For references to studies which discuss the technical terminology used in descriptive bibliography and editing, see entries 605-629. For lists of abbreviations commonly used for the titles of scholarly journals, see Meserole and Bishop, *Directory of Journals and Series in the Humanities* (848) and the lists provided in the current issues of the MHRA *Annual Bibliography* (10) and the MLA *International Bibliography* (11).

ABSTRACT   A brief summary of the contents of an article, chapter, dissertation, book, etc. For examples of reference works which provide abstracts see 16 and 820.

ADDENDA   Material added to a book in a special section, usually at the end. For example, see 1143.

A.L.A.   American Library Association.

ANALYTICAL BIBLIOGRAPHY   The study of texts with reference to the means by which they are produced and distributed, from the earliest records of the processes involved in their composition through all subsequent stages in their transmission. The results of this study are used in preparing DESCRIPTIVE BIBLIOGRAPHIES and CRITICAL EDITIONS. See 570–631.

ANNALS   An historical record arranged chronologically year by year. See 211, 324, and 453.

ANNOTATED BIBLIOGRAPHY   A bibliography whose entries include information about the contents of the works cited. This book is an annotated bibliography.

AUTHOR BIBLIOGRAPHY   A bibliography whose entries are limited to works by and/or about an individual author; see, for example, 244.

AUTHOR LIST   A bibliography, catalogue, or other reference source arranged alphabetically by authors' names; for example, see 268 and 369.

BIO-BIBLIOGRAPHY   A reference work which combines authors' biographies with bibliographies of writings by and/or about them. For example, see 170–182 and 311–315.

CALENDAR   A list arranged chronologically; see, for example, 264. The term is also used to refer to a list of manuscripts which includes descriptions of the physical features and, sometimes, the contents of each.

CATALOGUE   A list, often with accompanying descriptions, of works held in, offered for sale at, produced in, or in some other way related to a particular place such as a library, bookseller's shop, publishing house, country, etc. See, for example, 583, 779, and 1178. The term is sometimes also used to refer to any systematically arranged list including descriptive details; see, for example, 266.

CBEL   *Cambridge Bibliography of English Literature* (4).

CEAA   Center for Editions of American Authors.

CHAPBOOK   A cheap pamphlet, usually containing popular ballads, stories, or jests, sold by wandering peddlers or "chapmen"; popular especially in the 16th century.

CHECKLIST   A terse and/or tentative bibliography; see, for example, 295, 415, and 736.

CHEL   *Cambridge History of English Literature* (184).

CLASSIFIED ARRANGEMENT   The arrangement of a bibliography or other reference work in some order other than alphabetical—e.g., in logical categories such as the Dewey Decimal System, in categories determined by subject, location, time, etc. See, for example, 101 and 413.

CONCORDANCE   An index, usually arranged alphabetically, to the words appearing in a particular text or texts; see, for example, 1004.

CORRIGENDA   A list providing corrections of errors.

CRITICAL BIBLIOGRAPHY   See ANALYTICAL BIBLIOGRAPHY.

CRITICAL EDITION   A scholarly edition providing a corrected and emended text based upon all available evidence of an author's deliberate intention. For the principles followed in preparing such editions, see 617–629.

CUMULATIVE INDEX   An index which brings together previously published indexes into a single alphabetical list; see, for example, 181.

DAB   *Dictionary of American Biography* (962).

DAE   *Dictionary of American English on Historical Principles* (1081).

DESCRIPTIVE BIBLIOGRAPHY   A bibliography, based upon the conclusions of ANALYTICAL BIBLIOGRAPHY, which provides a detailed description of the works it lists (usually including such features as title page, gatherings, typography, paper, binding, etc.) and discriminates between *editions, impressions, states,* and *issues.* For definitions of these and other technical terms see 605–616; for examples of descriptive bibliographies, see 61 and 240.

DESCRIPTIVE CATALOGUE   A CATALOGUE which provides relatively full descriptions of the works it lists.

DEWEY DECIMAL CLASSIFICATION   A subject classification system in which 999 main classes are represented by three-digit numbers, and further subclassifications are indicated by numbers following a decimal point. Devised for library use but adapted to organize some reference works; for examples, see 870 and 1175.

DICTIONARY LIST   A list in which authors, titles, and subjects are arranged alphabetically; see, for example, 325 and 359.

DIRECTORY   A list, usually arranged alphabetically, of the names and addresses of a particular class of people or organizations; for examples, see 313 and 977.

DISSERTATION   An extended scholarly study usually written as part of the requirements for a doctoral degree.

DNB   *Dictionary of National Biography* (957).

EDITION   All copies of a printed work which depend upon any substantially unaltered single setting of type or other compositorial process, including copies produced by cast-metal plates, photo-offset, and the like. The term is sometimes loosely used to mean a reprinting, with or without minor alterations.

ENUMERATIVE BIBLIOGRAPHY   A bibliography whose entries provide only basic information—such as author, title, place, date, publisher, number of volumes, etc.—as opposed to the fuller and more precise details provided in a DESCRIPTIVE BIBLIOGRAPHY.

ERRATA   A list providing corrections of errors, usually added to the beginning or end of a book or loosely inserted in it.

FASCICLE   A separately published part of a book; very large works prepared over long periods of time are sometimes published in fascicles; see, for example, 1102.

FESTSCHRIFT   A collection of essays published in honor of a person and dedicated to him or her; the plural is FESTSCHRIFTEN.

FILMOGRAPHY   A primary and/or secondary bibliography devoted to cinemato-graphic materials.

GAZETTEER   A dictionary of geographical place names.

GREG NUMBER   The number of an entry in W.W. Greg's *Bibliography of English Printed Drama to the Restoration* (61).

HANDBOOK   A concise reference work intended as a convenient guide to a particular subject; see, for example, 205, 325, and 359.

HAND LIST   A preliminary, tentative list compiled for purposes of further investigation or checking.

HISTORICAL BIBLIOGRAPHY   The study of the history of books and the book-making and book-selling processes; see 590–604.

IMPRESSION   That part of an EDITION consisting of all copies of a work printed on a particular press at any one time that the type or plates remain in the press.

IMPRINT   The name of the publisher (and sometimes the printer), the place of publication, and the date; often given on the title page of modern books, though increasingly omitting the date.

INCIPIT   Latin for "begins"; used to refer to the opening line or lines of untitled works, usually those of the medieval period.

INCUNABULA   Books printed from movable type before 1500 or 1501; the singular is *incunabulum* or *incunable*.

INDEX   A list intended to facilitate access to the contents of some work or collection; for example, 38, 388 and 858.

IN PRINT   Said of books currently available from their publishers; books not so available (even though they may still be purchased from booksellers) are said to be OUT OF PRINT.

ISBN   International Standard Book Number. A ten-digit number system used by American, Canadian, and European publishers to assign unique identification numbers to the books they publish.

ISSN   International Standard Serial Number. An eight-digit number system used by American, Canadian, and European serial publishers to assign unique identification numbers to the serials they publish.

LC   Library of Congress. LC NUMBER refers to the call number assigned a book by the Library of Congress.

LIBRARY OF CONGRESS CLASSIFICATION   A subject classification system originally designed for the United States Library of Congress and now widely adopted by American libraries and used, also, as the basis for subject classification in some reference works—e.g., 817.

LITTLE MAGAZINES   Literary magazines of limited circulation intended to foster experimental creative writing; see 840-842.

MHRA   Modern Humanities Research Association.

MICRO-   Used of text reproduction in greatly reduced size requiring special enlargement machines to read. The major kinds are MICROFILM, which is stored on reels; MICROFICHE, which is film in separate sheets of various sizes; and MICROPRINT, which is in the form of 6- by 9-inch opaque cards. The general term for such reduced texts is MICROFORM or MICROTEXT.

MLA   Modern Language Association of America.

MONOGRAPH   A book, pamphlet, or other separate publication not intended as part of an indefinitely continuing work; cf. SERIAL.

MS   Manuscript. The plural is MSS.

NATIONAL BIBLIOGRAPHY   A list of books published in or related to a particular country; see 669–750.

NEW CBEL or *NCBEL   New Cambridge Bibliography of English Literature* (6).

OED   OXFORD ENGLISH DICTIONARY (1077).

OHEL   OXFORD HISTORY OF ENGLISH LITERATURE (183).

OUT OF PRINT   See IN PRINT.

PALEOGRAPHY   The study of older handwriting forms and styles, usually those before the 18th century.

PERIODICAL   A term used in this book to cover all kinds of SERIALS except newspapers.

PRIMARY   Used to refer to works *by* an author as opposed to SECONDARY works, which are *about* an author.

PRINTING   Synonym for IMPRESSION.

PROCEEDINGS   The records of the actions of an organization.

PROCTOR ORDER   The chronological-geographical arrangement adopted by

Robert Proctor in his *An Index to the Early Printed Books in the British Museum* (582).

REPRINT   A reproduction of an existing printed text in full size (not in MICRO-TEXT) by any kind of process except resetting the type.

RUNNING COMMENTARY   An annotated bibliography arranged in sentences and paragraphs which provide a coherent discussion of the works cited; see, for example, 15 and 255.

SECONDARY   See PRIMARY.

SERIAL   A magazine, journal, newspaper, or other similar publication which appears from time to time and is (or was) intended to continue indefinitely.

SERIES   A number of MONOGRAPHS, usually written by different authors, which are published under some general title—e.g., *American Literature, English Literature, and World Literatures in English: An Information Guide Series;* often prepared under a general editor and appearing in uniform format.

SHORT-TITLE   An abbreviated title, usually the first part of a more extensive title; a short-title catalogue (e.g., 688 and 700) provides less than full bibliographic information about the works it lists.

SINGLE-ALPHABET LIST   A list in which several kinds of items are arranged in one continuous alphabetical order—e.g., authors, titles, and subjects. See, for example, 266.

SMALL PRESS   A press of limited production and distribution facilities usually intended to foster the publication of experimental writing.

STATIONER   An early term for a publisher or bookseller.

STC NUMBER   Refers to the numbers of entries in the Pollard and Redgrave (688) and Wing (700) short-title catalogues.

SUBJECT BIBLIOGRAPHY   A bibliography devoted to a particular subject; see, for example, 480 and 541.

TEXTUAL BIBLIOGRAPHY or TEXTUAL CRITICISM   The application of the methods and conclusions of ANALYTICAL BIBLIOGRAPHY in the preparation of CRITICAL EDITIONS; see 617–629.

THESIS   A scholarly study usually written as part of the requirements for a bachelor's or master's degree; also used as a synonym for DISSERTATION.

TRANSACTIONS   The published records of a group or of a meeting of some association.

UNION CATALOGUE or UNION LIST   A CATALOGUE or list of the combined holdings of more than one library or other repository; more generally, any catalogue or list which locates copies.

UNIVERSAL DECIMAL CLASSIFICATION   An adaptation of the DEWEY DECIMAL CLASSIFICATION system for bibliographic organization, particularly in the sciences; see 834 for an example of a reference work so organized.

VARIORUM EDITION   An edition of a literary work which includes a more or less comprehensive record of scholarly comment on the text; also, loosely used as a synonym for a CRITICAL EDITION which provides a record of variant readings.

WING NUMBER   The number of an entry in Wing's *Short-Title Catalogue* (700).

WOODWARD AND McMANAWAY NUMBER   The number of an entry in G.L. Woodward and J.G. McManaway's *A Checklist of English Plays, 1641–1700* (88).

Reference Sources in
English and American
Literature

I. English Literature

A. Bibliographical Materials

1. General

1 HOWARD-HILL, TREVOR H. *Index to British Bibliography.* Vol. 1– ,
Oxford, 1969– .

Vol. 1, *Bibliography of British Bibliographies,* 1969, covers literary bibliographies, published as monographs, parts of monographs, or periodical articles after 1890, when these deal with English manuscripts, books, and printing and publishing in England. Arrangement is classified with categories such as "General and Period Bibliographies," "Forms and Genres," "Subjects," and "Authors." Includes an index of authors, compilers, editors, publishers, and subjects.
Vol. 2, *Shakespearian Bibliography and Textual Criticism: A Bibliography,* 1971, records bibliographies and textual studies of Shakespeare (excluded from vol. 1) and provides supplementary material to vol. 1 on pp. 179–322. Includes an index of authors, compilers, editors, publishers, and subjects.

2 NORTHUP, CLARK S. *A Register of Bibliographies of the English Language and Literature. With Contributions by Joseph Quincy Adams and Andrew Keogh.* New Haven, Conn., 1925. Rptd., N.Y., 1962.

A comprehensive bibliography of some 12,000 bibliographies on English language and literature published up to 1922, with some annotations. Arranged under two main headings: "General" and "Individual Authors and Topics." Includes English and American author bibliographies and bibliographies on topics such as "Drama," "Manuscripts," "Printing and Publishing," "Quakers," etc. Extensive subject-author index.

3 VAN PATTEN, NATHAN. *An Index to Bibliographies and Bibliographical Contributions Relating to the Work of American and British Authors, 1923–1932.* Stanford, Calif., 1934. Rptd., N.Y.

A continuation of Northup's *A Register of Bibliographies.* Arrangement is alphabetical by subject. Index to authors and compilers.

4 *The Cambridge Bibliography of English Literature.* Ed. FREDERICK W. BATESON. 5 vols. *Vol. I: 600–1660; Vol. II: 1660–1800; Vol. III: 1800–1900; Vol. IV: Index.* Cambridge, 1941. *Vol. V: Supplement, 600–1900,* ed. GEORGE WATSON, Cambridge, 1957.

A selective but very comprehensive bibliography of primary and secondary materials on English literature, including background materials, genres, and individual authors. Although much of this bibliography has been incorporated in or superseded by the *New Cambridge Bibliography*, 6, it remains useful for some classes of materials not included in the later work at all and for some valuable scholarship omitted in the more recent bibliography. Arrangement within vols. I–III and V is chiefly by genres and subgenres; author bibliographies are usually given within these classes, and the arrangement of secondary materials in author bibliographies is chronological by the first published work of each scholar cited. Relatively very full coverage is provided for primary materials and, also, for secondary materials on minor figures and background areas. Vol. IV provides an extensive subject-title index to vols. I–III.

5 *The Concise Cambridge Bibliography of English Literature 600–1950.* Ed. GEORGE WATSON. 2nd ed. Cambridge, 1965.

A compression by rigorous selection of the *CBEL* 1940 and the *Supplement* 1957, plus a section covering 1900–1950. About 400 'major' writers are selected.

6 *The New Cambridge Bibliography of English Literature.* Ed. GEORGE WATSON, *et al.* 5 vols. Cambridge, 1969– . *Vol. I: 600–1660*, 1974; *Vol. II: 1660–1800*, 1971; *Vol. III: 1800–1900*, 1969; *Vol. IV: 1900–1950*, 1972; *Vol. V: Index*, in progress.

A selective but very comprehensive bibliography of the primary and secondary materials of English literature, including cultural and economic background, genres, and individual authors. Based upon the earlier *CBEL*, the *New CBEL* generally incorporates and updates that work. However, some classes of materials provided in the earlier *CBEL* have not been included while other classes have been added or greatly enlarged; furthermore, vols. I–III have been criticised for the standards the editors employed in determining what was to be included and what omitted. The arrangement of the bibliography volumes is classified, chiefly by genre; except for figures like Shakespeare, author bibliographies are usually given under genre headings. Arrangement of secondary materials in author bibliographies and elsewhere is chronological by date of the first published work of each scholar, so that, for example, if a scholar has published 6 studies of Tennyson between 1935 and 1960, all will be listed together with other scholarship published on Tennyson in 1935. As with the earlier *CBEL*, the *New CBEL* provides coverage that is particularly useful for background material (e. g., publishing history, philosophy, children's literature) and minor figures; the author bibliographies are particularly full for primary materials, including manuscripts. Each of the 4 published volumes has a brief author-subject index of limited usefulness; vol. 5, when published, will be a detailed index volume.

7 BATESON, FREDERICK W. *A Guide to English Literature*. 2nd ed. London, 1967. N.Y., 1968.

Essentially a highly selective annotated bibliography of materials for students of English literature. Arrangement is by periods, exclusive of the Old English period. Each period is provided with a short essay followed by an annotated bibliography of selected primary and secondary materials. Includes brief lists of literary criticism and an introduction to research tools.

8 *Writers and Their Work*. London, 1950– .

A series of pamphlets (now over 250) published for the British Council and the National Book League by Longmans, Green & Co. on individual British authors of all periods and on topics as diverse as the metaphysical poets and the detective story. The pamphlets for 20th century writers include some relatively minor figures. Each pamphlet includes a selective bibliography of primary and secondary material.

9 STAMM, RUDOLF. *Englische Literatur*. Bern, 1957.

A survey of the research done during the period 1935 to 1955 on English literature from 1500 to 1900. Valuable for its tracing of the development of scholarly treatments of literary problems from pioneer studies through the period covered. Very fully documented. Includes an index of authors' and scholars' names.

10 *Annual Bibliography of English Language and Literature 1920–* . 1– (1921–).

Published by the Modern Humanities Research Association, London. Comprehensive annual bibliography of books, articles, and reviews of scholarship on English and American literature. Classified arrangement with categories such as "Bibliography," "Biography," "Language, Literature and the Computer," "Old English," "Nineteenth Century," and the like. Materials on American literature are not segregated but treated within the other categories. There is an index of subjects, including names of literary figures, and a second index of authors, editors, compilers, and translators of the scholarly works listed. Review citations are given immediately beneath the entry of the book reviewed. Each volume includes a list of abbreviations used for journal titles.

11 *MLA International Bibliography of Books and Articles on the Modern Languages and Literatures*. [1922– . See annotation].

Comprehensive annual bibliography of books and articles relating to all modern languages and literatures. Title, scope, and method of publication have varied. From 1922–1969 published annually in the June issues of PMLA. The bibliographies for 1921–1955 were titled "American Bibliography" and included only American scholarship; bibliographies for 1956–62 were titled "Annual Bibliography" and gradually became more international in scope and coverage. Separately published since 1969. Presently

15

published in 4 vols.: I (General, English, American, Medieval, Neo-Latin, Celtic Literatures and Folklore), II (European, Asian, African, and Latin American Literatures), III (Linguistics), and IV (Articles on Pedagogy in Foreign Languages). Arrangement is classified; categories include broad divisions ("English Literature," "American Literature," etc.) and, within these, sub-categories such as "Literary Criticism and Literary Theory," "Eighteenth Century," "Whitman," etc. Within literary period categories arrangement is classified first by some general topics ("Bibliography," "Poetry," "Fiction," etc.) and then alphabetically by author or, occasionally, by such topics as "Oxford Movement," etc. There are no subject indexes, but general works and festschriften are analyzed and there is an elaborate system of cross-references. Each vol. has an index of the authors of books and articles cited and a master list of abbreviations used for the titles of the some 2,600 periodicals now surveyed in compiling the bibliography. Titles of journals now abstracted in *MLA Abstracts* are asterisked, and all items abstracted are preceded by an asterisk.

12 RZEPECKI, ARNOLD N. ed. *Literature and Language Bibliographies from the American Year Book, 1910–1919.* Ann Arbor, Mich., 1970.

Ten annual bibliographies covering ancient and modern languages and literature, including English and American, brought together in a single volume. The bibliographies record only scholarship by Americans, but are valuable because they cover a period before the beginning of the MLA bibliography. Subject index; personal name and main entry index.

13 "Current Literature [year]." *English Studies*, 7–   (1925–   ). [Title and scope have varied.]

Annual surveys of selected recent scholarship on English literature, arranged under headings such as "Drama," "Essay and Prose," etc. Covers scholarship on literary history and theory, and new editions.

14 The American Bibliographic Service. *Quarterly Check-List of Literary History.* Darien, Conn., 1958–1975.

A quarterly check-list of monographic publications on English, American, French, and German literary history. Arranged alphabetically by author. Entries give title, publisher, and price information. Each issue includes a directory of publishers. The 4th yearly issue includes an author-editor-translator index for all four quarterly issues. The American Bibliographic Service publishes quarterly check-lists on a variety of subjects.

15 *The Year's Work in English Studies.* 1–   (1921–   ).

An annual running commentary on important books and articles published on English and American literature for the past year. Arrangement is classified, with categories for general materials, linguistics, major literary periods, and special categories for Chaucer and Shakespeare. Coverage of American literature began in 1954. Highly selective; attempts to cover only the more important scholarship.

16 *Abstracts of English Studies.* 1–   (1958–   ).

Abstracts of articles on American, English, and British Commonwealth literature and on English language appearing in about 1,100 journals. Published 10 times yearly. Monthly and annual indexes: monthly indexes are brief subject guides; annual indexes include an index of journals and monographs abstracted, a subject index of people and topics treated in the abstracts, and an index to authors of articles abstracted. Scope and arrangement of individual numbers have varied.

17 *[Year] MLA Abstracts of Articles in Scholarly Journals.* 1– (1972–   ).

A separately published 3 vol. annual edition of abstracts prepared by writers contributing to some 250 journals and festschriften; vol. 1 includes abstracts of writings on English and American literature. Arrangement follows the arrangement of the *MLA International Bibliography.* Includes a subject index.

18 McNamee, Lawrence F. *Dissertations in English and American Literature: Theses Accepted by American, British and German Universities 1865–1964.* N.Y., 1968. *Supplement One 1964–1968,* 1969; *Supplement Two 1969–1973,* 1974.

A comprehensive list of dissertations on English and American literature accepted by German, British, and American universities from 1865 to 1973. The supplementary volumes include British Commonwealth universities. Arrangement is classified: there are 35 main lists covering such topics as "Chaucer," "The Eighteenth Century," "The English Novel," "Comparative Literature," "Literary Criticism, Rhetoric, and Genre," etc. These lists are elaborately sub-classified. The main volume lists more than 14,000 dissertations, and the supplements add about 10,000 more. In the main volume there is a list of universities covered, the subject codes used, and an index to major literary authors; appendixes give a cross index of authors arranged alphabetically by subject author, and an index of authors of dissertations.

19 Habicht, Werner, ed. *English and American Studies in German: Summaries of Theses and Monographs, A Supplement to Anglia.* Tübingen, 1969–   .

An annual publication of abstracts covering as completely as possible all German doctoral dissertations and monographs on (1) Language, (2) English literature, (3) American literature. The abstracts, written in English, are prepared by the authors of the works abstracted. Annual volumes include separate indexes for authors and for literary figures and other subjects treated.

20 Mummendey, Richard. *Die Sprache und Literatur der Angelsachsen im Spiegel der Deutschen Universitätsschriften 1885–1950: Eine Biblio-*

graphie. Bonn, 1954. Simultaneously published as *Language and Literature of the Anglo-Saxon Nations as Presented in German Doctoral Dissertations 1885–1950: A Bibliography.* Charlottesville, Va., 1954.

The preface, table of contents, and section headings are given in German and English. A classified list of some 2989 German dissertations on English language and literature written between 1885 and 1950. Seriously incomplete, but of use because it supplies fuller bibliographic details, including form and place of full or partial publication, than other dissertation catalogues. Arranged under such headings as "History of genres," "History of motifs and subjects," "Romanticism, 1785–1830," "The Literature of the U.S., The Colonial Period," etc. Includes a name and subject index.

21 HOWARD, PATSY C. *Theses in English Literature 1894–1970.* Ann Arbor, Mich., 1973.

A bibliography of unpublished baccalaureate and masters' theses. Arranged alphabetically by names of English literary figures, with relevant theses listed alphabetically by author beneath each name. Separate indexes for subjects and thesis authors.

For references to other English literature bibliographies see entries **183, 184,** and **187–91.**

2. Period

a. Medieval

22 ROBINSON, FRED C. *Old English Literature: A Select Bibliography.* Toronto, 1970.

A selective list of scholarly books and articles, excluding works on nonliterary writing and Latin writing of the Anglo-Saxon period. Article citations have brief annotations; reviews are listed for most books. Index to scholars cited.

23 "Old English Bibliography for [year]." *Old English Newsletter,* 4– (1971–).

An annual bibliography of books, articles, dissertations, and reviews of books on Old English literature and language. Arranged as a classified list with such headings as "Linguistic," *"Beowulf,"* "Old English Prose," "Reviews," etc. Previously distributed as a mimeographed list at the annual meeting of the Old English Group of the Modern Language Association.

23a "The Year's Work in Old English Studies [year]." *Old English Newsletter,* 5— (1972–).

18

An annual critically annotated bibliography of selected important books and articles on Old English literature and language. Annotations are initialled.

23b BIDDLE, MARTIN, *et al.* "[Old English] Bibliography for 1971– ." *Anglo-Saxon England*. 1– (1972–).

Includes history, art, archaeology, numismatics, etc.

24 FISHER, JOHN H., ed. *The Medieval Literature of Western Europe: A Review of Research, Mainly 1930–1960*. N.Y., 1966.

A survey of the tools for research and of the most important research arranged in chapters such as Old English, Middle English, and Medieval Celtic literatures. Each chapter is divided into appropriate sections such as background studies, the different genres, individual authors, etc. The Index of Proper Names includes medieval authors and modern scholars.

25 GREENFIELD, STANLEY B. "Old English and Middle-English Bibliographical Guides" in David M. Zesmer, *Guide to English Literature from Beowulf Through Chaucer and Medieval Drama*. N.Y., 1961, pp. [287]–381.

Selective bibliographies emphasizing recent studies in English. The critical annotations are quite full. Cross references are given and Zesmer's index includes the items in the two bibliographies.

26 MATTHEWS, WILLIAM. *Old and Middle English Literature*. Goldentree Bibliographies. N.Y., 1968.

Highly selective lists of the more important scholarship on various topics and individual authors including Anglo-Latin and Anglo-French. Chaucer is represented only by a brief list of major studies. (There is a separate bibliography for Chaucer in the Goldentree series.) The scholarship is primarily British and American with some important continental studies.

27 WELLS, JOHN E. *A Manual of the Writings in Middle English 1050–1400*. New Haven, Conn., 1916. *Supplements*. 9 vols. 1919–1951.

A handbook to works in Middle English which attempts to describe "all the extant writings in print from single lines to the most extensive pieces, composed in English between 1050 and 1400." Arranged in two parts. The first part consists of a series of chapters covering such topics as "Romances," "Homilies and Legends," "Dramatic Pieces," "Chaucer," etc. Within these categories entries are provided for individual works; entries give "the accepted views of scholars" on questions of dating, MSS features and locations, dialects employed, form used, and sources. Entries for longer works can also include an abstract. The second part of the *Manual* is headed "Bibliographic Notes" and is arranged to follow the topics and citations in the first part; entries provide citations to editions and to secondary scholarship.

28 SEVERS, JONATHAN B. and ALBERT E. HARTUNG. *A Manual of the Writings in Middle English, 1050–1500.* 1967– . Hamden, Conn., 1967.

An extensive revision of Wells' *Manual,* 27. Each of the vols. covers a particular topic or group of topics – e. g., Romances, Saints' Legends, Malory and Caxton, Middle Scots Writers, etc.; the arrangement of each vol. follows the two-part order of Wells' *Manual,* but the scope now includes the entire 15th century (and in some cases extends into the 16th as well). Incorporates and corrects the material in Wells' *Manual* and is intended to be a definitive bibliography of all known creative and didactic writing in Middle English. Particularly valuable for its coverage of secondary scholarship after 1945, including citations to reviews. Each vol. has an index to Middle English authors, works, printers, and subjects.

29 TUCKER, LENA L. and ALLEN R. BENHAM. *A Bibliography of Fifteenth Century Literature, With Special Reference to the History of English Culture.* Seattle, Washington, 1927.

An annotated bibliography of primary and secondary materials on 15th century English literature and culture. Arrangement is by categories such as "Bibliography," "Political Background," "Cultural Background," etc. The category "Literature" includes general materials, drama, individual authors, and anonymous works. Author-title-subject index.

30 CALDWELL, HARRY B. and DAVID L. MIDDLETON. *English Tragedy, 1370–1600: Fifty Years of Criticism.* San Antonio, Texas, 1971.

A bibliography arranged in two main parts: nondramatic verse tragedy and dramatic tragedy. Each part is arranged chronologically by author (anonymous works by title) and citations to relevant criticisms are given beneath each author's name. Includes an appendix titled "Works in Need of Further Scholarship" and separate indexes for primary and secondary authors.

31 ROUSE, RICHARD H. *Serial Bibliographies for Medieval Studies.* Berkeley, Calif., 1969.

A comprehensive annotated list of serial bibliographies which pertain to medieval studies. Arrangement is classified by subject; literature and language serial bibliographies are covered in Section IX. Entries give the most recent volume of the bibliography, the approximate time lag between the dates of coverage and dates of publication, the approximate number of items the bibliography contains, and the approximate number of journals it surveys. An asterisk indicates those bibliographies which are most thorough. Indexes of titles and editors.

32 *International Medieval Bibliography.* 1– (1968–).

Quarterly lists of articles, notes, and review articles in journals and festschriften on all medieval subjects including literature. Arrangement is clas-

sified; there are author and subject indexes. The quarterly issues are cumulated in an annual volume; the 1970 cumulation covered some 1426 journals
and 135 festschriften.

33 *International Guide to Medieval Studies: A Quarterly Index to Periodical Literature.* 1– (1961–).

Includes both articles and reviews. Arrangement is by author in a single-
alphabet list, with a subject index. Some descriptive annotations. Annual
cumulation with author index.

34 The American Bibliographic Service. *Quarterly Checklist of Medie-
valia: An International Index of Current Books, Monographs, Bro-
chures, and Separates.* 1– (1958–).

Arranged as a single-alphabet author list with a subject index. Coverage
is international, but selective.

35 "Bibliography of American Periodical Literature." *Speculum,* 9–47
(1934–1972).

Lists articles published in the U.S.A. and, until 1959, Canada. Arrangement
varies, sometimes by author, sometimes classified in categories like "Art and
Architecture," "Chaucer," "Language," and the like. Published quarterly;
the extensive reviews and lists of books received in each quarterly issue are
useful supplements to the bibliography and are not limited to American
publications.

36 BROWN, CARLETON and ROSSELL H. ROBBINS. *The Index of Middle
English Verse.* N.Y., 1943.

An index of 4365 first lines from some 2,000 MSS, with some annotation.
Cites both MS and printed texts. Subject-title index.

37 ROBBINS, ROSSELL H. and JOHN L. CUTLER. *Supplement to The Index
of Middle English Verse.* Lexington, Ky., 1965.

Arranged to parallel the original *Index of Middle English Verse.* Corrects
or adds about 2300 entries. Appendixes provide a conversion table for poems
re-numbered from the *Index* and corrigenda for the subject-title index of the
original. Subject-title index.

38 BORDMAN, GERALD. *Motif-Index of the English Metrical Romances.*
Helsinki, 1963.

A subject index, by key terms in alphabetical order, to motifs in English
metrical romances. Corrects and supplements the relevant entries in Stith
Thompson, **1018**. There is a very full index to the terms used in the entries.

39 STRATMAN, CARL J. *Bibliography of Medieval Drama.* 2nd ed. rev.
and enl. 2 vols. N.Y., 1972.

A bibliography of primary and secondary materials on medieval drama.
Arranged in ten chapters, each covering a topic such as "Festschriften," "Latin

Drama," "English Drama," etc. Entries for primary materials include *STC* numbers, SR entries, and MS locations. Important works are marked with an asterisk. Index to critical and scholarly material cited.

39a HOULE, PETER J. *The English Morality and Related Drama: A Bibliographical Survey*. Hamden, Conn., 1972.

59 English morality plays are treated in alphabetical order. Editions, summaries stating main theme and position of the play in the morality canon and a bibliography of criticism on each play are given. There is a list of general critical material at the end.

40 JOLLIFFE, P. S. *A Check-List of Middle English Prose Writings of Spiritual Guidance*. Toronto, 1974.

A classified list of tracts and other medieval writings in prose concerning spiritual guidance; arranged alphabetically by first word within fifteen major categories. Entries provide information on manuscript locations. Includes a bibliography, and indexes to authors and titles, to incipits, to manuscripts, and to acephalous works.

40a HENINGER, S. K., JR. *English Prose, Prose Fiction, and Criticism to 1660. A Guide to Information Sources*. Gale Information Guide Library series. Detroit, Mich., 1975.

An annotated guide to the major works in English prose from its beginnings to 1660. Arranged chronologically within genre classes (religious writings, travel literature, essays, translations, etc.); entries provide both citations to primary works (giving modern edition if available) and to secondary scholarship with annotations. Author index.

41 BRUCE, JAMES D. "A Select Bibliography of Arthurian Critical Literature." Chapter 7 of Vol. 2 of *The Evolution of Arthurian Romance*. 2 vols. Göttingen, 1923–24. 2nd ed., 1928. Rptd., 1958.

Highly selective secondary bibliographies of books and articles divided to parallel the divisions of the text. See also the bibliography of material on narrative lays (2nd ed., vol. 2, pp. 175–288) and the bibliographical footnotes and references throughout the text in both volumes. Subject index.

42 PARRY, JOHN J. and MARGARET SCHLAUCH. *A Bibliography of Arthurian Critical Literature for the Years 1922–1929*. N.Y., 1931, and *A Bibliography of Arthurian Critical Literature for the Years 1930–1935*. N.Y., 1936.

Intended as supplements to Bruce's "A Select Bibliography of Arthurian Critical Literature." Each volume provides a secondary bibliography of books (including citations to reviews) and articles arranged alphabetically by author, with a subject-title index.

43 "A Bibliography of Critical Arthurian Literature for the Year [1936–62]." *Modern Language Quarterly*, 1–24 (1940–63).

Includes monographs, articles, and reviews. Arranged as an author list with subject index.

44 *Bulletin bibliographique de la société internationale arthurienne.* 1– (1949–).

Comprehensive bibliography of books, articles, dissertations, and reviews on medieval Arthuriana. Classified list with author and subject indexes.

45 "Bibliography of Editions and Translations in Progress of Medieval Texts." *Speculum*, 43– (1973–).

An alphabetical author-title list of work in progress including projects that have lapsed.

46 "Old English Research in Progress," "Middle English Research in Progress," "Chaucer Research in Progress." *Neuphilologische Mitteilungen,* 66– (1965–).

Annual bibliographies of reserarch in progress. Arrangement is by subject categories such as "Alfred," "Devotional Materials," "Piers Plowman," "Troilus and Criseyde," and the like.

For other medieval literature bibliographies see entries **66, 155, 171, 456,** and **457.**

b. Renaissance

47 LIEVSAY, JOHN L. *The Sixteenth Century: Skelton Through Hooker.* Goldentree Bibliographies. N.Y., 1968.

Highly selective, classified list of primary and secondary sources. Scottish writers and all playwrights of the period are scanted. An asterisk indicates a work of special importance. Index of authors and subjects.

48 TANNENBAUM, SAMUEL A. *Elizabethan Bibliographies.* 41 vols. N.Y., 1937–50. Reissued in 10 vols., Port Washington, N.Y., 1967.

A series of bibliographies covering primary and secondary materials on Ascham, Beaumont and Fletcher, Breton, Chapman, Daniel, Dekker, Drayton, Heywood, Jonson, Kyd, Lodge, Lyly, Middleton, Marlowe, Marston, Massinger, Montaigne, Mundy, Nashe, Peele, Randolph, Shakespeare, Shirley, Sidney, Marie Stuart, Tourneur, and Webster, *et al.* Author-title-subject indexes.

49 PENNEL, CHARLES A. *et al.,* ed. *Elizabethan Bibliographies Supplements.* London, 1967– .

Intended as a supplement to Tannenbaum's *Elizabethan Bibliographies,* but includes other authors for the period 1400–1700. Volumes are devoted to individual authors and include both primary and secondary materials. The bibliographies attempt completeness except for anthology reprintings, M. A.

theses, and American and English Ph. D. dissertations. Arrangement within each volume is chronological, with an author index.

49a WRIGHT, LOUIS B., *et al. Surveys of Recent Scholarship in the Period of the Renaissance Compiled for the Committee on Renaissance Studies of the American Council of Learned Societies.* First Series. N.Y., 1945.

A collection of annotated guides to Renaissance scholarship in all areas, originally published in various journals between 1941 and 1944. The English literature survey by Rosemund Tuve was originally published in *Studies in Philology*, 40 (1943).

50 GABLER, HANS WALTER. *English Renaissance Studies in German 1945–1967: A Check-List of German, Austrian, and Swiss academic theses, monographs and book publications on English language and literature, c. 1500–1650.* Heidelberg, 1971.

By scope and design a survey of the post-war trends of English Renaissance studies in German. An English title translation has been added to each entry, and a detailed index of English catch-words is appended. Esp. valuable for its inclusion of all dissertations and university publications in the field, including some not listed elsewhere.

51 "Recent Literature of the Renaissance: A Bibliography." *Studies in Philology*, 14–66 (1917–1969).

An annual selective bibliography of books, articles, and reviews, often annotated. Includes coverage of the European Renaissance after 1938. Classified arrangement, including separate categories for Spenser, Shakespeare, and Milton. Author-subject index.

52 "Renaissance Books." *Renaissance Quarterly,* 5–   (1952–   ). [Until 1966 the journal title was *Renaissance News*.]

A quarterly list of recent books published on all aspects of the Renaissance in Europe. Arranged as a classified list under headings such as "History," "Literature," "Philosophy," etc.

53 "Recent Studies in the English Renaissance." *Studies in English Literature 1500–1900.* 1—   (1961—   ).

Provides an annual running commentary on the year's work on non-dramatic literature of the Renaissance, including Milton; discussions of both books and articles. Highly selective; attempts to include only the more important scholarship.

54 "Recent Studies in the English Renaissance." *English Literary Renaissance,* 1–   (1971–   ).

Quarterly bibliographical articles surveying recent scholarship (from 1945 to the present) on individual Renaissance writers or (for anonymous works) titles. The surveys are in the form of running commentaries.

55 "Abstracts of Recent Articles." *Seventeenth Century News,* 1–
(1942–   ).

Quarterly issues often contain abstracts of selected recent articles on the
literature of the Seventeenth Century. Arrangement is classified, and includes categories for authors and for other subjects such as "Prose," "Drama," etc. Quarterly issues also include a separate commentary and abstracts
section titled "Neo-Latin News."

56 WILLIAMS, FRANKLIN B., JR. *Index of Dedications and Commendatory
Verses in English Books Before 1641.* London, 1962.

Alphabetical lists of dedicatees: personal, nonpersonal, anonymous, and
variant. Entries give the name of the work in which the dedication appears
by its *STC* number or other identification, and supplies the name of the
dedicatee and the source of biographical information about him..

57 CASE, ARTHUR E. *A Bibliography of English Poetical Miscellanies
1521–1750.* Oxford, 1935. Rptd., 1970.

A descriptive bibliography arranged chronologically by date of earliest known
edition. Entries give descriptions (including title pages in quasi-facsimile and
detailed annotations) of all earliest and subsequent editions to 1750, and
information on later editions is given in the notes. For a supplementary list
giving locations of copies in more than 14 American libraries, see Richard
C. Boys' "A Finding-list of English Poetical Miscellanies 1700–48 in Selected
American Libraries," *ELH,* 7 (June 1940), 144–62.

58 SPENCER, THEODORE. "A Bibliography of Studies in Metaphysical
Poetry, 1912–1938." In Theodore Spencer and Mark Van Doren's
Studies in Metaphysical Poetry: Two Essays and a Bibliography. N.Y.,
1939. Rptd., 1964.

Lists of scholarly and critical writing on metaphysical poetry appearing in
print since the publication of Grierson's edition of Donne in 1912 up to
May, 1938. Divided into sections covering general studies and twelve individual poets. Index to scholars cited.

59 BERRY, LLOYD E. *A Bibliography of Studies in Metaphysical Poetry,
1939–1960.* Madison, Wisc., 1964.

A continuation of Theodore Spencer's bibliography, arranged in the same
fashion.

60 FRANK, JOSEPH. *Hobbled Pegasus: A Descriptive Bibliography of
Minor English Poetry, 1641–1660.* Albuquerque, N. M., 1968.

An annotated descriptive bibliography of primary materials. In spite of the
title, includes some prose works. Annotations include Wing number and information on format, printing, literary form, and subject.

61 GREG, W. W. *A Bibliography of the English Printed Drama to the Restoration.* 4 vols. London, 1939–59. Rptd.

A descriptive bibliography, arranged chronologically. Attempts to include all editions up to 1700 of all plays written before 1643, or printed before 1660, in 10 English libraries. Entries give transcript of title page and full bibliographic descriptions of each work. Contents are described, and locations of copies examined are given. Various author, title, and subject indexes. Important introductory matter in vol. 4.

62 RIBNER, IRVING. *Tudor and Stuart Drama.* Goldentree Bibliographies. N. Y., 1966.

Highly selective, classified, primary and secondary bibliography covering bibliography and reference works, anthologies, play publication and production, the masque, and 22 dramatists. Shakespeare not included. Subject and author indexes. Items of special importance asterisked.

63 LOGAN, TERENCE and DENZELL S. SMITH. *The Predecessors of Shakespeare: A Survey and Bibliography of Recent Studies in English Renaissance Drama.* Lincoln, Neb., 1973.

A selective annotated bibliography of the scholarship on Renaissance drama published between 1923 and 1965. Arranged as a series of chapters covering Marlowe, Greene, Kyd, Nashe, Lyly, Peele, Lodge, Anonymous (18 plays) and Other Dramatists (Breton, Farrant, Forsett, Hughes, Kempe, Legge, Porter, and Wilson). The essays on the 7 major dramatists are arranged in 3 parts: (1) a general section on biography, guides, etc., (2) an annotated bibliography of criticism on individual plays, and (3) a canon of the writer's work, including apocrypha. For minor writers there are simple annotated bibliographies, arranged chronologically. Includes indexes to persons and plays.

63a LOGAN, TERENCE P. ed. *The Popular School: A Survey and Bibliography of Recent Studies in English Renaissance Drama.* Lincoln, Neb., 1975.

Discussions of dramatic writing 1593–1616, including annotated bibliographical essays on Dekker, Middleton, Webster, Heywood, Drayton, Barnes, Chettle, Day, Haughton, Rowley, etc. Includes a section on anonymous plays and separate indexes to persons and plays.

64 BERGERON, DAVID M. *Twentieth Century Criticism of English Masques, Pageants, and Entertainments: 1558–1642.* With a supplement on the folk play and related forms by Harry B. Caldwell. San Antonio, Texas, 1972.

65 "Some Recent Studies in Shakespeare and Jacobean Drama." *Studies in English Literature 1500–1900.* 1–   (1961–   ).

Provides an annual running commentary on the year's work on dramatic literature of the Renaissance. Includes discussions of both books and articles. Highly selective; attempts to include only the more important scholarship.

66 *Research Opportunities in Renaissance Drama.* 1– (1956–). Title for 1956–64: *Opportunities for Research in Renaissance Drama.* [The volume for 1964 appeared as a supplement to *Renaissance Drama.*]

Published annually as a report of the MLA Conference on Research Opportunities in Renaissance Drama. Each issue provides a survey of current and ongoing research. Since 1967 the volumes include a supplement for medieval drama.

67 JAGGARD, WILLIAM. *Shakespeare Bibliography: A Dictionary of Every Known Issue of the Writings of the Poet and of Recorded Opinion Thereon in the English Language.* Stratford-on-Avon, 1911. Rptd., N.Y., 1963.

A bibliography of primary and secondary materials arranged as a single-alphabet list. Secondary writings are entered under author's names and subject entries give cross references to appropriate author entries. Shakespeare's works are entered under his name. Locates some copies.

68 EBISCH, WALTHER and LEVIN L. SCHÜCKING. *A Shakespeare Bibliography.* Oxford, 1931. *Supplement 1930–1935*, Oxford, 1936. Rptd., N.Y., 1964.

A selective but quite full bibliography of books, articles, and reviews of books on Shakespeare published before 1936. Arrangement is in 14 major categories such as "Shakespeare Bibliography," "Shakespeare's Life," "Text: Transmission and Emendation," "Shakespeare's Sources," "Shakespeare's Stage and the Productions of His Plays," etc., followed by bibliographies arranged under the titles of Shakespeare's works. Some annotation. Index of authors.

69 SMITH, GORDON ROSS. *A Classified Shakespeare Bibliography 1936–1958.* University Park, Pennsylvania, 1963.

Continues the Ebisch and Schücking bibliography to 1958. Arrangement follows the categories used by Ebisch and Schücking with modifications and additions. Attempts to include everything written on Shakespeare that is recorded in an extensive number of bibliographies listed on pp. xlv-xlviii. Includes books, articles, and dissertations on Shakespeare's life, work, and background.

70 WELLS, STANLEY, ed. *Shakespeare: Select Bibliographical Guides.* London, 1973.

Provides a series of bibliographical essays on topics such as "Shakespeare's Text," "The Early Comedies," "The English History Plays," "Shakespeare in the Theatre," etc. The most discussed plays are given chapters to themselves. Each essay provides a running commentary on important primary and secondary materials; a list of the writings discussed is appended to each chapter.

71 "Shakespeare-Bibliographie [date]." *Jahrbuch der Deutschen Shakespeare-Gesellschaft.* [*Shakespeare Jahrbuch*, 1925–] 1– (1864–).

An index for the first 99 vols., *Gesamtverzeichnis für die Bände 1–99 des Shakespeare-Jahrbuchs* (1964), lists all the current and special bibliographies published in the yearbook. From 1965 on there are two German yearbooks, one published at Heidelberg (*Deutsche Shakespeare-Gesellschaft West: Jahrbuch [year]*), and one at Weimar (*Shakespeare Jahrbuch* [vol. number continued, year]). From 1969 on the annual bibliography in the Heidelberg yearbook is restricted to editions, and to publications in German, while the Weimar yearbook still contains the bibliography in its traditional form with full international coverage, listing books, articles, dissertations, reviews of books, etc. on Shakespeare and his time.

72 "Shakespeare: An Annotated World Bibliography for [year]." *Shakespeare Quarterly*, 1– (1950—).

A comprehensive annotated annual bibliography of books, articles, dissertations, and reviews of books on Shakespeare and his age. Arranged as a classified list with categories such as "Annuals, Bibliographies, Festschriften, and Series," "Books," "Dissertations," "Articles," "Current Stage and Screen Productions," etc. Indexes to Shakespeare's works, to subjects, and to names.

73 "The Year's Contributions to Shakespeare Study." *Shakespeare Survey: An Annual Survey of Shakespearian Study and Production*, 1– (1948–).

Highly selective running commentaries on the year's work on Shakespeare, arranged under topics such as "Critical Studies," "Shakespeare's Life, Times, and Stage," "Textual Studies," etc.

For other Shakespeare bibliographies see entries **1** and **785**.
For references to printed library catalogues of major Shakespeare collections see entries **1185a** and **1209**.

74 O'DELL, STERG. *A Chronological List of Prose Fiction in English Printed in England and Other Countries 1475–1640.* Cambridge, Mass., 1954. Rptd., N. Y., 1969.

Arranged chronologically by year and within each year alphabetically by author, with anonymous works by title. Entries provide relatively full bibliographic citations, including format, and give STC number and locations of copies. Author-title index.

75 ESDAILE, ARUNDELL. *A List of English Tales and Prose Romances Printed Before 1740.* London, 1912. Rptd., N. Y., 1971.

Divided into two parts, one covering the period 1475–1642, the other 1643–1739. Each part is arranged alphabetically by author or, in the case of anonymous works, by title or catchword title. Locates copies; when no copy has been located, provides a reference to the source from which the citation was taken.

76 MISH, CHARLES C. *English Prose Fiction 1600–1700: A Chronological Checklist.* Charlottesville, Va., 1967.

A chronologically arranged list of the seventeenth-century materials in Esdaile, **75**, with a few deletions and additions. Locates copies by supplying STC numbers or citing booksellers' catalogues. Index of authors and, for anonymous works, titles or catchwords.

77 SOUTHERN, ALFRED C. *Elizabethan Recusant Prose, 1559–1582: A Historical and Critical Account of the Books of the Catholic Refugees Printed and Published Abroad and at Secret Presses in England Together with an Annotated Bibliography of the Same.* London, 1950.

Includes an extensive bibliography on pp. 367–517.

c. Restoration and Eighteenth Century

78 BOND, DONALD F. *The Age of Dryden.* Goldentree Bibliographies. N. Y., 1970.

Highly selective, elaborately classified, primary and secondary bibliography covering bibliographies, reference works, poetry, drama, prose, criticism, and fine arts, with additional lists covering aspects of the historical and cultural background. Subject and author indexes. Items of special importance asterisked.

79 BOND, DONALD F. *The Eighteenth Century.* Goldentree Bibliographies. N. Y., 1975.

Highly selective primary and secondary bibliography of the literature and cultural background of 18th century England. Includes bibliographies for about 100 authors, and additional lists covering subjects such as historical, social, cultural, and intellectual background, the fine arts, science, periodicals, history, biography, autobiography, etc. Subject and author indexes. Items of special importance are asterisked.

80 TOBIN, JAMES E. *Eighteenth Century English Literature and Its Cultural Background: A Bibliography.* N. Y., 1939. Rptd. N. Y., 1967.

Classified bibliography of selected primary and secondary materials. Pt. 1 covers "Historical Background," "Social Thought," "Memoirs," "Criticism," "Poetry," "Prose," "Journalism," "Drama," "Extra-National Relations," and "Further Bibliographical Aids." Pt. 2 contains bibliographies of 169 individual authors. Index of 18th century authors, 18th century journals, and modern editors.

81 CORDASCO FRANCESCO. *Eighteenth Century Bibliographies.* Metuchen, N. J., 1970.

A compilation of 12 bibliographic pamphlets originally published separately. Includes bibliographies on Smollett (secondary materials, 1770–1945), Richardson, Sterne (secondary materials, 1895–1946), Fielding (secondary materials, 1895–1946), Dibdin (primary materials), the 18th century novel (secondary materials), Godwin, Gibbon, Young, and Burke (all secondary materials), with an additional bibliography of primary and secondary materials on Smollett.

82 "The Eighteenth Century: A Current Bibliography for [year]." *Philological Quarterly,* 5– (1926–). [Title has varied] The bibliographies for 1925–1970 are reprinted in R. S. Crane, *et. al., English Literature 1660–1800,* vols. 1–2 (Princeton, N. J., 1950–52), vols. 3–4 (1962), and vols. 5–6 (1972). Vols 2, 4, and 6 have index of authors, editors, subjects, and reviewers. From 1970 the annual bibliography has been reprinted as a monograph, with an author index, by the University of Iowa Press.

Comprehensive annotated bibliography of books, articles, and reviews arranged in classified lists such as "Literary Studies" and "Individual Authors."

83 "Recent Studies in the Restoration and Eighteenth Century." *Studies in English Literature 1500–1900.* 1– (1961–).

Provides an annual running commentary on the year's work on Restoration and Eighteenth-Century literature. Highly selective; attempts to include only the most important scholarship.

84 "Some New Books." "Some Recent Articles," etc. [titles vary]. *The Johnsonian Newsletter,* 1– (1940–).

The quarterly issues can contain annotated lists and comment on recent Eighteenth-Century scholarship.

85 FOXON, D. F. *English Verse 1701–1750.* 2 vols. Cambridge, 1975.

A catalogue of separately printed English poetry published in the first half of the 18th century. Contains about 10,000 entries which supply full bibliographical data and information on first lines, subjects, and locations of copies. Vol. 2 provides indexes to subjects, first lines, printers, booksellers, and publication dates.

85a COHANE, CHRISTOPHER. *English Poetry, 1660–1800: A Guide to Information Sources.*

A selective annotated guide announced for publication by Gale Research Co. of Detroit, Mich.

86 STRATMAN, CARL J., *et. al. Restoration and Eighteenth Century Theatre Research: A Bibliographical Guide, 1900–1968.* Carbondale, Ill.,
1971.

Comprehensive bibliography of books, articles, and theses. About 80 %
annotated. Includes 6560 entries elaborately classified into 780 subject
headings including 432 headings for the names of actors, musicians, playwrights, scene painters, stage managers, etc. Very full index; play titles are
listed under author's name.

87 "Restoration and 18th Century Theatre Research for [year]." *Restoration and 18th Century Theatre Research,* 1– (1962–   ).

A comprehensive, annotated, annual bibliography of books, articles, and
theses arranged as a classified list with categories ordered alphabetically; the
categories include names of playwrights and others connected with the
stage, and other categories such as "acting," "opera," "religious drama," etc.;
index to scholars. Includes American dramatists and drama.

88 WOODWARD, G. L. and J. G. MCMANAWAY. *A Checklist of English
Plays, 1641–1700.* Chicago, 1945. *Supplement,* by Fredson Bowers,
Charlottesville, Va., 1949.

89 GENEST, JOHN, ed. *Some Account of the English Stage from the Restoration in 1660 to 1830.* 10 vols. Bath, 1832. Rptd. N.Y., 1965.

Notes on plays, playwrights, and actors arranged in rough chronological
order. Vol. 10 includes notes on the Irish stage, a list of corrections, and an
index of play titles and actors.

89a LINK, FREDERICK M. *English Drama, 1660–1800: A Guide to Infor-
tion Sources.*

A selective annotated guide announced for publication by Gale Research
Co. of Detroit, Mich.

90 MACMILLAN, DOUGALD, ed. *Drury Lane Calendar, 1747–1776.* Oxford, 1938.

Provides a calendar of performances and receipt records. Index of actors,
authors, and others connected with Drury Lane.

91 LENNEP, WILLIAM VAN, *et al.,* eds. *The London Stage, 1660–1800: A
Calendar of Plays, Entertainments and Afterpieces Together with
Casts, Box-Receipts and Contemporary Comment.* 11 vols. Carbon-
dale, Ill., 1960–68.

Compiled from playbills, newspapers, and theatrical diaries. The 11 volumes
are arranged in 5 parts covering the periods 1660–1700, 1700–1729, 1729–
1747, 1747–1776, and 1776–1800; each part has an introductory essay followed by a chronologically arranged list of performances with supplementary
information about costs, kinds of performance, box receipts, etc. Each

volume has an index to titles, dramatists, composers, and other persons connected with the theatre.

92 HIGHFILL, PHILIP, JR., *et al. A Biographical Dictionary of Actors, Actresses, Musicians, Dancers, Managers, and Other Stage Personnel in London, 1660–1800.* Vol. 1–   Carbondale, Ill., 1973–   . In progress.

A biographical dictionary projected to reach 12 vols. Intended to include, when finished, information on about 8,500 persons connected with the Restoration and Eighteenth-Century stage in practically any capacity, including freaks, concessionaires, dressers, tailors, carpenters, barbers, etc. Arranged alphabetically by name of biographee. Entries attempt to include the following: dates of birth, christening, marriage, death, and burial; information on spouses and children; first and last stage appearance; occupation and roles; salaries; pseudonyms; assessments of professional worth drawn from contemporary reviews; creative contributions; and involvement in notable events on the stage. Entries can also include a portrait, and each volume contains an appendix providing reproductions of maps, views of London, theatre sites, theatre exteriors and interiors, etc.

93 MCBURNEY, WILLIAM H. and CHARLENE M. TAYLOR. *English Prose Fiction, 1700–1800 in the University of Illinois Library.* Urbana, Ill., 1965.

A list of 966 items held in the University of Illinois library, including 18th century editions of pre-1700 works. Arranged alphabetically by author, with anonymous and pseudonymous works by title. Provides dates of printing and names of printers, size of edition, references to bibliographies which list or describe the item, and the Illinois library call number.

94 MCBURNEY, WILLIAM H. *A Check List of English Prose Fiction, 1700–1739.* Cambridge, Mass., 1960.

An annotated bibliography of primary materials arranged chronologically. Locates copies. Includes a separate list of dubious or unauthenticated titles, a bibliography, and an author-title index.

95 BEASLEY, JERRY C. *A Check List of Prose Fiction Published in England, 1740–1749.* Charlottesville, Va., 1972.

An annotated bibliography of primary materials attempting to be as complete as possible. Arrangement is chronological by year and alphabetical by author (or title for anonymous works) within each year; translations are listed separately for each year after the list of original fiction. Includes a bibliography and an author-title index.

96 BLOCK, ANDREW. *The English Novel, 1740–1850: A Catalogue Including Prose Romances, Short Stories, and Translations of Foreign Fiction.* New ed., London, 1961. Rptd., 1968.

A list of primary materials including romances, short stories, and novels, both written in or translated into English, arranged alphabetically by author (anonymous works by title). [For important evaluative comment and caution, see *TLS*, 21 April, 1961, p. 256.]

97 BLACK, FRANK G. *The Epistolary Novel in the Late Eighteenth Century: A Descriptive and Bibliographical Study.* Eugene, Or., 1940.

98 MAYO, ROBERT D. *The English Novel in the Magazines, 1740–1815. With a Catalogue of 1375 Magazine Novels and Novelettes.* Evanston, Ill., 1962.

99 McNUTT, DAN J. *The Eighteenth-Century Gothic Novel: An Annotated Bibliography of Criticism and Important Texts.* N.Y., 1974.

100 BONHEIM, HELMUT W. *The English Novel Before Richardson: A Checklist of Texts and Criticism to 1970.* Metuchen, N.J., 1971.

A classified bibliography of primary and secondary materials arranged in three parts: a list of 24 authors who wrote before 1740 with their narrative prose titles and relevant criticism; a list of anthologies and bibliographies; and a list of relevant secondary literature. Index of subject authors and modern scholars.

100a SHAWCROSS, JOHN T. *English Prose and Criticism, 1660–1800: A Guide to Information Sources.*

A selective annotated guide announced for publication by Gale Research Co. of Detroit, Mich.

101 DRAPER, JOHN W. *Eighteenth-Century English Aesthetics: A Bibliography.* Heidelberg, 1931. Rptd., Amsterdam, 1967; N.Y., 1968.

A classified annotated bibliography arranged in categories such as "General Works on Aesthetics," "Architecture and Gardening," "Literature and Drama," etc. Within these categories arrangement is alphabetical by author. No index. Supplements to the main bibliography have been published by R. D. Havens in *Modern Language Notes*, 47 (1932), 118–20, and by W. D. Templeman in *Modern Language Notes*, 30 (1933), 309–16.

d. Romantic Movement

102 FOGLE, RICHARD H. *Romantic Poets and Prose Writers.* Goldentree Bibliographies. N.Y., 1967.

Highly selective bibliography of primary and secondary materials covering historical background, critical surveys, bibliography, and 14 major poets and prose writers. Items of special importance are asterisked.

103 JORDAN, FRANK, JR. ed. *The English Romantic Poets: A Review of Research and Criticism.* 3rd ed. N.Y., 1972. The 1st ed. (1950) and 2nd ed. (1956) were edited by T. M. Raysor.

A selective, annotated bibliography of primary and secondary materials in essay form. Contains a chapter on the Romantic Movement background and individual bibliographic essays on Wordsworth, Coleridge, Byron, Shelley, and Keats.

104 HOUTCHENS, CAROLYN W. and LAWRENCE H. HOUTCHENS, eds. *The English Romantic Poets and Essayists: A Review of Research and Criticism.* N.Y., 1957. Rev. ed., 1966.

Selective, annotated bibliographies in essay form covering bibliographies, editions, biographies, and criticism for Blake, Campbell, De Quincy, Hazlitt, Hunt, Lamb, Landor, Moore, Scott, and Southey. The 2nd ed., greatly enlarged, includes a chapter on Carlyle. Index to Romantic authors and modern scholars.

105 BERNBAUM, ERNEST. *Guide Through the Romantic Movement.* N.Y., 1930. Rev. and enl. ed., N.Y., 1949.

Arranged as a series of essays followed by selective primary and secondary bibliographies with brief, sometimes critical annotations. Covers topics such as "The Pre-Romantic Movement," "The Romantic Movement," and 16 major authors. Very brief index of authors and topics.

106 "The Romantic Movement: A Selective and Critical Bibliography for [year]." *English Language Notes,* 3– (1965–). From 1937–1949 published in *ELH*; from 1950–1964 in *Philological Quarterly.* Bibliographies for the years 1936–1970 have been reprinted in *The Romantic Movement Bibliography 1936–1970.* 7 vols. Ed. DAVID B. ERDMAN, A. C. ELKINS, JR., and L. J. FORSTNER. Ann Arbor, Mich., 1973.

An annual, selective, extensively annotated bibliography of books, articles, and reviews arranged as a series of classified lists covering general materials and the literatures of England, France, Germany, Spain, and Portugal. For each country the entries are grouped under such subcategories as bibliography, general works, environment, criticism, and individual authors. Vol. 7 of the 1973 reprinting provides three indexes: (1) author-main entry-reviewer, (2) subject index to personal names, and (3) topics.

107 "Bibliography for July, 1950–June, 1951," *Keats-Shelley Journal,* 1– (1952–). Title has varied. Beginning with volume 17 (1968) the bibliography has been issued separately. Bibliographies appearing in the first 12 volumes have been reprinted in D. B. GREEN and E. G. WILSON, eds. *Keats, Shelley, Byron, Hunt, and Their Circles: A Bibliography: July 1, 1950–July 30, 1962.* Lincoln, Nebraska, 1964.

Comprehensive bibliography of books, reviews, articles, phonograph recordings, and significant references on Keats, Shelley, Byron, Hunt, and their circles. Index to Romantic authors and titles and to modern scholars.

108 "Recent Studies in Nineteenth-Century English Literature." *Studies in English Literature 1500–1900,* 1– (1961–).

Provides an annual running commentary on the year's work on the literature of the Romantic Movement and the Victorian Period. Highly selective; attempts to cover only the more important scholarship.

109 REIMAN, DONALD H., ed. *The Romantics Reviewed: Contemporary Reviews of British Romantic Writers.* In 3 parts: *Part A: The Lake Poets,* 2 vols.; *Part B: Byron and Regency Society Poets,* 5 vols.; *Part C: Shelley, Keats, and London Radical Writers,* 2 vols. N.Y., 1972.

Reproductions of contemporary British periodical reviews of major and some minor Romantic writers. Arrangement within each part is alphabetical by title of periodical and chronological for the reviews published in each periodical. Vol. 2 of *Part C* includes an index to authors reviewed.

110 WARD, WILLIAM, S. *Literary Reviews in British Periodicals 1798–1820: A Bibliography With a Supplementary List of General (Non-Review) Articles on Literary Subjects.* 2 vols. N.Y., 1972.

A checklist of about 16,000 reviews and 1,000 literary articles for the period 1798–1820 in England. The basic index is arranged alphabetically by author reviewed (with anonymous works reviewed under the heading *anonymous*); relevant review citations are given beneath each author's name and the particular title of the work reviewed. Includes 3 appendices: (1) citations to general (non-review) articles on authors and their works, (2) citations to general and genre criticism, and (3) citations to reviews of operas.

e. Victorian Period

111 BUCKLEY, JEROME H. *Victorian Poets and Prose Writers.* Goldentree Bibliographies. N.Y., 1966.

Highly selective bibliography of primary and secondary materials covering social and political background, intellectual and literary history, anthologies of Victorian poetry and prose, and 31 individual poets and essayists. Items of special importance are asterisked.

112 JUCHHOFF, RUDOLF. *Sammelkatalog der biographischen und literarkritischen Werke zu englischen Schriftstellern des 19. und 20. Jahrhunderts (1830–1958). Verzeichnis der Bestände in deutschen Bibliotheken.* Krefeld, [1959].

A union list of books, dissertations, and parts of books (but not periodical articles) on English writers of the 19th and 20th centuries contained in 66 major German libraries. Arrangement is alphabetical by author, and for each author materials are listed in three categories: (1) autobiographies, letters, etc., (2) bibliographies, and (3) secondary materials. Includes a number of items not listed in bibliographies attempting exhaustive treatment of 19th and 20th century English authors.

113 EHRSAM, THEODORE G., *et al. Bibliographies of Twelve Victorian Authors.* N.Y., 1936. Rptd. N.Y., 1968.

Very full primary and secondary bibliographies, including doctoral dissertations, master's theses, contemporary reviews, and unpublished secondary materials. Attempts to be complete to July, 1934. Covers Arnold, E. B. Browning, Clough, Fitzgerald, Hardy, Kipling, Morris, C. Rossetti, D. G. Rossetti, Stevenson, Swinburne, and Tennyson. Additional materials provided in Joseph G. Fucilla's "Bibliographies of Twelve Victorian Authors: A Supplement," *Modern Philology,* 37 (1939), 89–96.

114 ALTICK, RICHARD D. and WILLIAM R. MATTHEWS. *Guide to Doctoral Dissertations in Victorian Literature 1886–1958.* Urbana, Ill., 1960. Rptd. Westport, Conn., 1973.

Comprehensive classified bibliography arranged in 9 categories: general topics, themes and intellectual influences, fiction, drama, poetry, literary criticism, periodicals, foreign relations, and individual authors. Index to authors of dissertations.

115 MADDEN, LIONEL. *How to Find Out About the Victorian Period: A Guide to Sources of Information.* Oxford, 1970.

Arranged as a series of chapters covering topics such as "General Guides to Literature," "English Literature," "Philosophy," "Science," etc. Each chapter provides an annotated bibliography on the subject it covers, often with sample pages of the reference works illustrated. The brief subject index is useful for locating sources of information on specific topics such as "Baptists," "Costume," "Record Repositories," etc.

116 "Victorian Bibliography for [year]." *Victorian Studies,* 1– (1958–). From 1933–57 published in *Modern Philology.* Bibliographies for the years 1932–64 have been reprinted in 3 vols.: *Bibliographies of Studies in Victorian Literature for the Thirteen Years 1932–1944.* Ed. WILLIAM D. TEMPLEMAN. Urbana, Ill., 1945. Includes an index of Victorian authors. *Bibliographies of Studies in Victorian Literature for the Ten Years 1945–1954.* Ed. AUSTIN WRIGHT. Urbana, Ill., 1956. Includes an index of Victorian authors, modern scholars, and selected topics. *Bibliographies of Studies in Victorian Literature for the Ten Years 1955–1964.* Ed. ROBERT SLACK. Urbana, Ill., 1967. Includes an index of Victorian authors, modern scholars, and selected topics.

Comprehensive annual bibliography of books, articles, dissertations, and reviews arranged in four lists: "Bibliographical Material," "Economic, Educational, Political, Religious, and Social Environment," "The Arts, Movement of Ideas, and Literary Forms," and "Individual Authors."

117 "Recent Publications: A Selected List." *Victorian Newsletter,* 1– (1952–).

Highly selective, annotated, semi-annual bibliography of books, articles, and reviews of books on the Victorian background and on individual authors.

118 TOBIAS, RICHARD C. ed. *Victorian Poetry and Prose.* Morgantown, W. Virginia, 1974.

Originally intended as an annual supplement to Faverty's *Victorian Poets* and DeLaura's *Victorian Prose* volumes. However, future plans call for no more separate volumes of this kind; an annual survey of scholarship on Victorian poetry and prose non-fiction will be continued in *Victorian Poetry.*

119 FAVERTY, FREDERICK E., ed. *The Victorian Poets: A Guide to Research.* Cambridge, Mass., 1956. Rev. ed., 1968.

Selective, annotated bibliographies of primary and secondary materials in essay form. Essays on general materials and on Arnold, the Brownings, Clough, Fitzgerald, Swinburne, Tennyson, the Pre-Raphaelites, and later Victorian poets. The first edition is still sometimes valuable for useful materials deleted in the second. Index of Victorian authors and modern scholars.

120 TOBIAS, RICHARD C. "The Year's Work in Victorian Poetry: [year]." *Victorian Poetry,* 1–10 (1963–72), 12–   (1974–   ).

Highly selective annual surveys of scholarship on Victorian poetry and poetics. "Poetry" is treated very broadly and taken to include discussions of the literary and poetic qualities in Victorian prose non-fiction. In 1974 coverage of Victorian prose was expanded, the title was changed to "The Year's Work in Victorian Poetry and Prose," and the survey became the joint product of a number of scholars.

120a CONOLLY, LEONARD and PETER WEARING. *English Drama in the 19th Century: A Guide to Information Sources.*

A selective annotated guide announced for publication by Gale Research Co. of Detroit, Mich.

120b "Nineteenth-Century Theatre Research: A Bibliography for [year]." *Nineteenth Century Theatre Research.* 1–   (1973–   ).

An annual bibliography appearing in the September issue. Biannual issues can also include notes of research in progress.

121 SADLEIR, MICHAEL. *Nineteenth Century Fiction: A Bibliographical Record Based on his Own Collection.* 2 vols. Cambridge, 1951. Rptd. N.Y., 1969.

A descriptive bibliography of fiction printed in the Romantic and Victorian periods; 3761 entries based largely but not exclusively on Sadleir's collection. Vol. 1 provides a list of novels arranged alphabetically by author, followed by a list of "comparative scarcities," illustrations of bindings, and an index of titles; vol. 2 contains a list of yellow-back novels, decriptions of series editions, illustrations of bindings, and an index of titles and authors.

122 WATT, IAN. *The British Novel: Scott Through Hardy*. Goldentree Bibliographies. Northbrook, Ill., 1973.

Highly selective bibliography of primary and secondary materials on the Victorian novel and novelists. Arranged as a classified list with headings "Bibliographies, Journals, and Surveys of Scholarship," "Literary Histories," "General Critical Studies and Collections," "Special Topics," followed by primary and secondary bibliographies of 84 novelists arranged alphabetically by name. There is a brief list of names and dates of minor novelists and an index to scholars cited.

123 STEVENSON, LIONEL, ed. *Victorian Fiction: A Guide to Research*. Cambridge, Mass., 1964. [A revision is in progress.]

Selective, annotated bibliographies of primary and secondary materials in essay form. Chapters on the Brontës, Bulwer-Lytton, Collins, Dickens, Disraeli, Eliot, Gaskell, Gissing, Hardy, Kingsley, Meredith, Moore, Reade, Thackeray, and Trollope. Index of Victorian authors and modern scholars.

123a DEVRIES, DUANE. *English Fiction in the Nineteenth Century: A Guide to Information Sources*.

A selective annotated guide announced for publication by Gale Research Co. of Detroit, Mich.

124 DELAURA, DAVID, ed. *Victorian Prose: A Guide to Research*. N.Y., 1973.

A selective, extensively annotated bibliography of primary and secondary materials on non-fiction. Chapters devoted to general materials, the Oxford movement, Victorian churches, unbelievers, and the critics; other chapters given to Macaulay, the Carlyles, Newman, Mill, Ruskin, Arnold, and Pater. An elaborately sub-divided table of contents is supplemented by an index to authors, subjects, and scholars.

124a WILSON, HARRIS W. *English Prose and Criticism in the 19th Century: A Guide to Information Sources*.

A selective annotated guide announced for publication by Gale Research Co. of Detroit, Mich.

125 FREDEMAN, WILLIAM E. *Pre-Raphaelitism: A Bibliocritical Study*. Cambridge, Mass., 1965.

A very full guide and bibliography, including an historical survey of scholarship and an annotated bibliography in four parts: sources for bibliography and provenance; individual figures; the Pre-Raphaelite movement; and Pre-Raphaelite illustrations. Very full index. For inaccuracies in content see F. L. Fennel, "The Rossetti Collection at the Library of Congress," *Bulletin of Bibliography*, 30 (Jan–Mar., 1973), 132–136.

For other Victorian period bibliographies see **108**, **173**, **839** and **839a**.

f. Transition

126 LAUTERBACH, EDWARD S. and W. EUGENE DAVIS. *The Transitional Age: British Literature 1880–1920.* Troy, N. Y., 1973.

Part II (pp. 75–314) provides a selective list of primary and secondary bibliographies of about 200 authors, arranged alphabetically by author. There is an index of names and terms.

127 "Bibliography, News, and Notes." *English Literature in Transition,* 1– (1957–).

Provides both annotated and unannotated bibliographies of primary and secondary materials relating to major and minor literary figures who flourished between 1880 and 1920. Until 1963 included only writers of fiction; thereafter, includes poets and dramatists. Provides frequent bibliographic surveys of individual writers, often annotated or in abstract form. There is a separately published *ELT Index* for vols 1–15 (1957–1972).

g. Modern

128 MELLOWN, ELGIN W. *A Descriptive Catalogue of the Bibliographies of 20th Century British Writers.* Troy, N. Y., 1972.

An annotated bibliography of bibliographies arranged alphabetically by subject authors. Covers English and Irish authors born after 1840 who published the larger part of their work after 1890. Includes both primary and secondary bibliographies. Index of compilers. Revision in progress.

129 TEMPLE, RUTH Z. and MARTIN TUCKER. *Twentieth Century British Literature: A Reference Guide and Bibliography.* N. Y., 1968.

A selective bibliography of primary and secondary materials in two parts. Part I is an annotated bibliography of reference materials covering bibliographies of bibliography, sources of bibliography, journals, history, autobiographical material, collections of essays, criticism, drama, the novel, and poetry. Part II provides some 400 author bibliographies, mostly of primary materials. An index to authors mentioned in Part I is included in Part II.

130 TEMPLE, RUTH Z. and MARTIN TUCKER eds. *A Library of Literary Criticism: Modern British Literature.* 3 vols. N. Y., 1966. Vol. 4, *Suppl.,* 1975.

A collection of selected critical comment on over 400 modern British authors and their works. Arranged alphabetically by authors' names (vol. 1, A–G; vol. 2 H–P; and vol. 3, Q–Z). Selected critical comments are given beneath each name. Each volume also has an appendix which provides a primary bibliography for the authors covered in the volume; if a separately published bibliography on an author exists, that also is cited. Vol. 3 includes a cross-reference index to authors and an index to critics.

131 POWNALL, DAVID E. *Articles on Twentieth Century Literature: An Annotated Bibliography 1954–1970.* 7 vols. N. Y., 1973.

Based on but not limited to the annotated bibliographies appearing in *Twentieth Century Literature*. Includes scholarly and critical articles, but not reviews. When completely published will consist of two parts: (1) articles on authors as subjects (arranged with general articles on the author first, then articles on individual works), and (2) general literary topics (arranged around subject headings to be listed in the front matter of the final volume). The annotations are in the form of brief abstracts.

132 "Current Bibliography." *Twentieth Century Literature*, 1– (1955–   ).

An annotated bibliography of articles on 20th century writers of all countries. Arranged as a classified list of topics (e. g., "American Literature," "Literary Theory," "Modern Literature," etc.) and authors' names. The annotations are brief abstracts.

133 "Annual Review Number." *Journal of Modern Literature*, 1– (1971—   ).

An annual annotated bibliography and review of scholarly books, articles, and dissertations mostly on the "Modernist" period in literature about 1885 to 1950. Covers scholarship on Continental and other literature, but emphasis is largely on British and American writers. Arranged in two main divisions: "General Subjects" and "Individual Writers." The "General" section is sub-divided into (1) reference and bibliography, (2) literary history, (3) themes and movements, (4) regional, national, and ethnic literatures, (5) comparative studies, two or more authors, (6) criticism of modern literature generally, (7) criticism of fiction, (8) criticism of poetry, (9) criticism of drama, and (10) film as literature. The individual writers section is arranged alphabetically by name of author and includes scholarship on authors as early as Hardy and as recent as John Fowles. In both the "General" and the "Individual Writers" sections entries range from simple citations to briefly annotated entries to full-length reviews.

134 KRAWITZ, HENRY. *A Post-Symbolist Bibliography.* Metuchen, N. J., 1973.

A bibliography of secondary writings on 19 post-symbolist writers, including Yeats, Eliot, and Stevens. Arranged in four main parts: (1) international studies, (2) national studies, (3) comparative studies, and (4) individual authors. Includes an index to authors.

134a SKAGGS, CALVIN. *Contemporary Poetry in America and England, 1950–1970: A Guide to Information Sources.*

A selective annotated guide announced for publication by Gale Research Co. of Detroit, Mich.

135 "Modern Drama: A Selective Bibliography of Works Published in English." *Modern Drama*, 3–12, 17–   (1960–69, 74–   ).

Annual bibliography (not published 1970–73) of books and articles on modern drama of all countries. Classified arrangement under broad headings such as "Bibliography and Reference," "American and Canadian," "British and Irish," etc.

136 BUFKIN, ERNEST C. *The Twentieth-Century Novel in English: A Checklist*. Athens, Ga., 1967.

A bibliography of primary materials arranged alphabetically by author. Intends to provide a listing of the novels of all major and many minor writers who have published the entirety or the greater part of their work in the twentieth century regardless of nationality.

137 WILEY, PAUL L. *The British Novel: Conrad to the Present*. Golden-tree Bibliographies. Northbrook, Ill., 1973.

Highly selective bibliography of primary and secondary materials on British novelists from Conrad to about 1950. Arranged as a classified list with headings such as "Bibliographies," "Histories of the Novel," "Studies of Theory," etc., followed by primary and secondary bibliographies of 44 novelists arranged alphabetically by name. Index of scholars cited.

138 DRESCHER, HORST W. and BERND KAHRMANN. *The Contemporary English Novel: An Annotated Bibliography of Secondary Sources*. Frankfurt, 1972.

A selective annotated bibliography of secondary scholarship on the modern English novel; includes English and foreign language books, articles, and reviews, both scholarly and popular, mostly published since 1954. Arranged in three parts: bibliographies and reference works, general studies, and individual authors.

138a RICE, THOMAS JACKSON. *English Fiction, 1900–1950: A Guide to Information Sources*.

A selective annotated guide announced for publication by Gale Research Co., of Detroit, Mich.

138b ROSA, ALFRED F. and PAUL A. ESCHHOLZ. *Contemporary Fiction in America and England, 1950–1970: A Guide to Information Sources*.

A selective annotated guide announced for publication by Gale Research Co. of Detroit, Mich.

For other bibliographies of modern literature see entries **112, 174, 176–182,** and **202.**

3. Form

a. Poetry

139 CRUM, MARGARET. *First-Line Index of English Poetry 1500–1800 in Manuscripts of the Bodleian Library, Oxford.* 2 vols. Oxford, 1969.

Entries are arranged alphabetically by first line and give also author, when known, title, last line, and MS source. Variants are cited and cross references are made to other versions of the same poem. There is a second list of unidentified poems with beginning lacking which is arranged by last line. Five indexes: (1) Bodleian MSS, (2) authors, (3) names mentioned, (4) authors of works translated, paraphrased, or imitated, and (5) composers. Coverage includes poetry in or acquired by the Bodleian through April 1961.

140 DYSON, A. E., ed. *English Poetry: Select Bibliographical Guides.* London, 1971.

A collection of selective annotated primary and secondary bibliographies on 20 English poets from Chaucer to T. S. Eliot, each compiled by a specialist. Each bibliography is arranged as a running commentary on the scholarship, followed by a list of the works discussed. No index.

140a BEALE, WALTER H. *English Poetry to 1660: A Guide to Information Sources.*

A selective annotated guide announced for publication by Gale Research Co. of Detroit, Mich.

For other bibliographies of British poetry see entries 36–38, 57–60, 85, 102–104, 111, 118–120, 125, 134, 134a, 151, 155, 176, and 177.

b. Drama

141 HARBAGE, ALFRED. *Annals of English Drama, 975–1700: An Analytical Record of All Plays, Extant or Lost, Chronologically Arranged and Indexed.* Rev. by SAMUEL SCHOENBAUM. London 1964. *Annals of English Drama 975–1700: A Supplement to the Revised Edition,* Evanston, Ill., 1966. *A Second Supplement to the Revised Edition,* Evanston, Ill., 1970.

A chronological list of plays arranged first by centuries and then by year. Within each year entries are by author and give title, date or approximate dates of first performance, type of play, the auspices under which the play was acted, the date of the first edition, and the date of the most recent modern edition.

141a WELLS, STANLEY, ed. *English Drama (excluding Shakespeare): Select Bibliographical Guides.* London, 1975.

Provides a series of bibliographical essays on the English drama from the earliest times to the present. Individual chapters are devoted to major authors and to periods. There is an introductory chapter on "The Study of Drama," dealing with reference books, works of dramatic theory, etc.

142 STRATMAN, CARL J., ed. *Bibliography of English Printed Tragedy, 1565–1900.* Carbondale, Ill., 1966.

A list of 1483 extant tragedies whose first editions were printed between 1565 and 1900 in England, Scotland or Ireland and their adaptations, but omitting Shakespeare's work. Arrangement is alphabetical by author with the editions of each work in chronological order. Each entry gives the full title, imprint, pagination, library locations and some commentary. Anonyma are arranged by title. The appendix lists extant English tragedies in MS (1565–1900) with location and catalogue number.

143 ARNOTT, JAMES F. and JOHN W. ROBINSON. *English Theatrical Literature, 1559–1900: A Bibliography Incorporating Robert W. Lowe's "A Bibliographical Account of English Theatrical Literature" Published in 1888.* London, 1970.

A descriptive bibliography of materials relating to the theatre of the British Isles, including Ireland and Scotland, with brief entries for foreign editions. Arranged as a classified list of subject headings; within each heading arrangement is chronological by date of publication. Author index, short-title index, and index of places of publication (excluding London).

144 STRATMAN, CARL J. *Britain's Theatrical Periodicals, 1720–1967: A Bibliography.* N.Y., 1972. [A revised ed. of *British Dramatic Periodicals, 1720–1960,* N.Y., 1962.]

A list of 1235 periodicals primarily concerned with drama and printed in England, Scotland, or Ireland. Arranged chronologically. Locates copies in about 150 libraries in England and America. Extensive name-title index.

144a PENNINGER, F. ELAINE. *English Drama to 1660: A Guide to Information Sources.*

A selective annotated guide announced for publication by Gale Research Co. of Detroit, Mich.

For other bibliographies of British drama see entries **39, 61–65, 86–92, 120a, 120b, 135, 152, 153, 168, 178, 196, 197, 201,** and **202.**

c. Fiction

145 BELL, INGLIS F. and DONALD BAIRD. *The English Novel 1578–1956: A Checklist of Twentieth-Century Criticisms.* Denver, Colorado, 1958.

A selective secondary bibliography of criticism on English novels from the Renaissance to the 20th century. Arranged alphabetically by author; for each author the novels are listed alphabetically by title under the author's name, with citations to relevant criticism listed beneath each title.

146 PALMER, HELEN H. and ANNE JANE DYSON. *English Novel Explication: Criticisms to 1972.* Hamden, Conn., 1973.

A selective secondary bibliography of criticism on English novels from the Renaissance to the 20th century. Arranged alphabetically by author; for each author the novels are listed alphabetically by title under the author's name, with citations to relevant criticism listed beneath each title. Covers criticism written 1958–1972. Author-title index.

147 DYSON, A. E. ed. *The English Novel: Select Bibliographical Guides.* London, 1974.

Highly selective critically annotated bibliographies of primary and secondary materials on 20 English novelists from Bunyan to Joyce. Arranged as a series of bibliographical essays followed by short lists of references.

For other bibliographies of British fiction see entries **74–76, 93–99, 121–123a, 136–138b, 161, 169,** and **179.**

d. Prose

For references to bibliographies of British prose non-fiction see entries **40, 40a, 77, 104, 111, 118, 120, 124, 124a, 925–930, 935,** and **939–941.**

4. Special Topics

(Regional Literature, Ethnic Literature, etc.)

148 EAGER, ALAN R. *A Guide to Irish Bibliographical Material, Being a Bibliography of Irish Bibliographies and Some Sources of Information.* London, 1964.

A bibliography of more than 3,500 enumerative bibliographies in books, periodicals, and unpublished manuscripts, covering all aspects of Ireland. Separate author and subject indexes.

149 BROWN, STEPHEN J., S. J., ed. *A Guide to Books on Ireland. Part I. Prose Literature, Poetry, Music and Plays.* Dublin, 1912.

An annotated bibliography of books (pamphlets and articles are excluded) in English dealing with Irish literature; includes both primary and secondary materials. Separate author indexes to general collections, to prose, to poetry, to music, and to plays by title and by subject.

150 BROWN, STEPHEN J., S. J. *Ireland in Fiction: A Guide to Irish Novels, Tales, Romances, and Folklore.* "New Edition." Dublin, 1919, Rptd., Shannon, 1969.

An annotated bibliography of more than 1700 novels whose subjects involve Ireland. Arranged alphabetically by author; most entries also provide a synopsis of the plot. Appendixes provide a selective annotated bibliography of reference works, a list of Irish publishers and publishers' series, a classified list of Irish fiction, and a list of Irish fiction in periodicals.

150a HARMON, MAURICE. *Modern Irish Literature 1800–1967: A Reader's Guide.* Dublin, 1967.

Introduction to Irish writing in English in four parts. Bibliographies.

151 O'DONOGHUE, DAVID. *The Poets of Ireland: A Biographical Dictionary.* London, 1892.

Bio-bibliographies of Irish poets, including many who never published book-length works. Arranged alphabetically.

152 MIKHAIL, E. H. *A Bibliography of Modern Irish Drama 1899–1970.* Seattle, Wash., 1972.

A bibliography of scholarship and critical writing on Irish drama 1899–1970. The entries (some 600) are arranged under four headings: bibliographies, books, periodicals, and unpublished material, and alphabetically by author within each section. No index.

153 MIKHAIL, E. H. *Dissertations on Anglo-Irish Drama. A Bibliography of Studies 1870–1970.* London, 1973.

Lists more than 500 dissertations on 24 dramatists (Samuel Beckett, Dion Boucicault, Oliver Goldsmith, James Joyce, Sean O'Casey, Bernard Shaw, George Shiels, W. B. Yeats, *et al.*) written between 1870 and 1970 at a large number of universities in Great Britain, Ireland, the U.S., Germany, France, and Canada.

154 LLOYD, D. M. ed. *Reader's Guide to Scotland: A Bibliography.* London, 1968.

A selective classified bibliography with a section on "Language and Literature" that is elaborately subdivided in chronological and genre categories. Includes indexes of personal names and corporate authors.

154a *Annual Bibliography of Scottish Literature.* Annual supplement of *The Bibliotheck.* 1– (1956–).

Bibliography of books, reviews, essays and articles in the field of Scottish literature. Authors covered include Dunbar, Boswell, David Hume, Adam Smith, Smollett, Carlyle, Hogg, Scott, MacDiarmid. The index is restricted to authors who have a major entry devoted to them.

155 GEDDIE, WILLIAM. *A Bibliography of Middle Scots Poets, With an Introduction on the History of Their Reputations.* Edinburgh, 1912.

A critically annotated bibliography of primary and secondary materials (books, parts of books, and articles) on medieval Scottish poetry. Arranged with general works first, then bibliographies of individual authors.

156 HANDLEY TAYLOR, GEOFFREY. *Scottish Authors Today.* London, 1972.

A bibliographical dictionary arranged in four main lists of authors: (1) born in and residing in Scotland, (2) born in Scotland and residing in the United Kingdom, (3) born in Scotland and residing overseas, and (4) non-natives residing or working in Scotland. Entries give very brief biographical information and citations by number code to one or more of 63 biographical sources.

158 BALLINGER, JOHN and JAMES IFANO JONES. *Catalogue of Printed Literature in the Welsh Department.* Cardiff, 1898.

A catalogue of books in the Welsh Collection of the Cardiff Free Public Library. Arranged as an author list with some subject entries--e.g., "Literature," "Drama," etc. Appendix of bardic names, pseudonyms, etc.

159 JONES, BRYNMOR. *A Bibliography of Anglo-Welsh Literature 1900–1965.* Llandysul, 1970.

A bibliography of primary and secondary material related to Anglo-Welsh literature written between 1900 and 1965. Arranged in three main parts: (1) Anglo-Welsh Literature--a primary bibliography of anthologies and the works of individual writers with bibliographic details of their writings given under each writer's name, (2) Bibliographical and Critical Works--arranged under two sub-headings, "General" and "Individual Authors," and (3) Children's Stories. Includes regional and general indexes.

160 HANDLEY-TAYLOR, GEOFFREY. *Authors of Wales Today.* London, 1972.

A biographical dictionary arranged in four main lists of authors: (1) born in and residing in Wales, (2) born in Wales and residing in the United Kingdom, (3) born in Wales and residing overseas, and (4) non-natives residing or working in Wales. Entries give very brief biographical information and citations by number code to one or more of 60 biographical sources.

161 LECLAIRE, LUCIEN. *A General Analytical Bibliography of the Regional Novelists of the British Isles 1800–1950.* Paris, 1954.

A primary bibliography of British regional novelists arranged in three chronological divisions (1800–1830, 1830–1870, 1870–1950), each with a brief introduction followed by bibliographies of individual authors. Includes indexes of authors' names (1) alphabetically and (2) by region, and an index of place names.

163 LAURENTI, JOSEPH L. *Bibliografía de la Literatura Picaresca: Desde Sus Origenes hasta el Presente. A Bibliography of Picaresque Literature: From Its Origins to the Present.* Metuchen, N.J., 1973.

A primary and secondary bibliography of picaresque literature in Europe and America, including both original languages and translations. Arranged as a classified list under categories such as "Bibliografias," "Antologias," "Generalidades," and names of individual authors. Index of names.

164 HAVILAND, VIRGINIA. *Children's Literature: A Guide to Reference Sources.* Washington, D.C., 1966.

A very full annotated bibliography of reference sources arranged under eight main headings: (1) "History and Criticism," (2) "Authorship," (3) "Illustration," (4) "Bibliography," (5) "Books and Children," (6) "The Library and Children's Books," (7) "International Studies," and (8) "National Studies." Includes citations to books, theses, articles, pamphlets, newspapers, recordings, catalogues, etc. Author-title-subject index. May be supplemented by Ann Pellowski's *The World of Children's Literature,* N.Y., 1968, an annotated world bibliography of children's literature with author-title-subject index.

167 MODDER, MONTAGU FRANK. *The Jew in the Literature of England.* N.Y., 1939. Rptd., 1960.

An historical study of the Jew in English literature from the middle ages through the 19th century. Includes a primary and secondary bibliography on pp. 381–426 (covering background matters and with a special section titled "Nineteenth Century Fiction of Jewish Interest"), a glossary, and an author-subject index.

168 COLEMAN, EDWARD. *The Jew in English Drama.* N.Y., 1943.

An annotated bibliography with classified arrangement: "Bibliography," "General Works," "Collections," "Individual Plays" (arranged in 3 chronological periods). Separate author and title indexes.

169 ROSENBERG, EDGAR. *From Shylock to Svengali: Jewish Stereotypes in English Fiction.* Stanford, Calif., 1960.

A study of the image of the Jew in English fiction of the 19th century, with some preliminary attention to earlier literary history. Eleven appendixes, including a chronological list of English fiction on Jewish themes, bibliographical notes (the notes to chapter I supply additional references to studies of the Jew in English literature), and an author-title-subject index.

B. Bio-Bibliographies

170 MYERS, ROBIN, ed. *A Dictionary of Literature in the English Language from Chaucer to 1940.* 2 vols. London, 1970–71.

Bio-bibliographies of about 3,500 authors. Arrangement is alphabetical by author, with cross references for pseudonyms. Volume 2 is a title index.

171 RUSSELL, JOSIAH C. *Dictionary of Writers of Thirteenth Century England.* London, 1936. Rptd. N.Y., 1971.

A biographical dictionary of about 350 writers in English and Latin, articles arranged alphabetically by the Christian name. Primary and secondary bibliographies are given.

172 KUNITZ, STANLEY J. and HOWARD HAYCRAFT. *British Authors Before 1800: A Biographical Dictionary.* N.Y., 1952. Rptd., 1956.

Provides short biographies of 650 authors followed by very brief bibliographies of primary and secondary materials. Includes 200 pictures of authors.

173 KUNITZ, STANLEY J. and HOWARD HAYCRAFT. *British Authors of the Nineteenth Century.* N.Y., 1936. Rptd., 1955.

Provides short biographies of about 1000 Nineteenth-Century British authors, with very brief bibliographies of primary and secondary materials. Includes 350 pictures of authors.

174 KUNITZ, STANLEY J. and HOWARD HAYCRAFT. *Twentieth Century Authors: A Biographical Dictionary of Modern Literature.* N.Y., 1942. Rptd., 1950. *First Supplement,* by Stanley J. Kunitz and Vineta Colby, 1955.

Provides brief biographies of 1850 British and American authors (and authors of other countries whose work has been translated into English), followed by very short bibliographies of primary and secondary materials. Includes 1700 pictures of authors. The *First Supplement* contains 700 new bio-bibliographies and updates the biographies in the original volume.

175 MILLETT, FRED B. *Contemporary British Literature: A Critical Survey and 232 Author-bibliographies.* 3rd rev. and enlgd. ed. by John M. Manly and Edith Rickert. N.Y., 1935. Rptd., 1968.

Divided into three main sections: a critical survey, concise biographical sketches with primary and secondary bibliographies, and a select bibliography of contemporary social, political, and literary history.

176 MURPHY, ROSALIE and JAMES VINSON, eds. *Contemporary Poets of the English Language.* Chicago, 1970. 2nd ed. rev. N.Y., 1975.

Bio-bibliographies of contemporary poets of all countries. Each entry gives a very brief biography, including usually a current address, followed by a list of primary materials, followed by a brief comment by the author himself or by a signed critical note. List of anthologies published since 1960 that include contemporary poetry in English.

177 *International Who's Who in Poetry 1974–75.* 4th ed. [1st ed. pub. 1958.] Totowa, N.J., 1974.

About 3000 bio-bibliographies of living poets. Compiled from information supplied by biographees; arranged alphabetically by poet's name. Entries provide biographical data and information on publications. Pseudonyms are cross-referenced. Appendixes provide portraits of poets, and lists of poetry awards, poetry societies, poetry magazines, and poetry on records and tapes.

178 VINSON, JAMES, ed. *Contemporary Dramatists.* N.Y., 1973.

Bio-bibliographies of contemporary dramatists of England, America, and Canada. Entries give a brief biography, often including a current address, followed by a list of primary materials, and, sometimes, brief reference to some secondary works. Manuscript locations are often given. Entries also include comments by the dramatist himself and/or signed critical comments by others.

179 VINSON, JAMES, ed. *Contemporary Novelists.* N.Y., 1972.

Bio-bibliographies of contemporary novelists of all countries. Each entry gives a brief biography, including a current address, followed by a list of primary materials and signed critical comment(s).

180 *The Writers Directory 1974–76.* N.Y., 1973.

A biennial guide to contemporary writers of fiction, poetry, plays, and non-fiction in English throughout the world. The main list is arranged alphabetically by author. Entries give the writer's full name, pseudonym if any, information about his writings, a list of his publishers, his current address, and other biographical information, including citations (by code) to other sources of biographical and bibliographical information about the writer.

181 HARTE, BARBARA and CAROLYN RILEY. *200 Contemporary Authors: Bio-Bibliographies of Selected Leading Writers of Today with Critical and Personal Sidelights.* Detroit, 1969.

A compilation of biographical sketches, containing primary and secondary bibliographies for individuals of particular current interest. The sketches are revisions based upon the original entries in *Contemporary Authors.* Arrangement is alphabetical by subject author. The volume also contains a cumulated index to vols. 1–20 of *Contemporary Authors.*

182 *Contemporary Authors: A Bio-Bibliographical Guide to Current Authors and Their Works.* 1–   (1962–   ).

Now issued semi-annually with cumulative index to all preceding volumes. Entries provide brief biographical information and primary and secondary bibliographic materials. Includes living writers of all countries. Biographies of deceased authors or authors who have passed normal retirement age and have not recently published a book or indicated a work in progress are reprinted in *Contemporary Authors: Permanent Series,* 1–   (1975–   ); these volumes are indexed in the regular cumulating indexes of *Contemporary Authors.*

For bio-bibliographies of Irish authors see entry **151**.

C. Histories

1. General Histories

183 *The Oxford History of English Literature.* Oxford, 1945–   .
BENNETT, H. S. *Chaucer and the Fifteenth Century.* 1947. Corrected ed., 1948. Rptd.
CHAMBERS, E. K. *English Literature at the Close of the Middle Ages.* 1945.
LEWIS, C. S. *English Literature in the Sixteenth Century Excluding Drama.* 1954.
WILSON, FRANK P. and GEORGE K. HUNTER. *The English Drama, 1485–1585.* 1968.
BUSH, DOUGLAS. *English Literature in the Earlier Seventeenth Century, 1600–1660.* 1945. 2nd ed. rev., 1962.
SUTHERLAND, JAMES R. *English Literature of the Late Seventeenth Century.* 1969.
DOBRÉE, BONAMY. *English Literature in the Early Eighteenth Century, 1700–1740.* 1959.
RENWICK, WILLIAM L. *English Literature, 1789–1815.* 1963.
JACK, IAN R. *English Literature, 1815–1832.* 1963.
STEWART, J. I. M. *Eight Modern Writers.* 1963.
Other volumes are in preparation.

A multi-volume comprehensive history of English literature, with each volume prepared by a single specialist. Except for vol. 12 which treats only 8 writers, each volume provides extensive historical coverage of the literature and the literary background of the era treated. Chapters are devoted to background materials, groups of authors, and individual authors, and each volume also contains (1) a chronological table in parallel columns for public events and literary history, (2) extensive but selective annotated bibliographies of primary and secondary materials, and (3) an author-title-subject index.

184 WARD, ADOLPHUS W. and ALFRED R. WALLER, eds. *The Cambridge History of English Literature.* 14 vols. Cambridge, 1907–27. *Index,* 1927. Rptd. without bibliographies.

A very comprehensive multi-volume history of English literature from the beginnings to the end of the 19th century. Each chapter is written by a specialist and includes bibliographies. Unusually extensive coverage is given to all aspects of literature and related areas. Most chapters are now out of date, but for some minor figures and some areas supplementary to literature this history is still useful.

185 SAMPSON, GEORGE. *The Concise Cambridge History of English Literature, With Additional Chapters on the Literature of the United States* of *America and the Mid-Twentieth-Century of the English-Speaking World by R. C. Churchill*. 3rd ed. Cambridge, 1970. (Original ed., 1941.)

A short one-volume history based upon the *Cambridge History of English Literature*. One chapter is given to each of the areas covered by the *CHEL* volumes, and the presentations follow the organization and to some extent even the wording of the *CHEL*. The revisions are largely additions and changes to the last part of the book dealing with the modern period and the literature of the United States.

186 *The History of Literature in the English Language*. 11 vols. London, 1969– . [In progress]
The Middle Ages, ed. W. F. BOLTON.
English Poetry and Prose, 1540–1674, ed. C. RICKS.
English Drama to 1710, ed. C. RICKS.
Dryden to Johnson, ed. R. LONSDALE.
The Victorians, ed. A. POLLARD.
The Twentieth Century, ed. BERNARD BERGONZI.
American Literature, 1, ed. M. CUNLIFFE.
American Literature, 2, ed. M. CUNLIFFE.

A multi-volume history of English and American literature, each volume arranged as a series of essays on individual authors, groups of authors, literary movements, and other topics, each essay written by a specialist. The essays include documentation and selective primary and secondary bibliographies. Each volume includes a chronological table.

187 DOBRÉE, BONAMY, gen. ed. *Introductions to English Literature*. 5 vols. London, 1938–1966.
RENWICK, WILLIAM L. and HAROLD ORTON. *The Beginnings of English Literature to Skelton, 1509*. 3rd ed., 1966.
PINTO, VIVIAN DE S. *The English Renaissance, 1510–1688. With a Chapter on Literature and Music by Bruce Pattison*. 3rd ed., 1966.
DYSON, HENRY and JOHN BUTT. *Augustans and Romantics, 1689–1830*. 3rd ed., 1961.
BATHO, EDITH C. and BONAMY DOBRÉE. *The Victorians and After, 1830–1914*. 3rd ed., 1962.
DAICHES, DAVID. *The Present Age, After 1920*. 1958. Rptd., 1969.

A multi-volume general history of English literature. Each volume provides first a narrative account of the literature and its backgrounds, followed by a bibliography arranged under a series of subject headings such as "Poetry," "Philosophy," "Scottish Literature," etc. Within these classes, arrangement is by author, with lists of primary writings of each author followed by a brief commentary.

188 FORD, BORIS, ed. *Pelican Guides to English Literature.* 7 vols. London, 1954–1963.
The Age of Chaucer. 1954. Rev. ed. 1961
The Age of Shakespeare. 1955. Rev. ed. 1961.
From Donne to Marvell. 1956. Rev. ed. 1962.
From Dryden to Johnson. 1957. Rev. ed. 1962.
From Blake to Byron. 1957, Rev. ed. 1962.
From Dickens to Hardy. 1958. Rev. ed. 1963.
The Modern Age. 1961. 3rd ed. 1973.

A multi-volume historically arranged critical guide to English literature. Each chapter written by an individual critic. The contents of each volume are divided into four main parts: (1) a literary survey, (2) a survey of cultural background, (3) discussions of individual writers and other literary topics, and (4) an appendix giving further general secondary readings and brief primary and secondary bibliographies for individual authors.

189 BAUGH, ALBERT C., *et al. A Literary History of England.* N.Y., 1948. 2nd ed., rev., 1967. Published both as a single volume and as four parts.
The Middle Ages, KEMP MALONE and ALBERT C. BAUGH.
The Renaissance, TUCKER BROOKE and MATTHIAS A. SHAABER.
The Restoration and Eighteenth Century, GEORGE SHERBURN and DONALD F. BOND.
The Nineteenth Century and After, SAMUEL C. CHEW and RICHARD D. ALTICK.

Each part is arranged as a series of narrative chapters covering literary background, movements, groups of authors, and individual writers, with primary and secondary bibliographic materials supplied in footnotes. The revised edition retains essentially the same text as the original, but supplies bibliographic supplements which update the original bibliographic notes.

190 CRAIG, HARDIN, ed. *A History of English Literature.* N. Y. and London, 1950. Rptd., 2 vols, 1962, and thereafter rptd. in 4 vols:
Old and Middle English Literature, from the Beginnings to 1485, George K. Anderson.
The Literature of the English Renaissance, 1485–1660, HARDIN CRAIG.
The Literature of the Restoration and Eighteenth Century, 1660–1798, LOUIS I. BREDVOLD.
The Literature of the Nineteenth and Early Twentieth Centuries, 1798 to the First World War, JOSEPH W. BEACH.

Each volume is arranged as a series of narrative chapters covering background, groups of writers, etc. Includes bibliographies which have been revised and somewhat enlarged for later editions.

191 SCHIRMER, WALTER F. *Geschichte der englischen und amerikanischen Literatur von den Anfängen bis zur Gegenwart.* 5., unter Mitwirkung von Arno Esch neubearb. Aufl., Tübingen, 1968.

A single-volume history of English and American literature which focuses on literary development, not on the details of authors' lives. Within main chronological divisions the arrangement is primarily by genres. Includes extensive primary and secondary bibliographic materials in the form of lists at the beginnings of chapters and in footnotes. Author and anonymous title index.

192 STANDOP, EWALD and EDGAR MERTNER. *Englische Literaturgeschichte.* Heidelberg, 1967, verbess. 1971.

A single-volume history of English literature. Focus is generally upon the detailed analysis of a few representative works of each major literary figure treated. No secondary bibliography, but editions are cited in footnotes.

193 LEGOUIS, EMILE and LOUIS CAZAMIAN. *Histoire de la littérature anglaise.* Paris, 1924. Engl. transl.: *A History of English Literature.* 2 vols. London & N.Y., 1926–27. Rev. ed. 1964. Rptd.

A short history of English literature. Arranged as a continuous narrative, with footnotes providing biographical sketches of authors and citations to primary and secondary materials. The emphasis is less on individual authors than on broad literary movements and tendencies. Index to literary authors and to titles of anonymous works.

2. Period and Genre Histories

193a GREENFIELD, STANLEY B. *A Critical History of Old English Literature.* N.Y., 1965.

194 COURTHOPE, W. J. *A History of English Poetry.* 6 vols. London, 1895–1910. Rptd. N.Y., 1962.

In the absence of a modern comprehensive history of English poetry, Courthope's six-volume study is still of value, though it extends only as far as the romantic movement. Vol. 6 includes a cumulative index.

195 CHAMBERS, E. K. *The Medieval Stage.* 2 vols. Oxford 1903. Rptd., 1967.

A very extensive pioneer history of the medieval theatre, with sections on minstrelsy, folk drama, religious drama, and the interlude. Includes 24 appendixes and a subject index.

196 YOUNG, KARL. *The Drama of the Medieval Church.* 2 vols Oxford, 1933. Rptd., 1967.

An exceptionally full history of medieval church drama, including discussion of church liturgy and of plays associated with the nativity, the resurrection, the passion, and other biblical subjects and legends. Includes 4 appendixes, a selected bibliography, and title-name-subject index.

197 CRAIG, HARDIN. *English Religious Drama of the Middle Ages.* Oxford, 1955. Rptd., 1968.

A general history of English medieval religious drama-origins, range and extent of liturgical drama, the stage, play cycles, etc. Includes a selective bibliography and an index to titles, names, and play subjects.

198 CHAMBERS, E. K. *The Elizabethan Stage.* 4 vols. Oxford, 1923. Rptd. with corr. 1951.

A very full account of the Elizabethan stage, with individual sections devoted to the court, the control of the stage, the play-houses, the companies, plays and playwrights, and anonymous works. Includes 13 appendixes, and separate indexes to plays, persons, places, and subjects. Very extensive documentation. See also Beatrice White's *An Index ... to 'The Elizabethan Stage' ... by Sir Edmund Chambers,* Oxford, 1934.

199 CHAMBERS, E. K. *William Shakespeare: A Study of Facts and Problems.* 2 vols. Oxford, 1930.

A detailed examination of the evidences related to Shakespeare's life and work, including much information on the Elizabethan stage, actors' companies, etc., with brief bibliographies at the beginning of each chapter. Subject index, and also indexed by Beatrice White's *An Index ... to 'The Elizabethan Stage' ... by Sir Edmund Chambers,* Oxford, 1934.

200 BENTLEY, GERALD EADES. *The Jacobean and Caroline Stage.* 7 vols. Oxford, 1941–68. Rptd., 1966–68.

Continues the detailed history of the stage begun by Sir Edmund Chambers, 195, 198, up to 1642. Vols. 1–2 give a history of London dramatic companies and biographies of actors; vols. 3–5 deal with plays and playwrights in alphabetical order (entries give detailed information on MSS, secondary scholarship, Stationers' Register entries, contemporary references, etc.); vol. 6 treats theatre buildings; and vol. 7 contains a chronological table of Jacobean and Caroline theatrical affairs (pp. 16–128) and an exceptionally full analytical index (pp. 129–390).

201 NICOLL, ALLARDYCE. *A History of English Drama, 1660–1900.* Rev. ed. 6 vols. Cambridge, 1952–59. Vol. 6 titled: *A Short-Title Alphabetical Catalogue of Plays Produced or Printed in England from 1660 to 1900.*

Vol. 6 provides a list of plays produced or printed in England between 1660 and 1900, arranged alphabetically by title, including cross-referenced alternate titles. Entries give author's name; volume and page references to where the work is discussed in the historical volumes; earliest date either of production, publication, or submission to the Lord Chamberlain's office; and occasionally other information.

202 NICOLL, ALLARDYCE. *English Drama 1900–1930*. London, 1973.

Pp. 451–1048 provide an extensive hand-list of English plays for the period 1900–1930. Arrangement is alphabetical by author. Entries include the title, kind of drama (e. g., comedy, burlesque), date of licensing, date and place of first performances, name of sponsoring society, etc. For a detailed explanation of the entries, see pp. 451–470. Addenda to the list are given on pp. 1049–53.

203 BAKER, ERNEST A. *The History of the English Novel*. 10 vols. London, 1924–39. Vol. 11 by Lionel Stevenson, N. Y., 1967.

The first 10 volumes, although now largely out-of-date, are still sometimes useful; each volume includes bibliographic material and is separately indexed. Volume 11 continues the history to the present and includes its own selected reading lists and bibliography and an index.

204 STEVENSON, LIONEL. *The English Novel: A Panorama*. Boston, 1960. Rptd.

A survey of the history of the English novel from the beginnings to Joyce Cary which contains a selective bibliography of secondary scholarship and a "chronological summary" of primary writings in fiction.

D. Handbooks and Chronologies

205 HARVEY, SIR PAUL. *The Oxford Companion to English Literature*. 4th ed., rev. by Dorothy Eagle. Oxford, 1967.

A handbook of information on English literature of all periods. Arranged as a dictionary list, with entries for authors (brief biographies and lists of writings), titles (plot summaries, indications of theme, etc.), characters, literary terms, and allusions, with extensive cross referencing.

206 EAGLE, DOROTHY. *The Concise Oxford Dictionary of English Literature*. 2nd ed. London, 1970.

An abridgment of Harvey **205**, but with additional articles on literary periods and some general literary subjects. Includes, also, more articles on contemporary English and American writers.

207 GILLIE, CHRISTOPHER. *Longman Companion to English Literature*. London, 1972.

A handbook to English literature arranged in two main parts: (1) a series of essays on very broad topics – e. g., "Society and the Arts," "Religion, Philosophy, and Myth," "Poetic Form Since 1350," etc. – with subdivisions such as "The Sonnet," "The Short Poem," etc., and (2) an alphabetically arranged handbook providing entries for authors (including very brief bibliographies of secondary scholarship), titles (including plot summaries) character name identifications (and pronunciation guides), and subjects related to literature.

208 BARNHART, CLARENCE L. *The New Century Handbook of English Literature.* Rev. ed., N.Y., 1967.

A comprehensive handbook of British and Commonwealth literature. Arranged as a single-alphabet list of entries for authors (brief biographies and works), titles (brief summaries and critical comment), character names, literary terms, allusions, etc. Includes guides to the British pronunciations of names.

209 WRIGHT, ANDREW H. *A Reader's Guide to English & American Literature.* Glenview, Ill., 1970.

A selective list of major authors, works of biography and criticism on them, and works of reference in English, American and some foreign literatures. Divided into English and American literature sections. Both sections are subarranged: general works, period divisions, then works by and about individual authors. There is an index of English and American authors.

210 BROWNING, DAVID CLAYTON. *Everyman's Dictionary of Literary Biography: English and American.* 3rd ed. rev. with supplement. London, 1969.

A biographical dictionary of about 2,300 English and American authors, mostly literary, of which some 650 were not included in earlier editions. Biographies are arranged alphabetically by writers' names and include citations of important primary works. Another useful reference work in this series is William Freeman's *Everyman's Dictionary of Fictional Characters.* 3rd ed. rev. by Fred Urquhart. London, 1969.

211 *Annals of English Literature, 1475–1950: The Principal Publications of Each Year Together with an Alphabetical Index of Authors and Their Works.* 2nd ed. rev. by Robert W. Chapman. Oxford, 1961.

A chronological list of English literary works arranged by year, with parallel columns giving writers' birth and death dates and events in foreign countries (including literary publications) that are significant for English literature. Author-title index.

212 HARDWICK, MICHAEL. *A Literary Atlas and Gazetteer of the British Isles.* Detroit, Mich., 1973.

A literary atlas of Great Britain arranged according to the British National Grid reference system (an explanation of the system is given on p. 8); each map is marked with numbered dots locating places of literary significance; explanatory notes are provided in a series of numbered notes related to each map. Includes two indexes to personal names: (1) arranged alphabetically and (2) arranged geographically by English county.

213 ALLIBONE, S. A. *A Critical Dictionary of English Literature and British and American Authors Living and Deceased from the Earliest*

Accounts to the Latter Half of the Nineteenth Century. 3 vols. Philadelphia, Pa., 1858. *Supplement* by J. F. Kirk, Philadelphia, Pa., 1891. Rptd. with *Supplement*, Detroit, 1965.

A dictionary of British and American authors. Arranged alphabetically by author, with extensive subject indexes. Entries give biographical information, excerpts from critical reviews with their sources, etc. The supplement continues the coverage to 1880. Taken together, Allibone and the *Supplement* provide information on about 83,000 authors and cite some 433,000 titles. Useful particularly for information on minor figures.

214 *Chambers's Cyclopaedia of English Literature.* 3 vols. Rev. ed. by David Patrick and J. L. Geddie. London, 1922–38.

An encyclopedia of English literature arranged chronologically by historical periods and within each period by genres and other topics. Entries for individual writers supply biographical data, critical comment, bibliographies, selections from the author's work, and, often, a portrait. Still useful for its inclusion of very many minor literary figures and other writers on theology, travel, history, etc. Volume 3 includes a separate list of American authors and a general index to authors and titles.

215 CAMPBELL, OSCAR JAMES and EDWARD G. QUINN. *The Reader's Encyclopedia of Shakespeare.* N.Y., 1966. Published in England with the title *A Shakespeare Encyclopaedia*, London, 1966.

An encyclopedic handbook to Shakespeare's life, work, and times. Arranged alphabetically. Entries for Shakespeare's works provide detailed information on texts, dates, sources, stage history, plus plot summaries, critical comment, and bibliographies. Other entries cover all aspects of Shakespeare, the Elizabethan background, his reputation and influence, etc. Articles frequently provide citations to sources used. Genealogical tables and a chronology of events surrounding Shakespeare's life. Select bibliography on pp. 983–1014.

216 SCHABERT, INA, ed. *Shakespeare-Handbuch: Die Zeit – Der Mensch – Das Werk – Die Nachwelt. Unter Mitarbeit zahlreicher Fachwissenschaftler und mit einem Geleitwort von Wolfgang Clemen.* Stuttgart, 1972.

A comprehensive handbook and survey of scholarship on Shakespeare and his time. Extensive coverage of the Elizabethan background – political, intellectual, theatrical, etc. – and of Shakespeare's life, work, and subsequent reputation. The treatment ranges from the very broadest matters to minute points of textual history. Arranged under wide subject headings elaborately subdivided; includes a very detailed analytic table of contents. Extensive bibliographic materials are provided at the end of each major part, and also for each of Shakespeare's plays. Index to names.

For other handbooks and chronologies see entries **358–360, 447, 448,** and **453.**

E. Anthologies

Of the many anthologies of English literature, the following are some representative standard works:

217 *The Norton Anthology of English Literature.* Gen. ed. M. H. Abrams. 3rd ed. 2 vols. N. Y., 1974.

218 *The Oxford Anthology of English Literature.* Gen. eds. FRANK KERMODE and JOHN HOLLANDER. 2 [or 6] vols. N. Y. and London, 1973.

219 *British and American Classical Poems* in continuation of LUDWIG HERRIG'S 'Classical Authors' newly ed. and annotated by HORST MELLER and RUDOLF SÜHNEL. Braunschweig 1966.

220 *The Works of the English Poets from Chaucer to Cowper.* Ed ALEXANDER CHALMERS. 21 vols. London, 1810. Rptd. with bibl. note by B. FABIAN. Hildesheim, 1969–72.

220a *The Oxford Book of Medieval English Verse.* Ed. Kenneth and Celia Sisam. Oxford, 1970.

221 *Poetry of the English Renaissance, 1509–1660.* Ed. by J. WILLIAM HEBEL and HOYT H. HUDSON. N. Y., 1929. Rptd.

222 *Prose of the English Renaissance, Selected from Early Editions and Manuscripts.* Ed. by J. WILLIAM HEBEL et al. N. Y., 1952.

223 *Eighteenth Century Poetry and Prose.* Ed. by LOUIS I. BREDVOLD et al. 2nd ed. N. Y., 1956.

224 *A Collection of English Poems, 1680–1800.* Ed. RONALD SALMON CRANE. N. Y., 1932.

225 *English Romantic Poetry and Prose.* Ed. with essays and notes by Russell Noyes. Rev. ed. with expanded bibliographies. N. Y., 1967.

226 *English Romantic Writers.* Ed. DAVID PERKINS. N. Y., 1967.

227 *Poetry of the Victorian Era.* Ed JEROME H. BUCKLEY and G. B. WOODS. 3rd ed. Chicago, 1965.

228 *Victorian Literature: Poetry.* Ed. DONALD J. GRAY and G. B. TENNYSON. N. Y., 1976. *Victorian Literature: Prose.* Ed. G. B. TENNYSON and DONALD J. GRAY. N. Y., 1976.

II. American Literature

A. Bibliographical Materials

1. General

240 BLANCK, JACOB N. *Bibliography of American Literature*. New Haven, Conn., 1955– . [Vol. 6: Longstreet to Parsons, publ. 1974.]

A multi-volume selective (though very full) descriptive bibliography of work (primarily *belles lettres*) by American authors since the Revolution who had died by the end of 1930. Arrangement is alphabetical by author. Under author is given a full description of all first editions in chronological order, briefer descriptions of first appearences of other work in books (not in periodicals), variant issues or states, and subsequent editions if containing authorial changes. There is a selective list of bibliographical, biographical and critical works about each. Locations are given only for copies collated. Each volume has its own initials, pseudonyms and anonyms index.

241 JOHNSON, MERLE D. *American First Editions*. 4th ed. by Jacob Blanck. N.Y., 1942.

A bibliography of first editions of about 200 American authors with extensive descriptive notes and brief lists of secondary bibliographic and biographical materials. The coverage has varied from the 1st to the 4th editions, with some authors deleted and others added.

242 FOLEY, P. K. *American Authors, 1795–1895: A Bibliography of First and Notable Editions Chronologically Arranged With Notes*. Boston, 1897. Rptd., Waltham, Mass., 1969.

A series of lists of works (primarily monographic) by literary authors. Originally intended as an aid to the collector of American authors' editions. Arrangement is alphabetical by author, and chronological within each author category.

243 NILON, CHARLES H. *Bibliography of Bibliographies in American Literature*. N.Y., 1970.

An extensive list of monographic and serial bibliographies dealing with American literature. Arranged in four sections: (1) general bibliographies, (2) author bibliographies, (3) genre bibliographies, and (4) "ancilla." The author bibliographies are arranged alphabetically by subject author and under that alphabetically by author of the bibliography. Very full author-title-subject index.

For a survey of the state of reference bibliography in American literature see G. Thomas Tanselle, "The State of Reference Bibliography in American Literature," *Resources for American Literary Study* 1 (1971), 3–16, and John T. Flanagan, "American Literary Bibliography in the Twentieth Century," in Downs, **669**.

244 HAVLICE, PATRICIA P. *Index to American Author Bibliographies.* Metuchen, N. J., 1971.

A checklist of author bibliographies published in periodicals. Arranged as an alphabet list of authors' names with the bibliographies listed beneath each name. Includes an index of compilers. Supplements Nilon, **243**.

245 DAVIS, RICHARD B. *American Literature Through Bryant, 1585–1830.* Goldentree Bibliographies. N.Y., 1969.

Highly selective bibliography of primary and secondary materials, classified in categories such as "General Bibliography," "Periodicals and Newspapers," etc., followed by bibliographies covering the colonial period, the revolutionary period, and the early national period. In each period category, primary and secondary bibliographies of individual authors are given under headings "Major Figures" and "Lesser Figures." Author-subject index.

246 CLARK, HARRY HAYDEN. *American Literature: Poe Through Garland.* Goldentree Bibliographies. N. Y., 1971.

A selective bibliography of primary and secondary materials on American literature, 1830–1914, excluding the novel and the drama. (In fact, some material on novelists such as Hawthorne and Twain is included). Arranged as a classified list covering "Bibliographies and Reference Works," "Background," "Literary History," followed by primary and secondary bibliographies of 44 major and minor American literary figures. Author-subject index.

247 GOHDES, CLARENCE. *Bibliographical Guide to the Study of the Literature of the U.S.A.* 3rd ed. rev. and enl. Durham, N.C., 1970.

An annotated bibliography of monographic materials useful to the student of American literature and civilization. Arrangement is classified, with categories such as "General Bibliographies," "American History," etc., and including categories for periods, genres, and themes in American literature. Two indexes: author-editor-compiler index and subject index. The listing of individual authors' bibliographies which was added as an appendix to the 2nd ed. has been omitted.

247a LEARY, LEWIS. *American Literature: A Study and Research Guide.* N. Y., 1976.

A critically annotated guide to American literary scholarship with special emphasis on what has appeared in the last 40 years. Arranged as a series of chapters on such topics as "Literary Histories," "Language," "Bibliographical

Guides," "Biographical Sources," and a chapter providing primary and secondary bibliographies for 28 individual writers. Includes a chapter on the research paper and an index of authors.

248 SPILLER, ROBERT E. *et al. Literary History of the United States.* 4th ed. rev. 2 vols. N.Y., 1974. Original ed. in 3 vols., 1948; 2nd ed. 3 vols. in 2, 1953; *Bibliography Supplement,* 1959; 3rd ed., 2 vols., 1963; *Bibliography Supplement II,* 1972.

The 2nd vol. of the 4th ed. is the *Bibliography.* It is a corrected reprint of the original bibliography vol. of 1948, followed by reprints of the supplements of 1959 and 1972, with a general index to all three parts. The *Bibliography Supplement II* of 1972 covers the period 1958–1970, adds some pre-1958 items, and includes an additional 16 authors. Chapters are in essay form and arranged in the following categories: (1) Guides to Resources; (2) Bibliographies: Literature and Culture, Period and Type, Background, American Language, Folk Literature; (3) Bibliographies: Movements and Influences, Writing other than English, Regionalism and Local Color, Transcendentalism, etc.; and (4) Bibliographies: Individual Authors, each covering separate works, collected works, edited texts and reprints, biography and criticism, primary sources, and secondary materials. Subject (including subject author) and title index.

249 REES, ROBERT A. and EARL N. HARBERT. *Fifteen American Authors Before 1900.* Madison, Wis., 1971.

Selective annotated bibliographies in essay form of primary and secondary materials on Adams, Bryant, Cooper, Crane, Dickinson, Edwards, Franklin, Holmes, Howells, Irving, Longfellow, Lowell, Norris, Taylor, and Whittier, followed by two bibliographic essays titled "The Literature of the Old South" and "The Literature of the New South." Author-subject index.

250 WOODRESS, JAMES, ed. *Eight American Authors: A Review of Research and Criticism.* Rev. ed. N. Y., 1971. First ed., 1956, with bibliographical supplement by J. Chesley Mathews, 1963.

Selected but very full annotated bibliographies of primary and secondary materials on Poe, Thoreau, Emerson, Hawthorne, Melville, Whitman, James, and Twain. The bibliographies are in essay form under the headings "Bibliographies," "Editions," "Biography," and "Criticism," with some additional headings for some authors. Index to scholars cited.

251 LEARY, LEWIS. *Articles on American Literature, 1900–1950.* Durham, N.C., 1954. Rptd., 1970.

A bibliography of articles and significant reviews on American literature. Arrangement is classified, with categories such as "Almanacs, Annuals, and Giftbooks," "Prose," etc.; within each section arrangement is alphabetical by subject, including authors as subjects.

252 LEARY, LEWIS. *Articles on American Literature, 1950–1967*. Durham, N.C., 1970.

A bibliography of articles and significant reviews continuing Leary's earlier work for the period 1900–1950.

253 "Articles on American Literature Appearing in Current Periodicals." *American Literature*, 1– (1929–).

Quarterly non-critically annotated bibliography of recent articles (not reviews). Presently arranged in four major chronological categories (1607–1800, 1800–1870, 1870–1920, and 1920-present) followed by a list of articles on general topics. Each quarterly issue also includes a section titled "Brief Mention," which is a critically annotated list of recent books on American literature; there is also a separate list for "Research in Progress." The bibliographies of articles for the period 1929–1967 have been collected and republished by Lewis Leary, **251**, **252**.

254 MARSHALL, THOMAS F. *Analytical Index to American Literature, Vols. 1–30 (1929–1959)*. Durham, N.C., 1963.

An index to the first 30 years of *American Literature*. Divided into two parts: authors-subjects and reviews.

254a *Resources for American Literary Study*. 1– (1971–).

Published semiannually. Individual issues can include (1) annotated checklists of critical and bibliographical scholarship on the significant works of major authors or the total works of minor figures, (2) evaluative bibliographical essays on major authors, genres, or trends, (3) catalogues of research materials in archives and libraries, (4) and other related matters such as newly edited materials, etc.

255 *American Literary Scholarship: An Annual [1963–]*. 1965– .

An annual selective running commentary on the year's work in American literary scholarship. Covers books, articles, and dissertations. Arranged as a series of essays on topics as narrow as individual authors and as broad as "Nineteenth Century Fiction," "Drama," and the like. Index of authors and scholars. Beginning with the volume published in 1975, there is a final chapter included on foreign (French, German, Italian, Japanese, and Scandinavian) contributions to American literary scholarship.

256 *American Literature Abstracts: A Review of Current Scholarship in American Literature*. 1–5 (1967–1972).

Abstracts of articles arranged in four literary periods and, within each period, alphabetically by author. The article abstracts are followed by a "Book Review Consensus" which provides a survey of reviewers' opinions of selected recent books on topics in American literature.

257 "Articles on American Studies [1954–73]." *American Quarterly*, 7–25 (1955–75).

A selective annual bibliography of articles on all aspects of American studies. Arrangement is classified and includes categories such as "Language" and "Literature," "Folklore," "Mass Culture," etc., and separate bibliographies titled "Writings on the Theory and Teaching of American Studies" and on "American Studies Dissertations." With the August, 1975, issue, the "Articles on American Studies" bibliography was terminated, and in its place appears a series of bibliographic and analytic articles on various aspects of American studies – e. g., "Film and American Studies," "Quantitative American Studies," etc. The bibliographies for 1954–68 have been cumulated in *Articles in American Studies 1954–1968*, 2 vols., Ann Arbor, Mich., 1973.

258 "Deutsche amerikanistische Veröffentlichungen [date]." *Jahrbuch für Amerikastudien*. 1–18 (1956–73). Continued as *Amerikastudien/American Studies*. 19–   (1974–   ).

Now published twice a year. *Amerikastudien/American Studies* presents articles on language and literature and on the cultural, social and political history of the U. S. It contains a review section, bibliographical essays, review articles and special bibliographies at irregular intervals, as well as the annual bibliography of publications in American studies from Austria, the German Democratic Republic, the Federal Republic, and Switzerland in the fall numbers.

260 WOODRESS, JAMES. *Dissertations in American Literature 1891–1966*. 3rd ed., rev. Durham, N.C., 1968.

A list of 4700 dissertations from all countries. Arranged as an alphabetical list of subjects; first individual author subjects, then general topics such as "Civil War," "Drama," "Fine Arts," "Foreign Relations," "Negro," "Religion," etc. Author index.

261 HOWARD, PATSY C. *Theses in American Literature 1896–1971*. Ann Arbor, Mich., 1973.

A bibliography of unpublished baccalaureate and masters' theses. Arranged alphabetically by names of American literary figures, with relevant theses listed alphabetically by author beneath each name. Separate indexes for subjects and thesis authors.

262 "American Studies Dissertations [1956–   ]." *American Quarterly*, 9–   (1957–   ).

An annual checklist of dissertations on all aspects of American studies. Arrangement is classified, including a category "Literature," and within each category dissertations are listed under the headings "New Listings" (work in progress), "Completed," and "Withdrawn" (dissertation project abandoned).

For references to other American literature bibliographies see entries **2, 3, 11–13, 15–19, 191, 316–319** and **653**.

2. Period

a. 1585–1830

263 JANTZ, HAROLD S. "Bibliography of Early New England Verse" in his *The First Century of New England Verse*. Worcester, Mass., 1944; rptd. N.Y., 1962, pp. 175–292.

A very full list of poetry, printed or in MS, by New England writers born no later than the 1670's. Anonymous verse is listed chronologically to 1700. Arrangement is alphabetical by author with some biographical material provided. The anonyma is at the end of the list.

264 LEMAY, J. A. LEO. *A Calendar of American Poetry in the Colonial Newspapers and Magazines and in Major English Magazines Through 1765*. Worcester, Mass., 1972.

An annotated list arranged chronologically. Each entry gives place and date of publication, first line of the poem, title of the poem, the number of lines, the author or pseudonym, and notes on the author, on reprintings, etc. Includes 4 indexes: (1) first line index, (2) name, pseudonym, and title index, (3) subject and genre index, and (4) periodical title index.

265 WEGELIN, OSCAR. *Early American Poetry: A Compilation of the Titles of Volumes of Verse and Broadsides by Writers Born or Residing in North America North of the Mexican Border*. 2nd ed., rev. and enl. 2 vols. N.Y., 1930. Rptd., 1965.

A descriptive bibliography arranged in two main lists, one for the period 1650–1799 and another for the period 1800–1820. Within each list, arrangement is alphabetical by author, followed by anonymous works by title. Entries give full description of the title page statement, format, and some library locations.

266 STODDARD, ROGER E. *A Catalogue of Books and Pamphlets Unrecorded in Oscar Wegelin's Early American Poetry 1650–1820*. Providence, R. I., 1969.

A single-alphabet author-short title list of 261 works not recorded in Wegelin **265**, with occasional annotations and correction of Wegelin's entries. Locates copies.

267 WEGELIN, OSCAR. *Early American Plays 1714–1830: A Compilation of the Titles of Plays and Dramatic Poems Written by Authors Born in or Residing in North America Previous to 1830*. 2nd ed. rev. N.Y., 1905. Rptd., N.Y., 1968. Originally published N.Y., 1900.

A bibliography of primary materials arranged in three lists: (1) anonymous plays alphabetically by title, (2) plays alphabetically by author, and (3) "Plays in MS." Many of the entries give title, title-page information, format, the number of pages, and a biographical sketch of the author. Index to titles of published plays.

268 HILL, FRANK P. *American Plays Printed 1714–1830: A Bibliographical Record.* Stanford, Washington, 1934. Rptd. N.Y., 1968.

Arranged as an author list (anonymous works by title). Based on Wegelin, 267, supplemented by a 1918 typescript list of plays in the collection of F. W. Atkinson. Entries give author's name and dates, titles of play, date of publication, format, and locations of copies in 10 American libraries. Includes a title index and a chronology.

269 WEGELIN, OSCAR. *Early American Fiction 1774–1830: A Compilation of the Titles of Works of Fiction, by Writers Born or Residing in North America, North of the Mexican Border and Printed Previous to 1831.* 3rd ed. N.Y., 1929. Rptd., Gloucester, Mass., 1963.

A primary bibliography arranged in three lists: (1) anonymous fiction alphabetically by title, (2) fiction alphabetically by author, and (3) addenda. Title index to works which originally appeared anonymously.

270 WRIGHT, LYLE H. *American Fiction 1774–1850: A Contribution Toward a Bibliography.* San Marino, Calif., 1939. 2nd rev. ed. 1969.

A checklist of fictitious narratives of all kinds (novels, tales, fictitious biographies, etc.). Arranged alphabetically by author (or title for anonymous works). Entries give some locations of copies.

271 "Seventeenth Century Americana." *Seventeenth Century News,* 1– (1942–).

Quarterly issues often contain abstracts of selected recent articles and dissertations on Seventeenth Century American authors and other literary subjects. Arrangement varies.

For another bibliography of early American literature see entry 320.

b. 1830–1875

272 WRIGHT, LYLE H. *American Fiction 1851–1875: A Contribution Toward a Bibliography.* San Marino, Calif., 1957. Rptd. with additions and corrections, 1965.

A checklist of 2,813 fictitious narratives of all kinds; continues Wright 270.

273 GROSS, THEODORE L. and STANLEY WERTHEIM. *Hawthorne, Melville, Stephen Crane: A Critical Bibliography.* N.Y., 1971.

Highly selective critically annotated bibliographies of primary and secondary materials. The bibliographies of each author are followed by an author-editor-compiler list of the items annotated in the bibliography.

c. 1875–1900

274 U.S. Copyright Office. *Dramatic Compositions Copyrighted in the United States, 1870–1916.* 2 vols. Washington, D. C., 1918. Rptd. N.Y., 1970.

A title list of about 60,000 plays submitted for copyright between 1817 and 1916. Lists plays both published and in manuscript. Author-editor-translator-pseudonym index.

275 WRIGHT, LYLE H. *American Fiction 1876–1900: A Contribution Toward a Bibliography.* San Marino, Calif., 1966.

A checklist of fictitious narratives of all kinds; continues Wright 270, 272.

276 EICHELBERGER, CLAYTON L., *et al. A Guide to Critical Reviews of United States Fiction, 1870–1910.* Metuchen, N. J., 1971. *Supplement,* 1974.

A selective bibliography of reviews of American fiction 1870–1910 arranged as an alphabetical list of the fiction writers' names; under each name are listed the titles of the writer's works and, beneath each title, citations to reviews. An appendix gives titles of anonymous works with review citations beneath each title. There is an index of titles. The *Supplement* adds some 9000 additional citations.

277 *American Literary Realism 1870–1910.* 1– (1967–).

The quarterly issues frequently include primary and secondary annotated bibliographies and other bibliographical studies of American literary figures who flourished in the period 1870–1910.

d. 1900–present

278 JONES, HOWARD M. and RICHARD M. LUDWIG. *Guide to American Literature and Its Backgrounds Since 1890.* 4th ed., rev. Cambridge, Mass., 1972.

A highly selective guide to the primary and secondary materials of modern American literature. Includes lists of readings on historical background and literary history, an outline of historical events, an annotated list of magazines, and a chronologically arranged sequence of 52 brief reading lists of primary materials covering the development of American literature from 1890, each with a short historical introduction.

279 BRYER, JACKSON, ed. *Sixteen Modern American Authors: A Survey of Research and Criticism.* Rev. and enl. ed. Durham, N.C., 1974. (Earlier ed., 1969, titled *Fifteen Modern American Authors,* without bibliography of William Carlos Williams.)

Selective annotated bibliographies of primary and secondary materials covering Anderson, Cather, H. Crane, Dreiser, Eliot, Faulkner, Fitzgerald, Frost, Hemingway, O'Neill, Pound, Robinson, Steinbeck, Stevens, Williams, and Wolfe, each divided into 5 parts: bibliography, editions, manuscripts and letters, biography, and criticism. Index of authors (titles indexed under authors' names) and scholars.

280 CURLEY, DOROTHY NYREN, MAURICE KRAMER and ELAINE FIALKA KRAMER, eds. *A Library of Literary Criticism: Modern American Literature*. 4th ed. 3 vols. N.Y., 1969.

A collection of critical comments on modern American writers and their works. Arranged alphabetically by name of author; beneath each author's name are given selected excerpts from reviews and critical writings about him with citations to the source of each excerpt. Includes an index to critics.

281 IRISH, WYNOT R. *The Modern American Muse: A Complete Bibliography of American Verse, 1900–1925*. Syracuse, N.Y., 1950.

A bibliography of 6,906 books of poetry arranged in twenty-five annual lists, each list arranged alphabetically by author. Entries give title, size of volume, pagination, illustrations, year, publisher or place of publication, and the LC order number when available. No index.

282 ZULAUF, SANDER and IRWIN H. WEISER. *Index of American Periodical Verse [year]*. Metuchen, N.J., 1973– .

An annual index to American poetry published in periodicals. The most recent index (published in 1975 and covering the year 1973) includes references to more than 170 periodicals publishing poetry written by some 3600 poets. Arranged alphabetically by name of poet or translator. Includes a list of periodicals indexed and separate author and title indexes.

283 TATE, ALLEN. *Sixty American Poets, 1896–1944, Selected with Preface and Critical Notes*. Rev. ed. Washington, D.C., 1954.

A brief checklist of some primary and secondary materials including translations and recordings. Locates copies of items not in the Library of Congress.

284 MALKOFF, KARL. *Crowell's Handbook to Contemporary American Poetry*. N.Y., 1973.

A critical handbook to American poetry after 1940. The introduction gives a general historical account of the development of major schools and movements in modern American poetry. The handbook itself is an alphabetically arranged series of entries for about 70 individual poets; each entry pro vides a brief biographical note, primary and secondary bibliographical information, and a critical analysis of the poet's work and his relationship to the various groups and movements in modern American poetry such as the Beats, the Deep Imagists, the Black Aestheticists, etc.

284a WHITE, WILLIAM. *American Poetry, 1900–1950: A Guide to Information Sources.*

A selective annotated guide announced for publication by Gale Research Co. of Detroit, Mich.

284b HURLEY, PAUL. *American Drama, 1900–1970: A Guide to Information Sources.*

A selective annotated guide announced for publication by Gale Research Co. of Detroit, Mich.

285 NEVIUS, BLAKE. *The American Novel: Sinclair Lewis to the Present.* Goldentree Bibliography. N.Y., 1970.

A highly selective classified list of primary and secondary material including listings for 48 individual novelists. Some brief critical annotation of secondary material. Author-subject index.

286 WOODRESS, JAMES. *American Fiction 1900–1950: A Guide to Information Sources.* Detroit, Mich., 1974.

An annotated bibliographical guide to sources of information on selected modern American fiction writers. Arranged in two main parts: (1) general bibliography, covering both general background and reference material and specialized source material, and (2) a series of bibliographical essays on 44 individual authors, arranged alphabetically by name of author, including both primary and secondary materials published through 1972. This is the first in a projected 26 volume series titled *American Literature, English Literature, and World Literatures in English: An Information Guide Series* to be published by Gale Research Co.

For other bibliographies of modern American literature see entries **131, 134a, 174,** and **176–180.**

3. Form

a. Poetry

286a SLOTE, BERNICE. *American Poetry to 1900: A Guide to Information Sources.*

A selective annotated guide announced for publication by Gale Research Co. of Detroit, Mich.

For bibliographies of American poetry see entries **176, 177, 263–266, 281–284a, 302, 305, 313,** and **314.**

b. Drama

287 LONG, E. HUDSON. *American Drama from Its Beginnings to the Present.* Goldentree Bibliographies. N. Y., 1970.

A highly selective classified list of primary and secondary material. Some brief critical annotation of secondary material. Asterisks mark particularly important work. Index to scholar-critics.

288 PALMER, HELEN H. and JANE A. DYSON. *American Drama Criticism: Interpretations, 1890–1965 Inclusive, of American Drama Since the First Play Produced in America.* Hamden, Conn., 1967. *Supplement I: To January, 1969,* 1970. *Supplement II,* 1976.

A bibliography of secondary materials on American dramatists. Arranged alphabetically by author, with critical materials arranged under the title of each play by that author. Author-title index.

289 GOHDES, CLARENCE L. *Literature and Theatre of the States and Regions of the U.S.A.: An Historical Bibliography.* Durham, N.C., 1967.

A bibliography of secondary materials on American theatre arranged geographically by state or region and within those categories by cities. Appendixes on Western theatre and on regionalism.

290 RYAN, PAT. *American Drama Bibliography: A Checklist of Publications in English.* Ft. Wayne, Indiana, 1969.

A classified bibliography with categories like "History and Reference" and "General Background," followed by bibliographies of secondary materials on individual American dramatists from colonial times to the present.

291 STRATMAN, CARL J. *Bibliography of the American Theatre, Excluding New York City.* Chicago, 1965.

A bibliography of secondary materials on all aspects of American theatre. Includes theses and dissertations. Some items are annotated; library locations are given for books. Arrangement is by geographical areas, with cities listed under state names, and materials arranged chronologically under city names. Includes an author-subject index.

292 STRATMAN, CARL J. *American Theatrical Periodicals, 1798–1967: A Bibliographical Guide.* Durham, N.C., 1970.

A list of about 685 serials (all but 85 located). Arranged chronologically by year of first publication between 1798 and 1967. Within each group the arrangement is alphabetical by title. Each entry gives the title, the editors, city of issuance, publisher, number of volumes, inclusive dates, title changes, frequency, library locations with annotations on the extent of holdings. There are addenda for 1839–1946 and a list of references. Charts are provided to illustrate the publication spans of the periodicals. Index of names, places, titles and subjects.

292a MARSHALL, THOMAS F., III. *American Drama to 1900: A Guide to Information Sources.*

A selective annotated guide announced for publication by Gale Research Co. of Detroit, Mich.

For other American drama bibliographies see entries **87, 135, 178, 267, 268, 274, 284b, 307,** and **1216.**

c. Fiction

293 HOLMAN, C. HUGH. *The American Novel Through Henry James.* Goldentree Bibliography. N.Y., 1966.

A selective bibliography of primary and secondary materials classified into "Bibliographies," "Reference Works," "American Literary History," "American Publishing and Bookselling," "The Novel as Form," "Histories of the American Novel," "Special Studies of the American Novel" (including various period and genre studies), "Collections of Studies of the American Novel," and primary and secondary bibliographies of 42 major and lesser American novelists. Author-subject index.

294 NEVIUS, BLAKE. *The American Novel: Sinclair Lewis to the Present.* Goldentree Bibliography. N.Y., 1970.

A selective bibliography of primary and secondary materials classified under "Bibliographies," "Reference Works," "Special Studies of the American Novel," "Collections of Studies of the American Novel," and followed by primary and secondary bibliographies of 48 contemporary novelists. Author-subject index.

295 GERSTENBERGER, DONNA L. and GEORGE HENDRICK. *The American Novel, 1789–1959: A Checklist of Twentieth-Century Criticism.* Denver, 1961. Vol. II, *The American Novel: A Checklist of Twentieth Century Criticism of Novels Written since 1789: Criticism Written, 1960–1968.* Chicago, 1970.

A selective checklist of secondary materials including both general studies and commentaries on individual authors. The materials dealing with individual authors are arranged alphabetically by author with the titles of the novels given beneath each author's name and the critical citations beneath each novel title. The general materials are arranged by literary period.

296 KIRBY, DAVID K. *American Fiction to 1900: A Guide to Information Sources.* Detroit, Mich., 1975.

An annotated guide to primary and secondary materials for the study of American fiction before the 20th century. Arranged in two main parts: (1) "General Aids" including both reference works and general critical studies and (2) 41 individual author bibliographies, each sub-arranged under such headings as "Principal Works," "Letters," "Critical Studies," etc. Author-title index.

For other bibliographies of American fiction see entries **136, 138b, 179, 269, 270, 273, 286, 301, 309a,** and **323.**

d. Prose

For bibliographies of American prose non-fiction see entries **931, 934, 936–938,** and **942–943.**

4. Special Topics (Regional Literature, Ethnic Literature, etc.)

297 Coan, Otis W. and Richard G. Lillard. *America in Fiction: An Annotated List of Novels That Interpret Aspects of Life in the United States, Canada, and Mexico.* 5th ed. Palo Alto, Calif., 1967.

An annotated bibliography of novels, volumes of short stories, and collections of folklore dealing with American civilization. Arranged in classified lists under broad headings such as "Pioneering," "Industrial America," "Minority Ethnic Groups," etc., each elaborately subclassified. Entries provide descriptive annotations. Includes an index of authors.

298 Bernard, Harry. *Le Roman Régionaliste aux États-Unis, 1913–1940.* Montréal, 1949.

A general study of regional fiction in America. Arranged geographically, with chapters on the South, the Mid West, etc. Includes plot summaries, critical comment, and lists of fiction at the end of each chapter. The short reference list at the end of the book includes unpublished dissertations.

299 Rubin, Louis D., Jr., ed. *A Bibliographical Guide to the Study of Southern Literature. With an Appendix Containing Sixty-Eight Additional Writers of the Colonial South.* Baton Rouge, 1969.

A series of selective lists of critical and scholarly commentary on various aspects of literary activity in the south and on individual authors. Each subject has a headnote putting the material into a context. For individual authors it frequently provides critical, biographical and bibliographical commentary. The appendix is similarly arranged.

300 Etulain, Richard W. *Western American Literature: A Bibliography of Interpretative Books and Articles.* Vermillion, S.D., 1972.

300a "Bibliography of New England." *New England Quarterly,* 1– (1928–).

A comprehensive annual bibliography of books and articles on all aspects of the northeastern United States, including extensive coverage of literary studies. Arrangement is classified. Author index.

301 DICKINSON, ARTHUR T. *American Historical Fiction*. Rev. ed. N.Y., 1963.

An annotated bibliography of more than 1,900 works of 20th-century American historical fiction. Includes a detailed subject index.

301a JAHN, JANHEINZ. *A Bibliography of Neo-African Literature from Africa, America, and the Caribbean*. London and Düsseldorf, 1965.

A bibliography of Neo-African literature, including Afro-American literature. The introduction, headings, and titles are given in English, French, and German. Arranged in two main parts – African and American – each geographically subdivided, and within these sub-classes anthologies first and then individual authors. Entries include information on editions, reprintings, illustrations, etc. Index to authors.

302 CHAPMAN, DOROTHY. *Index to Black Poetry*. Boston, 1974. [Original title, *Black Poetry Index*.]

An index to the works of about 5,000 black poets published in 94 books and 33 anthologies. Arranged as three separate indexes: first lines and titles, subjects, and authors.

303 TURNER, DARWIN T. *Afro-American Writers*. Goldentree Bibliography. N.Y., 1970.

A highly selective bibliography of primary and secondary materials. Arrangement is classified into "Aids to Research," "Background," "Literary History and Criticism" followed by primary and secondary bibliographies on about 135 authors, with an appendix titled "Selective Criticism of Africans and Afro-Americans as Characters." Author-subject index and supplement of additional recently published materials.

304 RUSH, THERESSA GUNNELS, *et al. Black American Writers Past and Present: A Biographical and Bibliographical Dictionary*. 2 vols. Metuchen, N.J., 1975.

Primary and secondary bibliographies of more than 2000 black American writers from the early 18th century to the present. Arranged alphabetically by subject author's name. Vol. 2 includes a general bibliography on black writing in America on pp. 799–859.

305 PORTER, DOROTHY B. *North American Negro Poets: A Bibliographical Checklist of Their Writings 1760–1944*. Hattiesburg, Miss., 1945. Rptd., N.Y., 1969.

This expansion of Arthur A. Schomburg's *Bibliographical Checklist* (N.Y., 1916) cites books and pamphlets, anthologies edited by negroes, and a few broadsides. Arrangement is alphabetical by author. Entries give title, publication data, number of pages, and some locations of copies.

306 MATTHEWS, GERALDINE O., *et al. Black American Writers, 1773–1949: A Bibliography and Union List.* Boston, Mass., 1975.

A union list of the holdings of about 60 repositories in Alabama, Georgia, North Carolina, South Carolina, Tennessee, and Virginia. Locates copies of the works of over 1600 black authors written prior to 1950 on all subjects. Arrangement is by broad subject categories – e.g., "Language," "Literature," "Religion," etc. Within these classes entries are arranged alphabetically by author and include the author's dates, a citation to the work, and library location symbols. There is an author index.

307 HATCH, JAMES V. *Black Image on the American Stage: A Bibliography of Plays and Musicals 1770–1970.* N.Y., 1970.

Arranged chronologically, mostly by decades after 1900, and alphabetically by author within chronological divisions. More than 2,000 entries of plays and musicals by black writers, or plays and musicals that have black characters or themes. Includes a bibliography and separate author and title indexes.

308 WHITLOW, ROGER. *Black American Literature: A Critical History.* Chicago, 1973.

Includes a bibliography of some 1,520 primary and secondary works relating to Afro-American literary history.

308a "Studies in Afro-American Literature: An Annual Annotated Bibliography, [year]." *Obsidian: Black Literature in Review, 1–* (1975–   ).

An annual annotated bibliography of secondary scholarship on Black American literature. Arranged in seven main sections: (1) interviews, (2) general studies, (3) studies in poetry, (4) studies in fiction, (5) studies in drama, (6) studies in narratives and autobiographies, and (7) studies of individual authors. Limited to U. S. publications.

309 MILLER, ELIZABETH W., ed. *The Negro in America: A Bibliography.* 2nd ed. by Mary L. Fisher. Cambridge, Mass., 1970.

A very full, annotated, classified bibliography of material on all aspects of the Negro in the U. S. A. published since 1954. See particularly the chapters on "Biography and Letters," "Folklore and Literature," "Theatre, Dance and the Arts," and "The Negro in Literature and the Arts." Chapter 21 provides a guide to further research by citing indexes, abstracts, serials, etc. Index to authors cited. No subject index, but the analytical table of contents can be used as a subject index.

309a CORRIGAN, ROBERT A. *Afro-American Fiction, 1853–1973: A Guide to Information Sources.*

A selective annotated guide announced for publication by Gale Research Co. of Detroit, Mich.

310 Hirschfelder, Arlene B., ed. *American Indian Authors: A Representative Bibliography.* N.Y., 1970.

An annotated list of primary and secondary materials on American Indian writers. Includes a preliminary list of Indian authors arranged alphabetically by tribe, and two supplements: (1) anthologies and (2) periodical publications.

For other references to bibliographies on these special topics see entries **257, 315, 806, 843, 865**, and **938.**

B. Bio-Bibliographies

311 Kunitz, Stanley J. and Howard Haycraft. *American Authors, 1600–1900: A Biographical Dictionary of American Literature.* N.Y., 1938. Rptd., 1949.

Provides short biographies of about 1300 American authors, with very brief bibliographies of primary and secondary materials. Includes pictures of authors.

312 Millett, Fred B. *Contemporary American Authors: A Critical Survey and 219 Bio-Bibliographies.* N.Y., 1940. Rptd., 1970.

Arranged to provide (1) a critical survey of contemporary literature, (2) 219 short biographies with brief primary and secondary bibliographies, and (3) selected lists of readings.

313 *A Directory of American Poets.* 2nd ed. N.Y., 1975.

A list of about 1500 contemporary poets and other contemporary writers who publish in the United States. Entries include current address(es), telephone number(s), teaching preference and experience, foreign languages spoken, and citations to works published including the latest book and its publisher.

314 *Coda: Poets and Writers Newsletter.* 1– (May, 1973–).

Published 7 times yearly. Planned as an extension of **313.** Provides new names and addresses of contemporary American writers and news of their activities. Updates other materials in **313.**

315 Shockley, Ann Allen and Sue P. Chandler. *Living Black American Authors.* N.Y., 1973.

An alphabetical list by author giving brief outline biographies, including works published and current addresses. There is a list of black publishers in an appendix. Index to book titles cited.

For other bio-bibliographies of American authors see entries **174, 176–182.**

C. Histories

315a JONES, HOWARD MUMFORD. *The Theory of American Literature.* 2nd ed. rev. Ithaca, N.Y., 1965.

A critical sketch of the development of American literary history. Chapters include extensive documentation. There is a "Postscript 1965" and a selected bibliography. Author-title-subject index. See also Franz H. Link, *Amerikanische Literaturgeschichtsschreibung: Ein Forschungsbericht,* Stuttgart, 1963.

*

1. General Histories

316 SPILLER, ROBERT E. *et al. Literary History of the United States.* 4th ed. rev. 2 vols. N.Y., 1974. Original ed. in 3 vols., 1948; 2nd ed. 3 vols. in 2, 1953; *Bibligography Supplement,* 1959; 3rd ed., 2 vols., 1963; *Bibliography Supplement II,* 1972.

A comprehensive history of American literature with accompanying bibliographic volume (see **248**). Individual chapters cover background materials, literary movements, groups of writers, and individual writers; each chapter is written by a specialist. A brief "Reader's Bibliography" is appended to the history vol. Includes an author-title-subject index.

317 QUINN, ARTHUR HOBSON, *et al. The Literature of the American People: An Historical and Critical Survey.* N.Y., 1951.

A single volume history of American literature from the beginnings to 1950. Arranged in 4 main chronological parts, each written by a specialist. Includes selective bibliographies for each part on pp. 987–1107 and an author-title-subject index.

318 TRENT, WILLIAM P. *et al. The Cambridge History of American Literature.* 4 vols. N.Y., 1917–1921. Rptd. 3 vols., 1933. Rptd. 1 vol.

A comprehensive history of American literature. Each chapter is written by a specialist and includes bibliographies. Very extensive treatment of the literature, of literary backgrounds, and of related subjects, with particularly full coverage of colonial and revolutionary literature. Although the bibliographies and most historical materials are now out of date, the history is still useful for its treatment of minor figures and matters peripheral to the literature.

319 LÜDEKE, HENRY. *Geschichte der amerikanischen Literatur.* 2. erweit. Aufl. Bern, 1963.

A comprehensive survey-history of American literature from the beginnings to the 20th century. The 1963 edition has an epilogue on recent literature. Chapters cover individual writers and broader topics. Includes a selective bibliography covering general works, literary periods, and individual authors. Separate author, title, and periodical indexes. See also Rudolf Haas, *Amerikanische Literaturgeschichte*, 2 Bde., 1973–74.

2. Period and Genre Histories

320 TYLER, MOSES COIT. *A History of American Literature, 1607–1765.* 2 vols. N.Y., 1878. Rptd. 2 vols. in 1. *The Literary History of the American Revolution, 1763–1783.* 2 vols. N.Y., 1897. Rptd. 2 vols. in 1.

A particulary full study of American literary history from the beginnings to 1783, especially valuable for minor figures. The 2nd volume of the *Literary History of the American Revolution* includes a bibliography of primary works cited; the 2nd volume of each set contains an author-subject index.

321 MATTHIESSEN, F. O. *American Renaissance: Art and Expression in the Age of Emerson and Whitman.* N.Y., 1941.

A critical study of American literature from 1800 to 1855, with particular emphasis on the inter-relationships between Emerson, Thoreau, Hawthorne, Melville, and Whitman. Includes a chronology and an author-title-subject index.

322 STRAUMANN, HEINRICH. *American Literature in the Twentieth Century.* 3rd ed. N.Y., 1965.

An attempt to describe the basic conceptions of life underlying the works of some major 20th century authors. Arranged in chapters with such titles as "The Quest for Tradition," "The Realm of Imagination," etc. Author-title-subject index.

323 QUINN, ARTHUR HOBSON. *American Fiction: An Historical and Critical Survey.* N.Y., 1936.

A critical history of American fiction from the late 18th century to the 1930's. Includes selective bibliographies on pp. 726–772. Author-title index.

D. Handbooks and Chronologies

324 HART, JAMES D. *The Oxford Companion to American Literature.* 4th ed. N.Y., 1965.

A dictionary of American literature with brief articles arranged alphabetically. Headings for authors, fictional characters, titles, genres, groups, periodical titles, place names, etc. For authors brief biographies and primary bibliographies are given. This edition adds articles on 223 authors previously unnoted. There is a "Chronological Index" giving year-by-year the major events of literary history in America and in a parallel column the major social events of the time. Coverage is 1577–1965. Since less important material has been dropped, earlier editions may still have some utility.

325 HERZBERG, MAX J. ed. *The Reader's Encyclopedia of American Literature.* N.Y., 1962.

A comprehensive one-volume handbook to American and Canadian literature. Arranged as a dictionary list of entries covering authors (biography and writings), titles (plot summaries and commentaries), character names, and other literary matters. There are signed articles on special topics (e. g., "Amerindian Literature," "Magazines," etc.) and many pictures of authors. A brief glossary of literary terms is provided in an appendix.

326 BURKE, W. J., and W. D. HOWE. *American Authors and Books 1640 to the Present Day.* 3rd ed. rev. by Irving Weiss and Anne Weiss. N.Y., 1973.

A dictionary of American literature providing very brief entries for authors (dates, publications, etc.), titles of novels, plays, and poems (some plot summaries), pseudonyms, publishing firms, newspaper and magazine titles, etc. Provides broader but less detailed coverage of American authors than **324**.

For other handbooks and chronologies see entries **209–211**, **213**, **358–360**, **447**, and **448**.

E. Anthologies

Of the many anthologies of American literature the following are some representative standard works:

327 *American Literature: A Period Anthology.* Gen. ed. OSCAR CARGILL. Rev. ed., 4 vols., N.Y., 1949.

I: *The Roots of National Culture: American Literature to 1830*, ed. Robert E. Spiller and Harold W. Bodgett; II: *The Romantic Triumph: American Literature from 1830–1860*, ed. Tremaine McDowell; III: *The Rise of Realism: American Literature from 1860 to 1900* ed. Louis Wann; IV: *Contemporary Trends: American Literature since 1900*, ed. John H. Nelson and Oscar Cargill.

328 HOLMAN, C. HUGH. *The Odyssey Surveys of American Writings.* 4 vols. N.Y., 1965–66.

I: *Colonial and Federal American Writing*, ed. George F. Horner; II: *The Romantic Movement in American Writing*, ed. Richard Harter Fogle; III: *The Realistic Movement in American Writing*, ed. Bruce R. McElderry, Jr.; IV: *Twentieth Century American Writing*, ed. William T. Stafford.

329 *American Life in Literature,* ed. JAY B. HUBBELL, rev. ed. N.Y., 1951.

330 *American Literature: An Anthology and Critical Survey,* ed. JOE LEE DAVIS *et al.* Chicago, 1948–49.

331 *The Growth of American Literature: A Critical and Historical Survey,* ed. EDWIN HARRISON CADY, N.Y., 1956.

332 *American Literature: Tradition and Innovation.* Ed. HARRISON T. MESEROLE, WALTER SUTTON, and BROM WEBER. 3 vols. Lexington, Mass., 1969.

III. Literary Forms: Bibliographies, Indexes, and Handbooks

348 RUTTKOWSKI, WOLFGANG. *Bibliographie der Gattungspoetik für den Studenten der Literaturwissenschaft. Bibliography of the Poetics of Literary Genres for the Student of Literature. Bibliographie de la poétique des genres littéraires pour l'étudiant de la littérature.* München, 1973.

A short-title catalogue of more than 3,000 books, dissertations and articles in English, French, and German, listing (1) literary dictionaries containing articles on genres, (2) works on literary genres in general, (3) works on particular genres. Index of genres and author index.

A. Poetry

1. Primary Materials

350 *Granger's Index to Poetry: Sixth Edition, Completely Revised and Enlarged, Indexing Anthologies Published through December 31, 1970.* Ed. WILLIAM JAMES SMITH. N.Y., 1973.

An index to collections of poetry (including selections from the Bible and Shakespeare's work) in 514 anthologies. There are title and first line indexes, an author index, and a subject index.

351 CHICOREL, MARIETTA. *Chicorel Index to Poetry in Anthologies and Collections in Print.* 4 vols. N.Y., 1974. [Vols 5, 5 A, 5 B, and 5 C of *Chicorel Index.*]

An index to poetry in over 1,000 anthologies and collections, including collections of one poet. Arranged as a single-alphabet index of authors, editors, translators, titles, and first lines. Volume 5C includes an index of subject descriptors (e. g., *satirical, women's, religious,* etc.) and an author index.

352 CHICOREL, MARIETTA. *Chicorel Index to Poetry in Anthologies and Collections: Retrospective Index to Out-of-Print Titles.* 4 vols. N.Y., 1975. [Vols. 6, 6 A, 6 B, and 6 C of *Chicorel Index.*]

Arranged as in volume 5; covers collections which have gone out of print since about 1967.

2. Secondary Materials

353 CLINE, GLORIA S. and JEFFREY A. BAKER. *An Index to Criticisms of British and American Poetry.* Metuchen, N.J., 1973.

An index to 2,862 criticisms of 1,510 poems by 285 English and American poets of all periods. Covers criticism primarily written between 1960 and 1970. Arranged in two parts: (1) a list of citations to criticism arranged by author, with general critical comment first followed by criticism of individual poems, and (2) a list of 1,865 citations to critical writings arranged alphabetically by critic's name. The citations in part 1 are brief name references to the full citations given in part 2. Includes a bibliography of books and journals analyzed and an index of poem titles cited.

354 KUNTZ, JOSEPH M. *Poetry Explication: A Checklist of Interpretations Since 1925 of British and American Poems Past and Present.* Rev. ed. Denver, Colo., 1962.

A selective checklist of explications of English and American poems of 500 lines or less. Arranged alphabetically by poet; for each poet poem titles are listed alphabetically, and beneath each title is given the checklist of explications. Explications cited are from both books and periodicals.

355 WALCUTT, CHARLES C. and J. EDWIN WHITESELL. *The Explicator Cyclopedia.* Vol. 1: *Modern Poetry*; vol. 2: *Traditional Poetry*; vol 3: *Prose.* Chicago, 1966–1969.

Abstracts of explicatory articles which have appeared in *The Explicator.* Each volume is arranged alphabetically by writer, with abstracts of articles on individual works of that writer given beneath. The prose volume includes both fiction and non-fiction.

356 "A Checklist of Explication." *Explicator*, 3– (1945–).

Annual checklist of explicatory writings, covering both books and articles. Arranged alphabetically by subject author, and, under the name of each subject author, alphabetically by critic.

There is now *The Explicator Cumulative Index I* covering the 1237 articles in vols. 1—20 of *The Explicator* and *The Explicator Cumulative Index II* covering the 786 articles in vols. 21–30.

357 COLEMAN, ARTHUR. *Epic and Romance Criticism.* Vol. 1. Searingtown, N.Y., 1973.

A checklist of interpretations, published between 1940 and 1972, of English and American epics, metrical romances, mock-epics, and epic-like poems such as "Howl," "Paterson," "The Wreck of the Deutschland," and "The Waste Land." Arranged alphabetically by poem title, with citations to relevant criticisms beneath.

358 PREMINGER, ALEX, ed. *Encyclopedia of Poetry and Poetics*. Princeton, N.J., 1965. Rev. and enl. ed., titled *Princeton Encyclopedia of Poetry and Poetics,* 1975.

The 1965 vol. provides a series of about 1,000 articles, some quite extensive, on all aspects of poetry and poetics. Entries are arranged alphabetically and include such topics as schools of poetry and technical terms, as well as outlines of the poetry of various countries. Many articles have bibliographies appended. There are no articles on individual poets. The rev. ed. of 1975 contains an 84 page supplement which rectifies omissions in the 1965 ed. and includes new entries for recent developments.

359 DEUTSCH, BABETTE. *Poetry Handbook: A Dictionary of Terms*. 4th ed. N.Y., 1974.

A handbook of poetic terms arranged as a dictionary list with extensive cross-referencing. Entries give brief definitions and can include historical information and illustrations taken from English poetry. An appendix provides an alphabetical index to poets cited.

360 SPENDER, STEPHEN and DONALD HALL, eds. *The Concise Encyclopedia of English and American Poets and Poetry*. N.Y., 1963.

An illustrated series of articles on poets writing in English, giving brief biographies with comment on the poet's work. There are 32 general articles on various aspects of poetry. Arrangement is alphabetical. There is an index of poets and a general index which includes names, subjects and specialized terms explained in the course of an article. An appendix titled "For Further Reading" provides lists of primary and secondary works arranged under authors' names and subject headings.

For other poetry bibliographies and indexes see entries 36–38, 57–60, 85, 102–104, 107, 109, 111, 118–120, 125, 134, 134a, 139–140a, 151, 155, 176, 177, 263–266, 281–284a, 302, 305, 313, 314, 489, 769, 771, and 775.

B. Drama

1. Primary Materials

361 SAMPLES, GORDON. *The Drama Scholars' Index to Plays and Film-scripts: A Guide to Plays and Filmscripts in Selected Anthologies, Series and Periodicals*. Metuchen, N.J., 1974.

A selective index to plays and filmscripts of all countries published in 121 anthologies and collections and 39 periodicals not covered in **369**. The materials analyzed include some collections as early as 1700 and as extensive as *Bell's British Theatre;* analyzes many foreign periodicals not indexed elsewhere. Arranged as a single-alphabet list of authors, authors of original sources, film directors, historical characters, and titles, with main entries under author. Two appendixes give lists of collections and periodicals indexed.

361a The British Drama League. *The Player's Library: The Catalogue of the Library of the British Drama League.* 2nd ed. London, 1950. *First Supplement,* 1951. *Second Supplement.* 1954. *Third Supplement,* 1956.

A catalogue of the nearly 15,000 plays in the library of the British Drama League. Arrangement is alphabetical by author; entries give title, type of play, number of acts, scene settings required, appropriate costume, publisher's name, etc. The third supplement includes a separate catalogue of French plays. Contains a classified bibliography of books on the theatre and separate indexes to play titles and to names. The Drama League Player's Library also has collections of prompt books, periodicals, press cuttings, photographs, etc. not included in this catalogue.

362 BERGQUIST, GEORGE W. *Three Centuries of English and American Plays, A Checklist. England: 1500–1800; United States: 1714–1830.* N.Y., 1963.

This is an index to the Microprint edition of *Three Centuries of English and American Plays.* Arrangement is a single-alphabet list of authors and titles citing about 5500 plays in various editions and in manuscript. Author entries give full name, title, imprint, and, where possible, Greg and/or Woodward and McManaway numbers.

363 FIRKINS, INA TEN EYCK. *Index to Plays, 1800–1926.* N.Y., 1927. Rptd., 1971. *Supplement,* 1935.

An index to 7,872 plays in English periodicals, collections, and anthologies. Author and subject-title indexes. Appendixes list the collections and anthologies indexed. The *Supplement* indexes 3,284 plays.

364 THOMSON, RUTH G. *Index to Full Length Plays 1895 to 1925.* Boston, 1956.

A selected list, alphabetical by title, of 562 plays in English published in the period. There are author and subject indexes.

365 THOMSON, RUTH G. *Index to Full Length Plays 1926 to 1944.* Boston, 1946.

A selected list, alphabetical by title, of 1340 plays in English published in the period. There are author and subject indexes.

366 *Dramatic Index.* Vols. 1–41 (1909–1952). The quarterly issues of the *Dramatic Index* were annually cumulated as Part II of the *Annual Magazine Subject Index.* Rptd. as *Cumulated Dramatic Index, 1909–1949.* 2 vols. Boston, 1965.

An index to primary and secondary materials on drama appearing in periodicals. Texts of plays are cited under their title or under "Dramas." The reprint edition is a single-alphabet reproduction of all the entries in the original 41 vols., and three appendixes: (1) an author list of books about the drama, (2) a title list of published play texts, and (3) an author list of published play texts.

367 IRELAND, NORMA O. *Index to Full Length Plays 1944 to 1964.* Boston, 1965.

An index to 1187 plays in English published between 1944 and 1964. Arranged as a single-alphabet author-title-subject list.

368 CONNOR, JOHN M. and BILLIE M. CONNOR. *Ottemiller's Index to Plays in Collections: An Author and Title Index to Plays Appearing in Collections Published Between 1900 and Mid-1970.* Metuchen, N. J., 1971.

An index to 8912 copies of 3049 plays by 1644 writers in 1047 collections. Arranged as an author list, with separate lists for collections analyzed and a title index. Entries provide the author's name and dates, the title of the play, the date of first production, cross references to variant titles, and code symbols which refer the user to citations in the list of collections analyzed. Plays of unknown authorship are entered under the heading *anonymous*; foreign titles are indexed both in the original language and in English if the play has been translated.

369 KELLER, DEAN H. *Index to Plays in Periodicals.* Metuchen, N. J., 1971. *Supplement,* 1973.

An index to plays published in 103 periodicals, mostly contemporary, but a few from earlier periods. Arranged as an author list; entries give author's dates, play title, brief description of the play, and citation to the journal in which the play has appeared. The main volume includes a supplementary list for the period 1969–1971. The 1973 *Supplement* indexes an additional 37 periodicals not included in the basic volume and adds citations to 2,334 plays.

370 CHICOREL, MARIETTA. *Chicorel Theatre Index to Plays in Periodicals.* N. Y., 1973. [Vol. 8 of *Chicorel Index.*]

An index to plays appearing in 159 periodicals from the 19th century to the present. Arranged as a single-alphabet list of periodical titles, play titles, authors, translators, adapters, and editors of play scripts, followed by lists of periodicals indexed, play titles, authors, editors, translators, adapters, and subject indicators.

371 PATTERSON, CHARLOTTE. *Plays in Periodicals: An Index to English Language Scripts in Twentieth Century Journals.* Boston, 1970.

An index to over 4000 plays printed in 97 English language periodicals published between 1900 and 1968. Arranged alphabetically by title. Entries give author (translator, adaptor), play length, size and mixture of cast, and citation to the periodical in which the play was published. Includes an index to authors and a separate "cast analysis" index to the plays, arranged by the number of male, female, child, and extra parts required.

372 DuBois, William R. *English and American Stage Productions: An Annotated Checklist of Prompt Books 1800–1900 From the Nisbet-Snyder Drama Collection Northern Illinois University Libraries.* Boston, 1973.

A checklist of "over 2,000 prompt books and prompters' editions of plays mostly published in England and the United States from the last quarter of the eighteenth century to the end of the nineteenth .... Almost 700 items contain handwritten annotations of stage directions, changes, cuts, costuming, scenery, etc., and as such are unique in depicting nineteenth-century theatrical productions." Arranged alphabetically by author, with an addendum of 100 plays arranged by title. Entries give bibliographic details (a date may be "an informed guess"), some descriptive features of the copy, a note if the copy is marked, and an indication of earliest recorded N.Y. or London production. Separate author, title, and name indexes.

2. Secondary Materials

372a *Encyclopedia dello Spettacolo.* 9 vols. Roma, 1954–1962. *Aggiornamento 1955–1965,* 1966. *Appendice di Aggiornamento: Cinema,* 1963. *Indice-Repertorio,* 1968.

A very comprehensive encyclopedia of theatre and related arts – opera, ballet, film, television, radio, circus, etc. Arranged alphabetically. Articles are generally long, include bibliographies, and are signed by the specialists who wrote them. Very fully illustrated. The *Indice-Repertorio* is a general alphabetical index (with a special Greek section first) of more than 145,000 title entries, each giving an indication of the art form (drama, ballet, etc.), the author, and the date.

373 Baker, Blanch M. *Theatre and Allied Arts: A Guide to Books Dealing with the History, Criticism, and Technic of the Drama and Theatre and Related Arts and Crafts.* Rev. ed. N.Y., 1952. Rptd., 1967.

An annotated bibliography of about 6,000 books on theatre published mostly between 1885 and 1948. Generally does not include works which have not been written in or translated into English. Author and subject indexes.

374 Chicorel, Marietta. *Chicorel Bibliography to the Performing Arts.* N.Y., 1972. [Vol. 3 A of *Chicorel Index.*]

A buying guide to materials in the performing arts. Arranged as a classified list of about 8000 entries under more than 300 subject headings such as "actors," "black drama," "staging," "costume," "Shakespeare," etc. Entries give full bibliographic data, including price and ISBN.

375 LOWE, CLAUDIA J. *A Guide to Reference and Bibliography for Theatre Research.* Columbus, Ohio, 1971.

An annotated guide to 675 general and specialized reference works, arranged as a classified list with categories such as "Bibliographies," "Special Collections," "Theses," "Indexes," "Biographical Sources," "Annuals and Directories," and the like. An appendix includes additional items for fine arts and music. Author-title index.

376 SANTANIELLO, A. E. *Theatre Books in Print: An Annotated Guide to the Literature of the Theatre, the Technical Arts of the Theatre, Motion Pictures, Television and Radio.* 2nd ed. N.Y., 1966.

A classified bibliography of books on all aspects of drama and theatre throughout the world. Within each class arrangement is alphabetical by author. The entries give author, title, imprint, number of pages, price, and provide a descriptive annotation. Author and editor index.

377 ANGOTTI, VINCENT L. *Source Materials in the Field of Theatre: An Annotated Bibliography and Subject Index to the Microfilm Collection.* Ann Arbor, Mich., 1967.

An annotated bibliography of the materials compiled on microfilm at Ann Arbor. Arranged alphabetically by author; the bibliography includes monographs, serials, manuscripts, journals, and diaries in English, French, German, Italian and Latin. Entry gives author, title, imprint, number of text pages, and a descriptive annotation analyzing the work. Subject index.

378 THE DRAMA BOOKSHOP. *Annotated Bibliography of New Publications in the Performing Arts.* 1– (1970–).

Published three times a year. Arrangement is classified in large categories such as "Books on Theatre and Drama," "The Mass Media and the Popular Arts," etc., with sub-categories such as "General Reference Works," "Shakespeare," "Costume," "The Actor and His Craft," etc.

379 SCHOOLCRAFT, RALPH NEWMAN. *Performing Arts in Print: An Annual Bibliography.* N.Y., 1973.

An annotated guide to about 12,000 books on all aspects of the performing arts, including theatre, drama, moving pictures, TV, radio, and the mass media. Includes only books in print in America; no plays or collections of plays are included except Shakespeare.

380 COLEMAN, ARTHUR and GARY R. TYLER. *Drama Criticism: A Checklist of Interpretation Since 1940.* Vol. 1, *English and American Plays.* Denver, Colo., 1966.

A bibliography of British and American dramatic criticism in 1050 periodicals and 1500 books published between 1940 and 1964. Provides two main
lists: (1) plays other than Shakespeare's, arranged by author and within
each author category by title, and (2) plays of Shakespeare. Citations to
criticisms are given beneath the title of each play.

381 ADELMAN, IRVING and RITA DWORKIN, eds. *Modern Drama: A Checklist of Critical Literature on Twentieth Century Plays.* Metuchen,
N. J., 1967.

An index of articles and parts of books on English, American, and European
dramatists of the twentieth century. For each dramatist, citations to general
studies are given first, followed by lists of commentaries arranged under
the headings of individual plays. Available bibliographies are also cited.

382 BREED, PAUL F. and FLORENCE M. SNIDERMAN. *Dramatic Criticism
Index: A Bibliography of Commentaries on Playwrights from Ibsen
to the Avant-Garde.* Detroit, Mich., 1972.

A list of nearly 12,000 citations to critical comments in English on the
work of modern playwrights, including some late 19th century writers.
Arrangement is alphabetical by playwright. Indexes some 630 books and
200 periodicals. Includes an index to titles and an index to critics.

383 SALEM, JAMES M. *A Guide to Critical Reviews.* 4 parts in 5 vols.
Metuchen, N. J., 1966–1971. Part I, 2nd ed., 1973.

Lists of critical reviews of plays primarily in the New York *Times* and in
magazines, not in scholarly journals. Each list is alphabetical by author
(anonymous works by title). Part I covers American drama, 1909–1969;
Part II covers the Broadway musical from 1920–1965; Part III covers
British and continental drama from Ibsen to Pinter; and Part IV covers
the screenplay. Each part has an author and a title index.

383a SAMPLES, GORDON. *How to Locate Reviews of Plays and Films: A
Bibliography of Criticism from the Beginnings to the Present.* Metuchen, N. J., 1976.

An annotated bibliography of sources of criticism on drama and cinema.
Arranged in two main parts, plays and film, each organized in categories
such as "Chronology of Study Guides," "Newspaper Indexes," "Criticism
Checklists," etc. Author-title index.

384 *The New York Times Directory of the Theatre.* N. Y., 1973.

Provides separate title and personal name indexes to all the theatre reviews
printed in the New York *Times* from 1920 to 1970. Includes supplementary
information on the New York *Times* theatre critics, theatre awards, and
reprints of *Times* articles on the awards.

385 BECKERMAN, BERNARD and HOWARD SIEGMAN, eds. *On Stage: Selected
Theatre Reviews from the New York Times 1920–1970.* N. Y., 1973.

A collection of reviews of New York stage plays reproduced by photo-offset from the New York *Times*. Separate indexes to authors of plays reviewed and to play titles.

386 "Dramatic Index." *Bulletin of Bibliography*, 6–21 (1909–1953).

A subject index, in each issue of the periodical, to material in about 150 periodicals relating to the drama and the theatre: actors, play synopses, reviews, portraits, scholarly articles, critical articles, etc.

386a "Nineteenth-Century Theatre Research: A Bibliography for [year]." *Nineteenth Century Theatre Research*, 1–   (1973–   ).

An annual bibliography appearing in the September issue. Biannual issues can also include notes of research in progress.

387 "Bibliographie." *Revue d'Histoire du Théâtre*, 12–   (1959–   ).

Each issue includes a bibliography covering all aspects of drama in England, America, and Europe.

388 *Theatre/Drama & Speech Index.* 1–   (1974–   ).

A triannual publication of two indexes: (1) *Theatre/Drama Index*, an index to articles appearing in about 60 jourals, arranged as a classified list with author, subject, title, name, and illustration indexes, and (2) *Speech Communication Index*, an index to articles appearing in about 30 journals, arranged as a classified list, with author, subject, and name indexes.

389 *Theatre Documentation.* 1–   (1968–   ).

A journal publishing bibliographies, indexes, accounts of theatre and film collections, and other information on theatre research. Includes a list of scholarly works in progress.

390 HARTNOLL, PHYLLIS, ed. *The Oxford Companion to the Theatre.* 3rd ed. London, 1967.

A dictionary list of articles arranged alphabetically by subject. Covers all aspects of the theatre throughout the world. Information about individual plays is given under the entry for the playwright. Includes extensive surveys of the theatre of individual nations and articles on such topics as "National Drama," "Incidental Music," "Trickwork," etc. Long articles are signed. Appendixes include a selective bibliography of books on the theatre and illustrations with notes. Published also in abridged form as *The Concise Oxford Companion to the Theatre*, London, 1972.

391 *McGraw-Hill Encyclopedia of World Drama.* 4 vols. N.Y., 1972.

An encyclopedia of world drama from the beginnings to the present. Arranged alphabetically. Entries include terms – e. g., "Boulevard Comedy," "Mystery Play," etc. – but most entries are for individual playwrights. Entries for major dramatists give a brief biography, a general critical survey of the dramatist's work, summaries of major plays, a list of plays written, and primary and secondary bibliographies. Entries for lesser playwrights give brief summaries of life and work. Includes many illustrations, both portraits of individual playwrights and scenes from plays. Vol. 4 includes an index of play titles (identified by name of author); in the index foreign titles are given both in their original language and in English.

392 GASSNER, JOHN and EDWARD QUINN, eds. *The Reader's Encyclopedia of World Drama*. London, 1970.

An encyclopedia of the drama of all times and places. Entries for plays (both plot summaries and critical comment), playwrights (biographical information and critical evaluations), genres (including minor genres such as *noh* theatre and *auto sacramentale*), and national drama (providing historical surveys for each country); other entries are provided for dramatic terms and related subjects. Includes an appendix of basic documents on dramatic theory from Aristotle to Dürrenmatt.

392a ANDERSON, MICHAEL, *et al.*, eds. *Crowell's Handbook of Contemporary Drama*. N. Y., 1971. Rptd. with the title *A Handbook of Contemporary Drama*, London, 1972.

A handbook to modern drama arranged alphabetically. Includes author, title, and subject entries. Entries can include highly selective bibliographies, dates of composition and first performances of plays, definitions, etc. No index.

392b MATLAW, MYRON, ed. *Modern World Drama: An Encyclopedia* N. Y., 1972.

393 BOWMAN, WALTER P. and ROBERT H. BALL. *Theatre Language: A Dictionary of Terms in English of the Drama and Stage from Medieval to Modern Times*. N. Y., 1961.

A dictionary providing brief explanations of the meanings of about 5000 terms generally used in American and British theatre.

394 SHARP, HAROLD S. and MARJORIE Z. SHARP. *Index to Characters in the Performing Arts*. 6 vols. N. Y., 1966–1973.

Part I (vols. 1–2) covers non-musical plays; Part II (vols. 3–4) covers operas and musicals; Part III (vol. 5) covers ballet; and Part IV (vol. 6) covers radio and television. Each part consists of a single alphabet list of character names (30,000 in Part I, covering 3,600 plays). Entries identify the character by the production in which he appears and refer the reader by a code symbol to a list of the productions at the end of the volume where each play, opera, ballet, or radio or television program is described in detail. Character names include descriptive names (e. g., Shrew) as well as given and family names.

395 KINDERMANN, HEINZ. *Theatergeschichte Europas*. 1–   (Salzburg, 1957–   ).

A comprehensive history of theatre in Europe, including England, from the beginnings to the present. By 1974, 10 volumes had been finished, bringing the history up to the beginning of the 20th century. Each volume is heavily documented and includes a bibliography; all volumes also provide chronological tables, extensive illustrations, a separate subject index, and an index to places, names, and titles.

396 LITTO, FREDRIC M. *American Dissertations on the Drama and the Theatre: A Bibliography.* Kent, Ohio, 1969.

A list of 4,565 dissertations on the performing arts: drama, legitimate stage, opera, film, radio, TV, dance, etc. Each entry in the list has a reference code, and the list is followed by a series of indexes to authors, to key-words, and to subjects, all keyed to the reference code. The key-word index provides a computer-generated concordance to "every significant word in every dissertation title in the Bibliography" except such words as *drama, theatre,* and *Shakespeare.* The subject index is arranged alphabetically by country, and under each country by time period; within each period arrangement is by such topics as "Individual Playwrights," "Audience," etc.

For other drama bibliographies and indexes see entries **39, 39a, 61–65, 86–92, 120a, 120b, 135, 141–144a, 152, 153, 168, 196, 197, 200–202, 267, 268, 274, 284b, 287–292a, 307, 770, 775,** and **784.**

C. Fiction

1. Primary Materials

397 WRIGHT, R. GLENN, ed. *Chronological Bibliography of English Language Fiction in the Library of Congress Through 1950.* 8 vols. Boston, 1974.

A chronological index to all the works of English language fiction in the PZ3 section of the Library of Congress. Arrangement is by nationalities of authors and within these categories chronological by year of publication. Under each year Library of Congress author cards are reproduced (in reduced size) alphabetically by author and for each author by title. Includes a list of foreign authors whose works have been translated into English, an index of translators, and a list of pseudonym identifications. Reproduces more than 130,000 Library of Congress cards. See also Wright, **398, 398a.**

398 WRIGHT, R. GLENN, ed. *Author Bibliography of English Language Fiction in the Library of Congress Through 1950.* 8 vols. Boston, 1973.

An author index to all the works of English language fiction in the PZ3 section of the Library of Congress cards. Includes information on nationalities of authors, identifications of pseudonyms, and a bibliography of primary and secondary sources. See also Wright, **397, 398a.**

398a WRIGHT, R. GLENN, ed. *Title Bibliography of English Language Fiction in The Library of Congress Through 1950.* 9 vols. Boston, 1976.

A title index to all the works of English Language fiction in the PZ3 section of the Library of Congress. Contains a complete listing of works that have been translated into English, accompanied by an Index of Translators. Pseudonym index. See also Wright, **397, 398.**

399 COTTON, GERALD B. and ALAN GLENCROSS. *Cumulated Fiction Index, 1945–1960.* London, 1960. Rptd., 1964.

A subject index to more than 25,000 works of fiction arranged under some 3000 alphabetically listed subject headings, with extensive cross-referencing. Entries give only author and short title.

400 SMITH, RAYMOND F. *Cumulated Fiction Index, 1960–1969.* London, 1970.

A subject index to about 18,000 works of fiction arranged under about 3000 subject headings. Covers fiction published 1960–1969, and is intended to be a continuation of the Cotton and Glencross index. Subject categories are arranged alphabetically, with extensive cross-referencing. Entries give only author and short title.

401 FIDELL, ESTELLE and ESTHER V. FLORY. *Fiction Catalogue.* 8th ed. N.Y., 1971.

A critically annotated bibliography of 4315 titles arranged alphabetically by author. Annotations include plot summaries and review quotations. Title and subject index.

402 BAKER, ERNEST. *A Guide to Historical Fiction.* N.Y., 1914. Rptd., 1969.

An annotated bibliography of historical fiction arranged by subject country and within each country by historical period treated. Annotations are usually plot summaries; juvenile fiction is identifed as such. Includes an index to authors, titles, historical names, places, events, and allusions.

402a McGARRY, DANIEL D. and SARAH HARRIMAN WHITE. *Historical Fiction Guide: Annotated Chronological and Topical List of Five Thousand Selected Historical Novels.* N.Y., 1963.

403 KERR, ELIZABETH. *Bibliography of the Sequence Novel.* Minneapolis, Minn., 1950.

404 SUMMERS, MONTAGUE. *A Gothic Bibliography.* London, 1941. Rptd., N.Y., 1964.

405 CLARKE, I. F. *The Tale of the Future from the Beginning to the Present Day: An Annotated Bibliography.* 2nd ed. London, 1972.

406 GOVE, PHILIP B. *The Imaginary Voyage in Prose Fiction: A History of Its Criticism and a Guide for Its Study, with an Annotated Check List of 215 Imaginary Voyages from 1700 to 1800.* N.Y., 1941. Rptd. London, 1961.

407 SIEMON, FREDERICK. *Science Fiction Story Index 1950–1968.* Chicago, 1971.

408 TUCK, DONALD H. *Encyclopedia of Science Fiction and Fantasy: A Bibliographic Survey of the Fields of Science Fiction, Fantasy and Wierd Fiction Through 1968.* Vol. 1– . Chicago, 1974– .

Intended to comprise three main volumes, with periodic supplements. A bio-bibliography arranged alphabetically by author's name; vol. 1 covers *A* through *L*.

409 BARZUN, JACQUES and WENDELL H. TAYLOR. *A Catalogue of Crime.* N.Y., 1971.

An extensively annotated bibliography of mystery and detective fiction.

410 HAGEN, ORDEAN A. *Who Done It? A Guide to Detective, Mystery and Suspense Fiction.* N.Y., 1969.

411 COOK, DOROTHY E. and ISABEL S. MONRO. *Short Story Index: An Index to 60,000 Stories in 4320 Collections.* N.Y., 1953. Four Supplements, 1950–1969.

The basic list is a single-alphabet author-title-subject index to 60,000 stories in 4,320 collections. The supplements provide additional indexes to more than 30,000 stories in more than 600 collections.

412 CHICOREL, MARIETTA. *Chicorel Index to Short Stories in Anthologies and Collections.* 4 Vols. N.Y., 1974 [Vols. 12, 12 A, 12 B, and 12 C of *Chicorel Index.*]

An index to more than 60,000 short stories in about 1,300 anthologies and collections of stories by individual writers. Arranged as a single-alphabet list by author, title, and collection title. Volume 12C contains an index of subject descriptors for countries, literary periods, and literary types (e. g., *mystery, folk tales*, etc.) and a list of collections analyzed.

2. Secondary Materials

413 COTTON, GERALD B. and HILDA MARY MCGILL. *Fiction Guides.* London, 1967.

A highly selective annotated bibliography of secondary materials on English and American fiction, excluding individual authors. Arranged as a classified list with headings such as "Comprehensive Guides," "American Fiction," "Humor and Satire," and the like. Author-title index.

414 ADELMAN, IRVING and RITA DWORKIN. *The Contemporary Novel: A Checklist of Critical Literature on the British and American Novel Since 1945.* Metuchen, N. J., 1972.

A bibliography of secondary criticism arranged alphabetically by authors of novels. For each author general works are listed first, then studies of individual novels, and, last, bibliographical studies.

415 "The Gothic Novel: A Checklist of Modern Criticism." *Bulletin of Bibliography,* 30 (1973), 45–54.

416 *Modern Fiction Studies: A Critical Quarterly.* 1–   (1955–   ).

In each year, two of the issues are usually devoted to a particular modern novelist, and these issues usually include a selective bibliography for that author. A cumulative index to vols. 1–20 (1955–1975) is in preparation.

417 *Studies in the Novel.* 1–   (1969–   ).

Individual issues often include bibliographic checklists on particular novelists or on general topics – e. g., American negro novelists. These include both original bibliographic checklists and checklists supplementary to existing bibliographies.

418 THURSTON, JARVIS A., *et al. Short Fiction Criticism: A Checklist of Interpretations Since 1925 of Stories and Novelettes (American, British, Continental), 1800–1958.* Denver, 1960.

An index to criticisms of short fiction; analyzes some 200 periodicals and "thousands of books." Arranged alphabetically by author; under each author's name his works are listed alphabetically by title, with citations to relevant criticisms given beneath each title. Includes only citations to criticisms written in English. No index.

419 WALKER, WARREN S. *Twentieth-Century Short Story Explication: Interpretations, 1900–1966 Inclusive, of Short Fiction Since 1800.* 2nd ed. Hamden, Conn., 1968. *Supplement, 1967–1969,* 1970. *Supplement, 1970–1972,* 1973.

A checklist of explicatory comment on short stories of all countries. Arranged as an author list, with short story titles given beneath each author's name, and a checklist of explications beneath each story title. Index to short story authors.

420 "Annual Bibliography of Short Fiction." *Studies in Short Fiction,* 1–   (1963–   ).

A checklist of explicatory comments on short stories of all countries. Arranged as an author list, with short story titles given beneath each author's name, and a checklist of explications beneath each short story title.

For other fiction bibliographies and indexes see entries **74–76, 93–99, 121–123a, 136–138a, 145–147, 150, 161, 169, 179, 269, 270, 273, 275, 276, 286, 293–298, 301, 309a, 323, 355, 491–495,** and **784.**

D. Prose

There are references to bibliographies and indexes for prose non-fiction in entries **40, 77, 104, 111, 118, 120, 124, 124a, 355** and **925–943.**

IV. General and Comparative Literature

A. General Literature

1. Dictionaries of Literary Terms

430 SHIPLEY, JOSEPH T., ed. *Dictionary of World Literary Terms: Criticism, Forms, Technique.* Rev. ed., London, 1970.

A dictionary in three main parts: (1) a list of literary terms with brief definitions; (2) a series of essays on literary criticism in various countries arranged alphabetically by country and historically within each country; (3) lists of critical readings arranged alphabetically by country. The earlier edition of this work, titled *Dictionary of World Literature: Criticism, Forms, Technique,* 1953, covers a similar range of material arranged as a single-alphabet list; this earlier edition has been reprinted in Totowa, N.J., 1968 and 1972.

431 HOLMAN, C. HUGH. *A Handbook to Literature.* Based on the Original by William Flint Thrall and Addison Hibbard. 3rd ed., N.Y., 1972.

A dictionary list of over 1360 literary terms with definitions. Terms in small capitals used within the definitions have their own definitions elsewhere in the book. Definitions range from one or two lines to essays of several pages. An appendix includes an outline history of English and American literature in parallel column arrangement from 1607 onwards.

432 ABRAMS, M. H. *A Glossary of Literary Terms.* 3rd ed. N.Y., 1971.

A dictionary of literary terms arranged as a series of essay-definitions of relatively broad topics – e. g., *aestheticism, meter, ode.* Less inclusive terms (e. g., *art-for-art's-sake, iambic, irregular ode*) are defined as part of the definition of the broader topics. Entries include illustrations and citations to works of relevant secondary scholarship. There is an index to all terms defined which incorporates also a guide to the pronunciation of the terms.

432a BECKSON, KARL and ARTHUR GANZ. *Literary Terms: A Dictionary.* N.Y., 1975.

A revised edition of *A Reader's Guide to Literary Terms* (1960). Limited to literary terms (no author or title entries); a dictionary providing definitions for such terms as *incremental repetition, objective correlative, theatre of cruelty, structuralism,* etc. Entries sometimes include citations to publications where further information can be found.

433 FOWLER, ROGER, ed. *A Dictionary of Modern Critical Terms.* London, 1973.

A list of critical terms in alphabetical order; entries give definitions, comments on works that use the terms, and lists of relevent readings. Serves both as a dictionary and as an introduction to readings on critical terminology.

434 SCOTT, ARTHUR F. *Current Literary Terms: A Concise Dictionary of their Origin and Use.* London, 1965.

A dictionary of the principal terms used in all branches of literary study and all literatures; the definitions often include illustrations, and etymological histories are provided. Brief bibliography and index of authors quoted.

435 RUTTKOWSKI, W. V. und R. E. BLAKE. *Literaturwörterbuch in Deutsch, Englisch und Französisch mit griechischen und lateinischen Abteilungen für den Studenten der allgemeinen und vergleichenden Literaturwissenschaft.* Bern, 1969.

Trilingual tables of the most important literary terms in English, French, and German. Entries include antonyms, synonyms, and subterms, with cross-referencing. Includes some Italian and Spanish terms, and entries may also supply the etymologies for Greek or Latin root terms.

436 WILPERT, GERO von. *Sachwörterbuch der Literatur.* 5. Aufl., Stuttgart, 1969.

A dictionary of the most important literary terms. About 4,200 entries deal with terms in such areas as genres, stylistics, metrics, literary psychology, theatre studies, etc. Entries give definitions, examples, and international bibliographies.

2. Literary Handbooks, Encyclopedias, and Indexes

437 *Cassell's Encyclopaedia of World Literature.* Ed. Sigfrid Steinberg. Rev. and enl. ed. by J. BUCHANAN-BROWN. 3 vols. London, 1973.

A comprehensive encyclopedia of world literature, with signed articles by over 250 contributors. Arranged in 2 parts. Vol. 1 contains about 650 articles on world literary history and on other general topics such as literary genres arranged alphabetically by topic; vols. 2–3 provide about 9000 biographies of writers of all countries, arranged alphabetically by name (vol. 2, A–K; vol. 3, L–Z). Most articles include bibliographies, and each biographical entry includes a critical assessment of the author's work.

438 *Dizionario letterario Bompiani delle opere e dei personaggi di tutti i tempi e di tutte le letterature.* 9 vols. Milano, 1949–52. *Dizionario letterario Bompiani degli autori di tutti i tempi e di tutte le letterature.* 3 vols. Milano, 1956–57. *Appendice.* 2 vols. 1964–66.

Dictionnaire des oeuvres de tous les temps et de tous les pays: Littérature, philosophie, musique, science. 5 vols. and index vol. Paris, 1952–

67. Rptd. *Dictionnaire biographique des auteurs de tous les temps et de tous les pays.* 2 vols. Paris, 1957–58. Rptd., 1964. *Dictionnaire des personnages littéraires et dramatiques de tous les temps et de tous les pays: Poésie, Théâtre, Roman, Musique.* Paris, 1960, Rptd., 1964, 1970.

Kindlers Literatur Lexikon. Ed. WOLFGANG VON EINSIEDEL *et al.* 7 vols. Zürich, München, 1965–72.

Three parallel but independently produced dictionaries of world literature of all times. All are international in scope and very comprehensive, but each tends to emphasize the literature and literary outlook of the country in which it was produced. The Italian *Bompiani* has separate sets of volumes for author and for title and character entries, although the title-character series (1949–52) also has entries for literary topics at the beginning of the first volume and volume 9 includes a synoptic view of the development of world literature, an index to titles in their original languages, an index of authors, and an index of illustrators. The French version, called the "Laffont Bompiani," is arranged in three sets of volumes, one for authors, one for titles, and one for characters, with cross-referencing. Like the Italian *Bompiani*, it is richly illustrated. The German *Kindlers Lexikon* is arranged by title only; volume 7 provides an appendix of articles on the literatures of individual countries, areas, and languages, and includes indexes to authors, anonyma, titles, and essays, plus a list of sources used. The title entries in all three dictionaries provide summaries, background information, and bibliographies which can include citations to editions, translations, secondary scholarship, film productions, etc. Articles in all three dictionaries are signed.

439 *Dizionario Universale della Letterature Contemporanea.* 4 vols. plus *Index.* Milano, 1959–1962.

A comprehensive encyclopedic dictionary of modern world literature and related arts for the period 1870–1960. Arranged alphabetically. Includes entries for authors (and other artists and writers having some connection with the world of literature) and survey articles on modern literature in different parts of the world. Articles include primary and secondary bibliographies. The *Index* volume contains a year-by-year chronological table covering the period 1870–1961, and indexes to authors, titles, translations, foreign works not translated into Italian, literary surveys by country or period, etc.

440 WILPERT, GERO von, ed. *Lexikon der Weltliteratur.* Band I: *Biographisch-bibliographisches Handwörterbuch nach Autoren und anonymen Werken.* Stuttgart, 1963; 2. erw. Aufl., 1975. Band I: *Hauptwerke der Weltliteratur in Charakteristiken und Kurzinterpretationen.* Stuttgart, 1968.

An extensive dictionary of world literature of all times, divided into two main parts. Volume 1 is arranged as an author list (anonymous works by title); entries give a brief biographical sketch, followed by a list of the author's works and brief citations to secondary sources. Volume 2 is arranged as a title list; entries give author, date of publication, a summary and/or descriptive comment, and sometimes a reference to a relevant work of secondary scholarship. Includes a list of authors whose works have been cited in the volume.

441 SHIPLEY, JOSEPH T., ed. *Encyclopedia of Literature.* 2 vols. N.Y., 1946.

A series of survey histories of the literatures of the world, arranged alphabetically by name of country. The history of each national literature includes a bibliography. Volume 2 includes a biographical dictionary of significant world literary figures.

442 BENET, WILLIAM ROSE. *The Reader's Encyclopedia.* 2nd ed. N.Y., 1965. Rev. ed., 2 vols., 1966.

A dictionary list of articles on writers, works, and literary terms of all nations and all periods. Articles include brief biographies of writers, short plot summaries, and definitions of terms.

443 WALZEL, OSKAR, hrsg. *Handbuch der Literaturwissenschaft.* 22 (ungezählte) Bde. u. vier Lieferungen. Potsdam, 1923–[42]. Rptd. Darmstadt, 1957 ff.

444 SEE, KLAUS von, hrsg. *Neues Handbuch der Literaturwissenschaft.* Frankfurt, 1972–   .

445 EPPELSHEIMER, HANNS WILHELM. *Handbuch der Weltliteratur, von den Anfängen bis zur Gegenwart.* 3. Aufl. Frankfurt, 1960.

446 FLEISCHMAN, WOLFGANG B. *Encyclopedia of World Literature in the 20th Century.* 3 vols. N.Y., 1967. [An English version, rev. and enl., of the Herder *Lexikon der Weltliteratur im 20. Jahrhundert*, 2 Bde., Freiburg, 1960–61.]

A general encyclopedia of modern world literature. Its some 14,000 articles are arranged alphabetically and include entries for topics such as "Expressionism," "Symbolism," and "Psychology and Literature," as well as surveys of the literature of individual countries and entries for individual authors. Articles are signed and include bibliographies; many articles are illustrated.

447 WARD, A. C. *Longman Companion to Twentieth Century Literature.* London, 1970.

A dictionary list of articles on Twentieth-Century writers, mainly English, but including some Commonwealth and American writers, and some writers in languages other than English when they are of international reputation and when their works have been translated into English. Includes biographical entries, plot summaries, character identifications, and articles on topics such as "Drama," "Biography," "Censorship of Books," "Literary

Criticism," etc. Also includes entries for such matters as literary terms, allusions, and the like.

448 POLLARD, ARTHUR, ed. *Webster's New World Companion to English and American Literature.* N. Y., 1973.

A dictionary list of articles on authors and literary terms. The entries for individual authors provide a brief biography and a list of works; an appendix provides a brief list of secondary materials on each author.

449 *Columbia Dictionary of Modern European Literature.* Ed. Horatio Smith. N. Y., 1947.

A dictionary of 1167 articles on European literature from about 1870 to the present. The bulk of the dictionary consists of author entries; these provide a biographical and critical survey and invariably include secondary bibliographies. There are also 31 articles on the literatures of different European countries. All articles are initialled.

450 HARVEY, Sir PAUL and J. E. HESELTINE. *The Oxford Companion to French Literature.* Oxford, 1959. Rptd.

A dictionary list of about 6,000 entries for authors, titles, and subjects related to French literature. Authors treated are mostly literary figures, but include also historians, savants, statesmen, philosophers, etc. Entries for authors give dates and provide a brief account of the author's life and work. Title entries supply summaries of plots and, sometimes, literary comment. Subject entries include historical, geographical, social, economic and political matters. Coverage is up to 1939. Much cross-referencing. No secondary bibliographies are provided in the entries, but there is an appendix which gives a general list of books and periodicals, with "pointers to the study of French literature and its background," and a second appendix of maps.

450a GARLAND, HENRY and MARY GARLAND. *The Oxford Companion to German Literature.* London, 1976.

Concise biographies, synopses of works, entries on literary movements and styles, background. Alphabetical arrangement. Includes Austria and Switzerland.

451 KOEHMSTEDT, CAROL L. *Plot Summary Index.* Metuchen, N. J., 1973.

An index to the contents of 26 collections of plot summaries, including all the variant compilations in the *Masterplots* series. Provides citations to summaries of novels, plays, poems, and some nonfiction. Entries are arranged in two main alphabetical lists: (1) by title and (2) by author. Entries in both lists include code symbol references to collections in which summaries appear. The key to the code system given on pp. vii-ix provides, in effect, a brief bibliography of collections of plot summaries. No index.

452 FRENZEL, ELISABETH *Stoffe der Weltliteratur: Ein Lexikon dichtungsgeschichtlicher Längsschnitte.* 3. überarb. Aufl. Stuttgart, 1970.

A dictionary of subject-matter of world literature. Alphabetical entries treat themes and figures (historical and legendary) which have become literary 'raw material' – *e. g.* Antigone, Faustus, Don Juan, Susanna, Thomas à Becket. Different adaptations to literary uses are described; for example, Joan of Arc is discussed as literary subject-matter for ballads, poems, romances, dramas, historical novels, librettos for operas, etc. Most articles include short reading lists. No index. See also E. Frenzel, *Stoff- und Motivgeschichte,* 2 verbess. Aufl. Berlin, 1974, which contains a useful bibliography.

453 BRETT-JAMES, ANTONY. *The Triple Stream: Four Centuries of English, French, and German Literature, 1531–1930.* Cambridge, 1953.

A parallel column chronology of literary works in England, France, and Germany, with indexes for each language for the periods 1531–1900 and 1901–1930, and for authors.

454 KAISER, FRANCES E. *Translators and Translation: Services and Sources.* 2nd ed. N. Y., 1965.

Contains an annotated international list of current and retrospective bibliographies of translations.

455 *Index Translationum: Répertoire international des traductions; International Bibliography of Translations.* Paris 1932–40, N. S. 1949– .

Originally quarterly, now an annual bibliography of published translations. Entries are arranged by country. The text of each entry is in both French and English. Until vol. 6 (1954) index of authors, translators, and publishers; thereafter, only author index.

456 FARRAR, CLARISSA P. and AUSTIN P. EVANS. *Bibliography of English Translations from Medieval Sources.* N. Y., 1946.

An annotated bibliography of translations of writings mainly from the 4th through the 15th centuries in Europe, Western Asia, and Northern Africa, but including some Christian writings as early as the 1st century. Arranged as an author list of about 4000 entries which include information on the quality of the translation, its printings and reprintings, etc. Author-title-subject index.

457 FERGUSON, MARY ANNE HEYWARD. *Bibliography of English Translations from Medieval Sources, 1943–1967.* N. Y., 1974.

An annotated bibliography which continues Farrar and Evans' *Bibliography of English Translations from Medieval Sources,* but extends the scope to include Talmudic material, Aesop, the Dead Sea Scrolls, etc., and includes more subject categories. For more recent translations of medieval materials, consult the lists of editions and translations published in *Speculum,* 1973– .

458 OPPEL, HORST. *Englisch-deutsche Literaturbeziehungen.* 2 Bde. Berlin, 1971.

Helpful survey with very extensive bibliographies.

459 GALINSKY, HANS. *Amerikanisch-deutsche Sprach- und Literaturbeziehungen: Systematische Übersicht und Forschungsbericht 1945–1970.* Frankfurt, 1972.

Comprehensive survey and review of research. Index of names and subjects.

B. Comparative Literature

463 BALDENSPERGER, F. and WERNER P. FRIEDERICH. *Bibliography of Comparative Literature.* CHAPEL HILL, N.C., 1950. Rptd., N.Y., 1960.

A comprehensive bibliography of books, articles, and dissertations on all aspects of comparative literature in all countries. Arrangement is elaborately classified; no index. Topics covered range from the most general influences on English and American literature to the work of particular authors and the influence of particular themes, motifs, etc.

463a ALBÉRÈS, R.-M. *L'Aventure Intellectuelle du XXᵉ Siècle: Panorama des littératures européennes 1900–1970.* 4th ed. rev. Paris, 1969.

A survey history of European (including English) literature 1900–1968. Major divisions cover broad literary periods; within these, chapters are devoted to literary movements and individual writers. An appendix provides synoptic tables of literary and other developments 1880–1968, with categories such as "Symbolisme Poétique," "Christianisme Tragique," etc. Index to authors.

464 *Yearbook of Comparative and General Literature.* 1–18 (1952–70).

Each annual volume includes an elaborately classified bibliography of books, articles, and dissertations on all aspects of comparative literature. Intended to serve as a continuation and supplement to **463**.

465 *Bibliographie générale de littérature comparée.* 5 vols. Paris, 1950–60.

466 WEISSTEIN, ULRICH. *Einführung in die vergleichende Literaturwissenschaft.* Stuttgart, 1968.

A general guide to the study of comparative literature, including such topics as the definition of comparative literature, its history, the study of international literary influences and critical responses, themes and genres, etc. Fully documented; includes a bibliography. Index of personal names.

467 PICHOIS, CLAUDE et ANDRÉ-MARIE ROUSSEAU. *La littérature comparée.* Paris, 1967.

A general guide to comparative literature, including such topics as the history of comparative literary study, international literary exchanges, the comparative study of literary themes and genres, and the aesthetics of translation. Fully documented; includes a bibliography. No index.

468 PRAWER, S. S. *Comparative Literary Studies: An Introduction.* London, 1973.

A readable introduction attempting to establish a descriptive typology of problems in comparative literature. It concludes with a bibliography and a genral index.

469 FRIEDERICH, WERNER P. and DAVID H. MALONE. *Outline of Comparative Literature from Dante to O'Neill.* Chapel Hill, 1954.

Despite the title, really a general comparative history of world literature, with particular emphasis on international literary similarities, differences, and influences. Includes an index to names and topics.

470 STALLKNECHT, NEWTON P. and HORST FRENZ. *Comparative Literature: Method and Perspective.* 2nd ed. Carbondale, 1971.

A series of essays on various aspects of the study of comparative literature. The chapter by Henry H. H. Remak titled "Comparative Literature: Its Definition and Function" includes a selected but relatively thorough and fully annotated bibliography of books and articles on comparative literature.

V. Literary Theory and Criticism

A. Bibliographical Materials

475 HALL, VERNON. *Literary Criticism Plato Through Johnson.* Goldentree Bibliographies. N. Y., 1970.

Highly selective bibliography of primary and secondary materials on literary criticism from the classical period through the 18th century. After preliminary lists of collections of criticism and general works, arrangement is by broad chronological periods (classical, medieval, renaissance, later criticism); within each period a list of general works is followed by primary and secondary bibliographies of individual critics arranged alphabetically by name. Index of scholars.

475a MURPHY, JAMES J. *Medieval Rhetoric. A Select Bibliography.* Toronto, 1971.

Lists more than 500 titles; partly annotated.

476 HARARI, JOSUÉ. *Structuralists and Structuralisms: A Selected Bibliography of French Contemporary Thought (1960–1970).* Ithaca, N. Y., 1971.

A classified list arranged under headings such as "Structuralism," "Literature," "Linguistics and Semiotics," etc., with sub-classes within these categories. Indexes to periodicals and to authors.

477 BAXANDALL, LEE. *Marxism and Aesthetics: A Selective Annotated Bibliography.* N. Y., 1968.

A selective annotated bibliography of books and articles in English on Marxist aesthetics. Arranged under various broad topics such as "Cinema," "Literature," "Theatre," etc., including entries for Great Britain and the United States; these in turn have sub-categories for literature, theatre, cinema, etc. Analytic table of contents; no index.

478 SHIBLES, WARREN A. *Metaphor: An Annotated Bibliography and History.* Whitewater, Wis., 1971.

A bibliography of books and articles on all aspects of metaphor. Arranged as an author list; entries give bibliographic citation and many also include an abstract. There are two indexes: (1) to general terms and names and (2) to ideas about metaphor.

478a "Selective Current Bibliography for Aesthetics and Related Fields."
Journal of Aesthetics and Art Criticism, 4–31 (1945–1973).

An annual selective bibliography of secondary materials on aesthetics. Arranged as a classified list with categories such as "architecture," "literature," etc.; within these categories arrangement is first books, then articles, each listed alphabetically by author.

479 MILIC, LOUIS T. *Style and Stylistics: An Analytical Bibliography.*
N. Y., and London, 1967.

An annotated bibliography of secondary materials on style and stylistics. Classified arrangement in five major categories: theory, methodology, applications, bibliographies, and general works; within each major division entries are arranged chronologically. Includes cross references and separate indexes for author-scholars, author-subjects, and topics.

480 BAILEY, RICHARD W. and DOLORES M. BURTON. *English Stylistics: A Bibliography.* Cambridge, Mass., 1968.

An annotated bibliography of primary and secondary materials related to the linguistic study of literary texts. Classified arrangement in three main categories: (1) bibliographical sources, (2) language and style before 1900, subdivided chronologically, and (3) stylistics in the 20th century, subdivided into sections on such topics as statistical analysis, translation, prose, poetry, etc. Separate indexes to literary authors and to critics.

481 "Annual Bibliography." *Style,* 1–   (1967–   ).

An annual bibliography of books, parts of books, dissertations, and articles dealing with the analysis of style. Recent issues often contain special bibliographies with annotations.

For other bibliographies of writings on critical theory and criticism see entries **101** and **124a**.

B. General Studies and Reference Collections

482 WELLEK, RENÉ and AUSTIN WARREN. *Theory of Literature.* 3rd ed.
rev. N. Y., 1956. Rptd.

Contains chapters on various aspects of critical analysis, including the relationship of literary study to other disciplines such as psychology, biography, history of ideas, etc. Provides an extensive bibliography on pp. 317–357, covering all aspects of literary theory and the relation of literature to other disciplines; citations are restricted to criticism written since about 1850. See also Wellek's *Concepts of Criticism,* ed. by S. G. Nichols, Jr., New Haven, Conn., 1963.

482a ELLIS, JOHN M. *The Theory of Literary Criticism: A Logical Analysis.*
Berkeley, Calif., 1974.

Less comprehensive than Wellek and Warren's *Theory of Literature*, but attempts to focus on the most central theoretical problems in literary criticism. Each chapter is documented, and there is a list of references at the end of the book. Index of names.

483 WEHRLI, MAX. *Allgemeine Literaturwissenschaft*. Bern, 1951.

A general discussion of the theory of literary study, with emphasis on the scholarship of the period 1930–1950. Provides an extensively documented survey of methods and approaches to the study of literature.

484 OPPEL, HORST. *Methodenlehre der Literaturwissenschaft*. Berlin, 1957. Rptd. from *Deutsche Philologie im Aufriss*. Hrsg. von Wolfgang Stammler. 3 Bde. 2 Aufl. Berlin, 1957–62; Register-Bd. L. M. Lechner *et al.*, 1969.

Oppel's article is not only a survey of methods of literary study, but also includes commentary on scholarship in literary theory and criticism. There are other articles of general interest, esp. in volume 1, section 1, of *Deutsche Philologie im Aufriß* on "Poetik," "Stoff- und Motivgeschichte" etc. with wide bibliographical coverage.

485 HYMAN, STANLEY EDGAR. *The Armed Vision: A Study in the Methods of Modern Literary Criticism*. N.Y., 1948. Rev. ed. abrdgd., 1955. Rptd.

A study of modern literary criticism with individual chapters on Yvor Winters, Van Wyck Brooks, Maud Bodkin, R. P. Blackmur, I. A. Richards, T. S. Eliot, Constance Rourke, Caroline Spurgeon, William Empson, Kenneth Burke, Edmund Wilson, and Christopher Caudwell. Includes a selected bibliography. The bibliography and the chapters on Wilson and Caudwell are omitted from the abridged edition. Hyman's *The Critical Performance: An Anthology of American and British Literary Criticism of Our Century*, N. Y., 1956, serves as a companion volume to *The Armed Vision*.

486 FRYE, NORTHROP. *Anatomy of Criticism*. Princeton, N. J., 1957. Rptd.

Extensive essays on four aspects of critical theory: (1) theory of modes, (2) theory of symbols, (3) theory of myths, and (4) theory of genres. Includes brief notes, a glossary, and an author-title-subject index.

487 KAYSER, WOLFGANG. *Das sprachliche Kunstwerk: Eine Einführung in die Literaturwissenschaft*. 17. Aufl. Bern, 1976. (Orig. ed., 1948).

A general introduction to literary study, with emphasis on the detailed analysis of individual literary works. Includes discussions of methods of interpretation, and the analysis of style and structure of literary works, illustrated by analyses of poems and representative prose selections in different languages. Extensive international bibliography with special emphasis on stylistic and poetic analysis.

488 ABRAMS, M. H. *The Mirror and the Lamp: Romantic Theory and the Critical Tradition.* London, 1953. Rptd.

A study of the development of English romantic poetic theory (and related ideas in philosophy, ethics, theology, and the sciences), considered against the background of eighteenth-century aesthetics. Describes the change from neoclassic to romantic criticism as a radical shift in the basic metaphors used in critical discourse.

489 FUSSELL, PAUL JR. *Poetic Meter and Poetic Form.* N. Y., 1965.

A general consideration of meter in English poetry, including a brief annotated bibliography of significant books and articles on meter. Has a subject index.

490 ALLOTT, MIRIAM, ed. *Novelists on the Novel.* London, 1959. Rptd.

An anthology of writings on the novel by novelists from Richardson to E. M. Forster, with introduction and connecting chapters. Arranged in three main parts, each subdivided into categories such as "The Ethics of the Novel," "Narrative Technique," "Characterization," "Style," etc. Analytic table of contents, an index of authors and titles, and an index to authors' treatments of different subjects.

491 HALPERIN, JOHN, ed. *The Theory of the Novel: New Essays.* N. Y., 1974.

Includes a selective annotated bibliography on theory of fiction and critical approaches to fiction.

492 STEVICK, PHILIP, ed. *The Theory of the Novel.* N. Y., 1967.

An anthology with a "Selected Bibliography" on pp. 407–428. Most of the writings cited were published after 1900 and deal with the theory of the novel generally, exclusive of particular novelists or special periods in the history of the novel.

493 BOOTH, WAYNE C. *The Rhetoric of Fiction.* Chicago, 1961.

An important analysis of narrative art and technique. Includes an extensive bibliography on various aspects of the theory and criticism of fiction, pp. 399–434. The bibliography is divided into five parts: (1) "General"; (2) "Technique as Rhetoric," subdivided into (a) "The Telling-Showing Distinction," (b) "Alternatives to Reliable Narration," and (c) "Realism and Technique"; (3) "The Author's Objectivity and the 'Second Self'"; (4) "Artistic Purity, Rhetoric, and the Audience"; and (5) "Narrative Irony and Unreliable Narrators," subdivided into (a) "General Discussions of Irony, Ambiguity, and Obscurity," (b) discussions of unreliability in specific authors, arranged alphabetically from Sherwood Anderson to Robert Penn Warren, and (c) "Some Sources of the Modern Unreliable Narrator."

494 LÄMMERT, EBERHARD. *Bauformen des Erzählens.* Stuttgart, 1955. Rptd.

A study combining both theoretical and historical analysis of the development of literary narrative. Extensive notes (pp. 255–84) and a bibliography of over 200 items.

495 ALDRIDGE, JOHN W. ed. *Critiques and Essays in Modern Fiction, 1920–1951.* N. Y., 1952.

Collection of representative essays and "A Selected Bibliography of Criticism on Modern Fiction" on pp. 553–610, sub-divided into three parts: (1) General Fiction Checklist, (2) Topic Checklists, and (3) Author Checklists.

496 MOULTON, CHARLES WELLS, ed. *The Library of Literary Criticism of English and American Authors.* 8 vols. Buffalo, N. Y., 1901–05. Rptd., N. Y., 1935–40; rptd. abrgd. and with add., N. Y., 1966, ed. MARTIN TUCKER.

A collection of critical comment on English and American authors arranged chronologically by literary period and covering the years 680–1904. For each author the entry provides a short biographical note followed by quotations from selected critical writings on the author and his works. Vol. 8 includes indexes to both literary authors and critics.

497 TUCKER, MARTIN, ed. *The Critical Temper: A Survey of Modern Criticism on English and American Literature from the Beginnings to the Twentieth Century.* 3 vols. N. Y., 1969.

A collection of selected critical comments on English and American writers and their works. Serves as a supplement to Moulton, **496**, covering the same literary period (680–1900) but providing selected critical excerpts from 20th century critics. Arranged chronologically by literary periods (American literature is included at the end of vol. 3). Within each period the names of literary figures are arranged in alphabetical order, with quotations from critical writings given beneath each name. Vol. 3 includes a cross-reference index to authors and an index to critics.

498 RILEY, CAROLYN, ed. *Contemporary Literary Criticism.* 1– . Detroit, Mich., 1973– .

Planned as a continuing series. Each volume provides a collection of passages from critical writings about the works of major and minor literary figures (including authors of such minor genres as mystery and science fiction) of all countries, who are now living or who died after 1959. Entries for each volume in the series are arranged A–Z by name of literary author; they include a brief biographical identification and quotations from relevant critical writings.

499 BROWN, CLARENCE A., ed. *The Achievement of American Criticism: Representative Selections from Three Hundred Years of American Criticism.* N. Y., 1954.

An anthology of some 65 works of American literary criticism from the preface to the *Bay Psalm Book* to the present, arranged chronologically in 4 main sections. A classified, selective bibliography of primary and secondary materials is provided on pp. 687–724.

500 ZABEL, MORTON D., ed. *Literary Opinion in America.* 2 vols. 3rd ed. rev. N. Y., 1962.

A collection of essays illustrating the methods and problems of literary criticism in 20th century America. Vol. 2, pp. 793–903, provides an extensive bibliography in the form of bibliographic appendixes such as "Recent Works of American Criticism," "Collections of Contemporary American Criticism," "A Supplementary List of Essays in Criticism: 1900–1950," and "A Note on Contemporary English Criticism."

501 STALLMAN, ROBERT W., ed. *Critiques and Essays in Criticism, 1920–1948.* N. Y., 1949.

Representative essays of modern British and American critics. Includes "A Selected Bibliography of Modern Criticism: 1920–1948," pp. 519–571.

502 CORBETT, EDWARD P. J., ed. *Rhetorical Analysis of Literary Works.* London, 1969.

A collection of rhetorical analyses of literary works. Includes a bibliography (pp. 233—272) of twentieth-century writings dealing both with the general theory and practice of rhetorical-critical analysis and with particular works of individual writers.

503 ERDMAN, DAVID V. and EPHIM G. FOGEL, eds. *Evidence for Authorship: Essays on Problems of Attribution with an Annotated Bibliography of Selected Readings.* Ithaca, N. Y., 1966.

A collection of essays on various problems of literary attribution, including both matters of theory and particular studies of English and American literature, arranged chronologically, with a special section on the detection of forgery. Provides an extensive annotated bibliography (pp. 397–523) arranged to follow the organization of the essays and including an additional section on statistical applications and computer studies. Separate indexes of subjects and of names and titles.

* * *

504 *The Critical Idiom Series.* London, Methuen, 1969– .

A series of volumes each dealing with a key term in the vocabulary of literary criticism. Volumes treat such terms as *romanticism, satire, plot, rhetoric, surrealism, the grotesque,* and *tragedy.* References are made, whenever appropriate, to more than one literature, and each volume includes a bibliography, often annotated, and an index to authors and titles, and, sometimes, to subjects.

Critical essays written in different periods of English literature and published by the Oxford University Press:

505 SMITH, G. GREGORY, ed. *Elizabethan Critical Essays*. 2 vols. 1904. Rptd.

506 SPINGARN, J. E., ed. *Seventeenth-Century Critical Essays*. 3 vols. 1908–9. Rptd.

507 ELLEDGE, SCOTT, ed. *Eighteenth-Century Critical Essays*, 2 vols. 1961.

508 JONES, EDMUND, ed. *English Critical Essays: Sixteenth, Seventeenth, and Eighteenth Centuries*. 1924. Rptd.

509 SMITH, D. NICHOL, ed. *Shakespeare Criticism: A Selection*. 1923. Rptd. [Criticism from 1623 to 1840.]

510 RIDLER, ANNE, ed. *Shakespeare Criticism 1919–1935*. 1936. Rptd.

511 RIDLER, ANNE, ed. *Shakespeare Criticism 1935—1960*. 1963. Rptd.

512 JONES, EDMUND D., ed. *English Critical Essays: Nineteenth Century*. 1916. Rptd.

513 JONES, PHYLLIS. M., ed. *English Critical Essays: Twentieth-Century*. First Series, 1933. Rptd.

514 HUDSON, Derek, ed., *English Critical Essays: Twentieth-Century*. Second Series. 1958. Rptd.

514a BEAVER, HAROLD, ed. *American Critical Essays*. 1959. Rptd.

* * *

There are a number of publishers' series devoted to printing collections of criticism on English and American authors. Among those, the most prominent are the following:

515 *The Critical Heritage Series*. London, Routledge & Kegan Paul, and N. Y., Barnes & Noble.
Reprintings of reviews and other critical writings published during the author's lifetime.

516 *Discussions of Literature*. London, Harrap, and Boston, Mass., D. C. Heath.
Modern critical writings on individual authors, literary works, or special topics.

517 *Macmillan Casebook Series*. London, Macmillan.
Reprintings of both earlier and more recent comment on an individual author's work.

518 *Contemporary Studies in Literature.* N. Y., McGraw-Hill.

Collections of modern critical writings on contemporary authors.

519 *Modern Judgments.* London, Macmillan.

Reprintings of criticism published in the past thirty years.

520 *Twentieth Century Views.* Englewood Cliffs, N. J., Prentice Hall.

Contemporary critical commentary on major writers. Key to the information in the series: *Reader's Index to the Twentieth Century Views ... Volumes 1–100.* Ed. Robert Mony. Englewood Cliffs, N. J., 1973.

520a *Twentieth Century Interpretations.* Englewood Cliffs, N. J., Prentice-Hall.

Collections of critical writings on great works of literature.

521 *Wadsworth Guides to Literary Study.* San Francisco, Wadsworth.

Selected criticism in chronological order, but major themes and problems may be approached with the help of a topical index.

522 *Penguin Critical Anthologies.* Harmondsworth, Middlesex, Penguin Books.

Contain selections from major writers on their own art, contemporary reception, later criticism and modern critical discussions and analyses. Bibliographies and glossarial indexes are added.

523 *Modern Essays in Criticism.* London & N. Y., Oxford University Press (Galaxy Books; Oxford Paperbacks).

Collections of recent essays on periods and *genres* of English literature, such as *The Elizabethan Drama, Eighteenth Century Literature*, etc. Emphasis is predominantly critical. As a rule the essays represent different points of view and divergent critical attitudes.

524 *Interpretationen.* Berlin, Erich Schmidt.

Collections of critical essays on English and American literature specifically written for this series. Volumes are differentiated by period and *genre* (*e. g. Der Moderne Englische Roman*, hrsg. Horst Oppel, 2. überarb. Aufl. 1971) and contain general introductions, interpretations of representative works in the context of the author's *oeuvre* and time, individual bibliographies and extensive general bibliographical appendixes.

525 Untitled series treating major literary *genres*. Düsseldorf, Bagel.

All contributions are originally written for the volumes in this series. They deal with English and American poetry, drama, novel, and short story; *genre* history is treated through a number of major individual works under such titles as *Das Englische Drama vom Mittelalter bis zur Gegenwart*, hrsg. Dieter Mehl, 2 Bde. 1970. Extensive notes and bibliographies in each volume.

109

Other series combine publication of an edited text with a collection of critical writings on it:

526 *Norton Critical Editions.* N.Y., W. W. Norton.

527 *Merrill Literary Casebook Series.* Columbus, Ohio, Charles E. Merrill.

528 *Crowell Literary Casebooks.* N.Y., Thomas Y. Crowell.

529 *Signet Classics.* N.Y., The New American Library; London, The New English Library.

For other collections of critical writings see entries **130** and **280**.

C. Histories of Literary Criticism

530 WIMSATT, WILLIAM and CLEANTH BROOKS. *Literary Criticism: A Short History.* N.Y., 1957.

Covers the history of literary criticism from the Greeks to the present. Does not provide a separate bibliography, but there is extensive bibliographic information provided in the footnotes.

531 ATKINS, J. W. H. *Literary Criticism in Antiquity.* 2 vols. Cambridge, 1934. *English Literary Criticism: The Medieval Phase.* Cambridge, 1943. Rptd. *English Literary Criticism: The Renascence.* 2nd ed., London, 1951. Rptd. *English Literary Criticism: 17th and 18th Centuries.* London, 1951.

Historical studies with chapters on topics such as "Medieval Poetics: Geoffrey of Vinsauf and John of Garland," "The Defense of Poetry: Willis, Lodge, Sidney," etc. Each volume includes a subject index. Somewhat fuller history than that provided by Saintsbury's *History of English Criticism* (Edinburgh, 1911), but does not take full advantage of scholarship published since Saintsbury. For a detailed analysis of the limitations of the 17th and 18th century criticism vol., see R. S. Crane, "On Writing the History of Criticism in England 1650–1800," *University of Toronto Quarterly,* 22 (1953), 376–91; rptd., *The Idea of the Humanities* (Chicago, 1967), vol. 2, pp. 157–75.

532 WEINBERG, BERNARD. *A History of Literary Criticism in the Italian Renaissance.* 2 vols. Chicago, 1961.

Vol. 2, pp. 1113–1158, provides a bibliography of primary and secondary materials; locates copies of scarce items.

533 WELLEK, RENÉ. *A History of Modern Criticism 1750–1950.* 5 vols. London, 1955– . [The 5th vol. has not yet appeared; it will cover the first part of the 20 th century.]

A very extensive history of modern criticism with exceptionally full documentation and some annotated bibliographies. Each volume has a chronological table and separate name and topic/term indexes.

535 SUTTON, WALTER. *Modern American Criticism.* Englewood Cliffs, N. J., 1963.

An historical survey of American literary criticism in the 20th century. Includes an index to critics.

536 O'CONNOR, WILLIAM VAN. *An Age of Criticism 1900–1950.* N.Y., 1952.

A short history of modern literary criticism. Includes a selected bibliography of works in which "extensive lists of books, articles, and reviews can be found." Author-title-subject index.

537 WEIMANN, ROBERT. *"New Criticism" und die Entwicklung bürgerlicher Literaturwissenschaft.* Halle, 1962.

A general history and critique of the "new criticism" from a Marxist point of view; includes an extensive bibliography on pp. 328–347, very full documentation, and an index to subjects as well as to names.

VI. Interdisciplinary Literary Materials

540 THORPE, JAMES E. ed. *Relations of Literary Study: Essays on Interdisciplinary Contributions.* N. Y., 1967.

A collection of essays by different scholars on the interdisciplinary study of literature, with bibliographies on the relations of literature to biography, to sociology, to myth, and to music. The individual essays on topics like the relationship of literature to psychology, etc. also contain bibliographic information in the form of footnotes.

541 *A Bibliography on the Relations of Literature and the Other Arts.* Compiled and issued by MLA Group IX, 1953– .

An annual bibliography (with some brief annotations) of secondary materials on the relationship of literature to music and the visual arts. Arrangement is classified under three main headings: "Theory and General," "Music and Literature," and "The Visual Arts and Literature." The bibliographies for the years 1952–1958 have been published in *Literature and the Other Arts: A Select Bibliography 1952–1958*, ed David Erdman, N. Y., 1959.

542 HENKEL, ARTHUR, und ALBRECHT SCHÖNE, hrsg. *Emblemata: Handbuch zur Sinnbildkunst des XVI. und XVII. Jahrhunderts.* Stuttgart, 1967. Ergänzte Neuausgabe, Stuttgart, 1976.

A compilation of 3713 emblems from 47 emblem books; the entries provide both the picture and associated texts. Arrangement is by emblem subject. Includes a descriptive bibliography of emblem books and indexes to mottoes, to the subject of pictures, and to significances of the emblems. An appendix gives reprintings of original indexes of some famous emblem books.

543 LURKER, MANFRED, *et al. Bibliographie zur Symbolkunde.* 3 Bde. Baden-Baden, 1964–68. Rptd. 1968.

An extensive bibliography listing bibliographies, periodicals, dictionaries, writings on the history and definition of symbol, selections from the literature of the 16th to the 18th century, ethnology, art, literature, music, types of symbols, symbolic figures. Author and subject indexes.

544 *Bibliographie zur Symbolik, Ikonographie und Mythologie. Internationales Referateorgan.* 1– (1968–).

Presents publications relevant to research in interdisciplinary topics which are difficult to correlate in their manifold ramifications. Signed abstracts written in German, English or French indicate the essentials of content, particular perspective of the author, state of investigation etc. Disciplines considered include prehistory, archaeology, classical studies ... literature, folklore studies, sociology, and philosophy. Extensive indexes of topics and authors. From 1970 on, each yearly volume contains an article dealing with one aspect of symbolism.

545 HERMAND, JOST. *Literaturwissenschaft und Kunstwissenschaft: Methodische Wechselbeziehungen seit 1900.* 2., verbess. Aufl., Stuttgart, 1971.

Review of research on the relations between literature and art since 1900. There are bibliographies at the end of each (sub)section and an index of names.

546 KIELL, NORMAN. *Psychoanalysis, Psychology, and Literature: A Bibliography.* Madison, Wis., 1963.

An extensive bibliography of writings on all aspects of the relationship between literature and psychology published after 1900. Includes a subject index.

547 "Bibliography for [year]." *Literature & Psychology*, 17– (1970–).

An annual selective annotated bibliography of articles on topics involving the relationship of literature and psychology. Bibliographies for 1964–67 were separately published.

548 GRIFFIN, ERNEST G. *Bibliography of Literature and Religion.* University of Alberta, 1969.

A list of books and articles in the field of literature and religion, mostly published in recent years. Arranged alphabetically by author. An index to 21 broad subjects (e. g., "Literature and Belief," "Religious Typology and Symbolism in Literature," etc.) is provided in the front matter.

549 LAURENSON, DIANA and ALAN SWINGEWOOD. *The Sociology of Literature.* London, 1972.

Contains a select bibliography (pp. 276–281) on the relations of literature to social theory and sociology.

550 EBISCH, WALTHER und LEVIN L. SCHÜCKING. "Bibliographie zur Geschichte des literarischen Geschmacks in England," *Anglia*, 63 (1939), 1–64.

A bibliography of writings dealing with the social conditions in which literary works are produced and read, including such topics as the author and his social position, his audience (court, bourgeoisie, women, clergy, family, etc.), literary agents, patrons, publishing firms, lending libraries, etc.

551 SCHÜCKING, LEVIN L. *Soziologie der literarischen Geschmacksbildung.* Bern, 1961.

552 CRUSE, AMY. *The Englishman and His Books in the Early 19th Century.* London, 1930.

553 CRUSE, AMY. *The Victorians and Their Books.* London, 1935.

554 CRUSE, AMY. *After the Victorians.* London, 1938.

555 ALTICK, RICHARD D. *The English Common Reader 1800–1900.* Chicago, 1957.

556 LEAVIS, Q. D. *Fiction and the Reading Public.* London, 1932. Repr. 1968.

557 "Relations of Literature and Society." Mimeographed bibliographies issued by MLA Group V annually from 1938 to 1946. Continued by *Literature and Society [1950–1965]: A Selective Bibliography.* University of Miami Publications in English and American Literature. Nos. 2, 4, and 9. Coral Gables, Fla., 1956, 1962, and 1967.

Selective bibliographies of books and articles on the relationship of literature and society. Arranged as two lists (books and articles), each alphabetical by author. The continuations in the University of Miami Publications provide an index to authors, scholar-critics, titles, and subjects.

558 LANDRUM, LARRY. "Recent Books in Popular Culture." *Indiana Social Studies Quarterly,* 26 (Winter, 1973–4), 76–83.

A survey of bibliographies, reference guides, and other materials relating to the study of "popular culture." Includes materials on literature, film, records, television, and musicals.

559 CAWELTI, JOHN G. "Recent Trends in the Study of Popular Culture," *American Studies: An International Newsletter,* 10 (Winter, 1971), 23–37.

A running commentary on scholarship in the area of "popular culture," including "The Popular Arts," "Mass Media and Communications," etc. Includes a brief bibliography.

560 *Popular Culture Methods.* 1– (1972–).

Published quarterly. Includes various checklists and bibliographies on popular culture materials.

561 DUDLEY, FRED A., ed. *The Relations of Literature and Science: A Selected Bibliography 1930–1967.* Ann Arbor, Mich., 1968.

A conflation of the bibliographies previously published in *Symposium,* 1951–1967, with earlier titles back to 1930. Arranged with general works first, then by period. Index of scholars, translators, editors, and critics.

562 "Relations of Literature and Science: Selected Bibliography for [year]." *Symposium,* 5–21 (1951–67).

Annual bibliography of books and articles on the relations of literature and science. Arranged with general materials first, then by period.

563 "Bibliography: Literature and Science." *Clio: An Interdisciplinary Journal of Literature,* 4– (1974–).

An annual bibliography of books and articles on the relations of literature and science; continues the bibliography formerly mimeographed and distributed annually at General Topics # 7 meetings of the Modern Language Association of America.

564 "Annual Bibliography for [year]." *Computers and the Humanities,* 1– (1967–).

Annual bibliography of books and articles on the use of computers and computer analysis techniques in the humanities. Arranged as a classified list with categories such as "History," "Language and Literature," etc.; within these categories arrangement is alphabetical by author.

VII. The Literary Text: Printing, Textual History, Analytic and Descriptive Bibliography, and Editing

A. General

570 GASKELL, PHILIP. *A New Introduction to Bibliography*. Oxford, 1972.

The successor to R. B. McKerrow, **571**; a comprehensive study of the processes of book production particularly as these relate to the transmission of literary texts. Treats the history of bookmaking from 1500 to the present and provides additional chapters on bibliographical applications to the identification, description, and analysis of texts, with appendixes on Elizabethan handwriting, bibliographical description, and textual transmission. Provides extensive documentation in footnotes and an annotated reference bibliography including such subjects as hand-printing and machine-printing technology, presswork, presses, composition, printing-house organization, type, paper, binding, decorating and illustrating, reproduction, and the book trade, as well as book identification, book description, and textual bibliography. Includes an exceptionally full subject index.

571 MCKERROW, R. B. *An Introduction to Bibliography for Literary Students*. Oxford, 1927.

572 *Esdaile's Manual of Bibliography*. 4th ed., rev. by Roy Stokes. London, 1967.

573 STOKES, ROY. *The Function of Bibliography*. N. Y., 1969.

574 TANSELLE, G. THOMAS. "The Periodical Literature of English and American Bibliography." *Studies in Bibliography*, 26 (1973), 167–191.

A general discussion of available periodical literature on English and American bibliography, with a list of the basic periodicals and their indexes.

575 BRACK, O. M. JR. and WARNER BARNES, eds. *Bibliography and Textual Criticism: English and American Literature, 1700 to the Present*. Chicago, 1969.

Collection of essays on various aspects of bibliography and textual criticism, all written between 1959 and 1968. Bibliography and subject index.

576 "A Selective Check List of Bibliographical Scholarship for [year]." *Studies in Bibliography*, 3–27 (1950–74). The checklists covering the years 1949–55 were republished with an index in *SB*, 10 (1957); the checklists covering the years 1956–62 were republished with an index in *Selective Check Lists of Bibliographical Scholarship, Series B,* Charlottesville, Va., 1966. The lists published for the years 1963–72 were subtitled "Series C." The publication of these checklists was discontinued because they would duplicate the material appearing in the *Annual Bibliography,* **592.**

577 *The Library: A Quarterly Journal of Bibliography* [Title has varied]. 1– (1899–).

Includes reviews and annotated lists of "Recent Books" and "Recent Periodicals" which often cite works related to analytic bibliography and editing. Earlier issues included reviews and lists of newly published books under headings such as "Records of Bibliography and Library Literature," "Reviews and Notices," etc.

578 "The Register.of Current Publications [year]." *Proof,* 1– (1971–).

An annual selective, descriptively annotated checklist of in-print monographs in the field of bibliographical and textual studies. Classified annual checklist: (1) edited primary works, (2) reprinted primary works, (3) author bibliographies and checklists, (4) subject bibliographies and checklists, (5) national bibliographies and checklists, (6) writing and autographs, (7) printing, binding, publishing, and bookselling, (8) copyright and intellectual property, (9) libraries and book collecting, (10) bibliographical and textual theory and practice, (11) concordances and indexes, (12) dictionaries, rhetorics, and guides to language, and (13) miscellaneous. Author-title-subject index.

579 *The Direction Line: A Newsletter for Bibliographers and Textual Critics.* Austin, Texas, and Leeds, England, 1975– .

A newsletter, published irregularly, containing information on work in progress, proposed investigations, and notes on bibliography and textual criticism.

B. Incunabula

580 HAIN, LUDWIG. *Repertorium Bibliographicum, In Quo Libri Omnes Ab Arte Typographica Inventa Usque Ad Annum MD.* 2 vols. in 4. Stuttgart, 1826–38. Rptd., Berlin, 1925.

A numbered list of books printed in the 15th century. Arranged alphabetically by author. The 16,299 entries give title, place and date of printing, printer, format and other information. Index of places and printers. Supplemented by the following works:

COPINGER, WALTER A. *Supplement to Hain's Repertorium Bibliographicum; Or, Collections Towards a New Edition of That Work.* 2 vols. in 3. London, 1895–1902. Rptd., Leipzig, 1926.

Provides corrections and almost 6,000 additions to Hain.

REICHLING, DIETRICH. *Appendices ad Hainii-Copingeri Repertorium Bibliographicum; Additiones ed Emendationes.* 7 vols. Monaco, 1905–11. *Supplementum . . . Cum Indice Urbium et Typographorum,* 1914.

581 PANZER, GEORG W. F. *Annales Typographici.* Vol. 1–11. Norimbergae, 1793–1803. Rptd. Hildesheim, 1963–64.

A bibliography of books printed from the beginning of printing to 1536. Arrangement is alphabetical by Latin place names, and, for each place, arrangement is chronological. Supplemented by the following:

BURGER, KONRAD. *Ludwig Hain's Repertorium Bibliographicum: Register, Die Drucker des XV. Jahrhunderts.* Leipzig, 1891.

BURGER, KONRAD. *Supplement zu Hain und Panzer: Beiträge zur Inkunabelbibliographie, Nummernconcordanz von Panzers lateinischen und deutschen Annalen und Ludwig Hains Repertorium Bibliographicum.* Leipzig, 1908. Rptd. Hildesheim, 1966.

582 PROCTOR, ROBERT. *An Index to the Early Printed Books in the British Museum, From the Invention of Printing to the Year 1500, With Notes on Those in the Bodleian Library.* 2 vols. London, 1898–99. *An Index . . . Part 2: 1501–1520.* 2 vols. 1903–1938. *Supplements.* 5 pts. 1900–1903.

A bibliography of incunabula in the British Museum. Arranged chronologically by the order of countries in which printing began in Europe; for each country arrangement is chronological by places and presses where printing began. This arrangement is known as "Proctor order." Numbered entries are brief but can give title, author, printer, publisher, and Hain number. Part 4 in vol. 2 of the 1898–99 volumes provides an index to towns, printers, and publishers, as well as lists of books in and not in Hain, authors of books published in the Netherlands, and books printed in England.

583 British Museum Department of Printed Books. *Catalogue of Books Printed in the XVth Century Now in the British Museum.* London, Part 1– , 1908– .

In progress. Arranged in Proctor order; 9 parts covering Germany, Switzerland, Austria-Hungary, Italy, France (with French-speaking Switzerland), and the low countries have been published. Parts covering Spain, Portugal, and England are in preparation.

584 OATES, J. C. T. *A Catalogue of the Fifteenth Century Books in the University Library, Cambridge.* London, 1954.

585 JOHN RYLANDS LIBRARY. *English Incunabula in the John Rylands Library: A Catalogue of Books Printed in England and of English*

Books Printed Abroad Between the Years 1475 and 1500. Manchester, 1930.

586 GOFF, FREDERICK R. *Incunabula in American Libraries: A Third Census of Fifteenth-Century Books Recorded in American Collections.* N. Y., 1964. Supplemented ed., 1973.

The 1964 edition provides a list of some 12,000 entries for 15th century books in American collections. Entries give short title, place, printer, date, format, notes, and references to earlier citations, as well as locations of about 47,000 copies in 760 American collections. Includes (1) indexes of variant forms of authors' names, of printers, and of publishers, (2) concordances which relate the numbering in the *Third Census* to those used in the *Gesamtkatalog der Wiegendrucke*, Hain, Proctor, and Margaret Stillwell's *Second Census* of American incunabula of 1940. The supplemented edition of 1973 adds some 3,000 items to the basic list.

587 *Gesamtkatalog der Wiegendrucke.* Hrsg. v. d. Kommission für den Gesamtkatalog der Wiegendrucke. 7 Bde., 1 Lfg. Leipzig 1925–40. Bde. 1–7 als durchges. Neudruck, Stuttgart 1968. Bd. 8, Lfg. 1–   . Stuttgart, 1972–   .

The most comprehensive catalogue of incunabula which will eventually include all the relevant material. Alphabetical arrangement (authors, anonyma), thorough bibliographical descriptions and collations. Will become a world union list of incunabula (all locations are given for European and American libraries if there are less than 10 copies extant, a wide selection if there is a greater number).

588 *Der Buchdruck des 15. Jahrhunderts: Eine Bibliographische Übersicht.* Hrsg. v. d. Wiegendruck-Gesellschaft. Berlin, 1929–36.

International bibliography of scholarship on incunabula. Arranged according to countries. Includes both books and articles. Author index.

589 BESTERMAN, THEODORE. *Early Printed Books to the End of the 16th Century: A Bibliography of Bibliographies.* 2nd ed. Geneva, 1951.

A bibliography of bibliographies and library catalogues for books printed up to 1600/1640. Includes bibliographies printed separately, as parts of books, or as articles. Entries sometimes include brief annotations and give the number of pages in the bibliography. Separate indexes to authors, subjects, printing places, printers and booksellers, libraries, and private collections.

C. History of Printing and the Book Trade

1. Bibliographies

590 MYERS, ROBIN. *The British Book Trade from Caxton to the Present Day: A Bibliographical Guide Based on the Libraries of the National Book League and St Bride Institute.* London, 1973.

A classified, annotated bibliography of books relating to the history of the book trade in England (and, to some extent, on the Continent and in America). Arranged in categories such as "Authorship," "Bookbinding," "Bookselling," "History of the Book Trade," "Paper for Bookwork and Printing Ink," etc. The annotations are both descriptive and critical. Author-title index.

591 TANSELLE, G. THOMAS. "The Historiography of American Literary Publishing." *Studies in Bibliography*, 18 (1965), 3–39.

An extensively documented survey of available materials for research in the history of American publishing and American national bibliography.

592 *Annual Bibliography of the History of the Printed Book.* 1– (1973–).

An annual bibliography which attempts to record all books and articles of scholarly value which deal with printing history and associated arts and crafts from beginning of printing to the present. Arranged as a classified list with categories such as "General Works," "Paper, inks, printing materials," "Bookbinding," "Legal, economic, social aspects," etc. Two indexes: (1) author's names and anonyms and (2) geographical and personal names.

593 *Saint Bride Foundation Catalogue of the Technical Reference Library of Works on Printing and the Allied Arts.* London, 1919.

594 *Catalogue of Periodicals Relating to Printing in the Technical Library of the Saint Bride Institute.* London, 1951.

595 *Dictionary Catalog of the History of Printing from the John M. Wing Foundation in the Newberry Library.* 6 vols. Boston, Mass., 1961.

2. Historical Studies

596 PLANT, MARJORIE. *The English Book Trade: An Economic History of the Making and Sale of Books.* 3rd ed. London, 1974.

An extensive study of the history of book trade economics in England – employment conditions, unions, production costs, etc. References are provided at the ends of chapters; particularly valuable for its citations of early materials.

597 CLAIR, COLIN. *A History of Printing in Britain.* London, 1965.

An outline history of the development of printing in Great Britain from the time of Caxton. No bibliography, but some documentation within the chapters. Subject index.

598 BENNETT, H. S. *English Books and Readers 1475–1557.* Cambridge, 1952. *English Books and Readers 1558–1603.* Cambridge, 1965.

Useful supplements to the histories of the English book trade by Marjorie Plant and Colin Clair for the period 1475–1603. Short bibliographies and indexes.

599 HINMAN, CHARLTON. *The Printing and Proof-Reading of the First Folio of Shakespeare.* 2 vols. Oxford, 1963.

An elaborately detailed investigation of the evidences of printing house practice employed in preparing the first folio of Shakespeare. Provides an exceptionally full picture of Renaissance printing, including analysis of the work of individual compositors, the movement of individual pieces of type from forme to forme, and the like. Subject-title index.

600 MCKENZIE, DONALD F. "Printers of the Mind: Some Notes on Biblio-graphical Theories and Printing-House Practices." *Studies in Bibliography,* 22 (1969), 1–75.

An important article dealing with the problems of interpreting evidences about the history of printing.

601 TEBBEL, JOHN. *A History of Book Publishing in the United States. Vol. I: The Creation of an Industry 1630–1865.* N.Y., 1972; *Vol. II: The Expansion of an Industry 1865–1919.* 1975. [In Progress.]

A comprehensive history of American publishing. Extensively documented. Vol. II includes appendixes on American book title output and directories of publishers. Both vols. have author-title-subject indexes.

602 LEHMANN-HAUPT, HELLMUT, *et al. The Book in America: A History of the Making and Selling of Books in the United States.* 2nd ed. rev. and enl. N.Y., 1952.

603 WROTH, LAWRENCE C. *The Colonial Printer.* Portland, Me., 1938. Rptd., Charlottesville, Va., 1964.

604 SILVER, ROLLO G. *The American Printer 1787–1825.* Charlottesville, Va., 1967.

⁎

A general annotated bibliography of materials related to the book trade and the history of book production is given in **570**.

D. Descriptive Bibliography

605 BOWERS, FREDSON. *Principles of Bibliographic Description.* Princeton, N. J., 1949. Rptd., N. Y., 1962.

A comprehensive statement of the principles and practices of descriptive bibliography as these apply to printed books of all periods. Chapters and sub-sections cover such topics as the definitions of *edition, impression, issue,* and *state*; title page transcription; collational formulae; binding; typography; catchwords; etc. Includes an author-subject index.

606 DEARING, VINTON A. *Principles and Practice of Textual Analysis.* Berkeley, Calif., 1974.

A study of the principles and methodology by which the genealogy of variant texts is established, archetypal texts are deduced, and the archetypes emended. Also has chapters on the formal theory of textual analysis, on probabilistic methods, and on editing. Subject index.

606a BÜHLER, CURT F., *et al. Standards of Bibliographical Description.* Philadelphia, Pa., 1949.

Essays on standards and practices of bibliographical description for incunabula, and for early English and American literature. No index.

607 FOXON, DAVID F. *Thoughts on the History and Future of Bibliographical Description,* Los Angeles, 1970.

An historical analysis of the development of quasi-facsimile title page transcription and of the notation conventions for recto and verso of individual leaves in descriptive bibliography.

608 MERIWETHER, JAMES B., and JOSEPH KATZ. "A Redefinition of 'Issue.'" *Proof,* 2 (1972), 61–70.

Argues that the term *state* should be used to refer to variants in an impression that are associated with the printing history of the book; *issue* should be used to refer to variants which are associated with the publishing history of the book.

609 TANSELLE, G. THOMAS. "Tolerances in Bibliographical Description." *The Library,* 23 (1968), 1–12.

A general discussion of the kinds of accuracy and range of tolerances possible in descriptive bibliography; suggests a system of various "levels" of acceptable precision related to the purpose of the bibliographic description.

610 TANSELLE, G. THOMAS. "A System of Color Identification for Bibliographical Description." *Studies in Bibliography,* 20 (1967), 203–34.

Proposes a system of bibliographic color identification based on the U. S. National Bureau of Standards' *The ISCC-NBS Method of Designating Colors and a Dictionary of Color Names* (Washington, D. C., 1965) and the

ISCC-NBS Centroid Color Chart (Standard Sample No 2106). The system proposed combines descriptive words and centroid numbers. Includes an extensive bibliographic note on the literature of color description.

611 TANSELLE, G. THOMAS. "The Bibliographical Description of Patterns." *Studies in Bibliography*, 23 (1970), 71–102.

Analyzes problems in the bibliographic description of patterns in binding cloth and endpapers and proposes systems for the description of both. Includes sample photographs of patterns in bindings and endpapers and indicates the sources for them and for other such illustrations. Extensively documented.

612 TANSELLE, G. THOMAS. "The Bibliographical Description of Paper." *Studies in Bibliography*, 24 (1971), 27–67.

A comprehensive survey of problems in the bibliographic description of paper, with recommendations for the treatment of such matters as paper sizes, wire and chainlines, watermarks (and the application of radiography to their study), paper bulk, tensile strength, permeability, smoothness, chemical makeup, etc. Includes extensive documentation.

613 TANSELLE, G. THOMAS. "The Identification of Type Faces in Bibliographical Description." *Papers of the Bibliographical Society of America*, 60 (1966), 185–202.

An analysis of the problems in treating type size and type design in descriptive bibliography. Includes extensive documentation. See also Tanselle's "The Use of Type Damage as Evidence in Bibliographical Description," *The Library*, 23 (1968), 328–51.

614 TANSELLE, G. THOMAS. "The Recording of Press Figures." *The Library*, 21 (1966), 318–25.

Proposes a notation system to be used by descriptive bibliographers for recording press figures in eighteenth-century English books.

615 TANSELLE, G. THOMAS. "Book-Jackets, Blurbs, and Bibliographers." *The Library*, 26 (1971), 91–134.

Provides information on the early history of book-jackets and the importance of their inclusion in descriptive bibliographies. Illustrated. Provides a checklist of examples of book-jackets, an author index, a publisher index, and a series index.

616 JONES, JOHN BUSH, ed. *Readings in Descriptive Bibliography*. Kent, Ohio, 1974.

A collection of readings on descriptive bibliography. Includes a brief "Checklist of Further Readings."

E. Editing

617 THORPE, JAMES. *Principles of Textual Criticism.* San Marino, Calif., 1972.

A general discussion of the principles underlying modern editing, with examples drawn from the Renaissance to the present. Chapters include "The Ideal of Textual Criticism," "The Treatment of Accidentals," "The Establishment of the Text," etc. Index to topics and authors.

618 BOWERS, FREDSON. *Bibliography and Textual Criticism.* Oxford, 1964.

A collection of six lectures on the uses of analytic bibliography in editing texts. Index of names, titles, and subjects.

619 Modern Language Association of America, Center For Editions of American Authors. *Statement of Editorial Principles.* N.Y., 1972.

A broad statement of the editorial principles adopted by the Center for Editions of American Authors governing the choice of copy-text, collation of texts, reporting collation results, preparing notes and introductions, proofreading, etc. Includes a brief bibliography of writings on editorial principles and on textual problems. For brief evaluations of the CEAA editions, see Hershel Parker's "The CEAA: An Interim Assessment," *Papers of the Bibliographical Society of America*, 68 (1974), 129–48.

620 TANSELLE, G. THOMAS. "Greg's Theory of Copy-Text and the Editing of American Literature." *Studies in Bibliography*, 28 (1975), 167–229.

A detailed analysis and exposition of Greg's theory of copy-text, with consideration of its critics, of proposed alternate theories, and of the relation of Greg's theory to the procedures adopted by the Center for Editions of American Authors. Extensively documented. For the article upon which Tanselle's paper is based, see W. W. Greg, "The Rationale of Copy-Text," *Studies in Bibliography*, 3 (1950), 19–36.

621 BOWERS, FREDSON. "Multiple Authority: New Problems and Concepts of Copy-Text." *The Library*, 27 (1972), 81–115.

A discussion for the procedure for constructing a copy-text in cases where no single document can serve as copy-text. Supplements but does not conflict with Greg's copy-text theory. For further discussion of this problem see Bowers' "Remarks on Eclectic Text" published in *Proof*, 4 (1974).

622 TANSELLE, G. THOMAS. "Some Principles for Editorial Apparatus." *Studies in Bibliography*, 25 (1972), 41–88.

A consideration of the uses and conventions of textual notes, emendations, line-end hyphenation, and historical collation.

623 GOTTESMAN, RONALD and SCOTT BENNETT. *Art and Error: Modern Textual Editing.* Bloomington, Indiana, 1970.

A collection of essays and studies on problems of editing English and American literary texts. Includes a selective annotated list of further readings.

❊ ❊ ❊

Various problems of editing the texts of particular literary periods have been the subject of a series of conferences on editing held at the University of Toronto.

624 RICHARD J. SCHOECK, ed. *Editing Sixteenth-Century Texts,* Toronto, 1966.

625 D. I. B. SMITH, ed. *Editing Seventeenth-Century Prose.* Toronto, 1972.

626 D. I. B. SMITH, ed. *Editing Eighteenth-Century Texts.* Toronto, 1968.

627 JOHN D. BAIRD, ed. *Editing Texts of the Romantic Period.* Toronto, 1972.

628 JOHN M. ROBSON, ed. *Editing Nineteenth-Century Texts.* Toronto, 1967. (Includes a bibliography).

629 FRANCES G. HALPENNY, ed. *Editing Twentieth-Century Texts.* Toronto, 1972.

F. Encyclopedias of the Book and the Printing Industry

630 GLAISTER, GEOFFREY ASHALL. *A Glossary of the Book: Terms Used in Papermaking, Printing, Bookbinding, and Publishing With Notes on Illuminated Manuscripts, Bibliophiles, Private Presses, and Printing Societies.* London, 1960. [Published with the title *An Encyclopedia of the Book,* Cleveland, Ohio, 1960.]

An encyclopedic dictionary covering all aspects of book making, with entries for persons, societies, techniques, tools, processes, and the vocabulary of the book trade. Includes much historical information. Extensively illustrated (the entry for *Marbling,* for example, includes sample marbled papers). Includes appendixes of type specimens, Latin place names used in early printed books, contemporary private presses, proof correction symbols, and a list of readings.

631 STRAUSS, Victor. *The Printing Industry.* Washington, D. C., 1967.

An encyclopedic guide to the modern printing industry. Arranged as a series of articles on broad topics – e. g., "Printing Processes and Methods," "Printing Presses," etc. – with extensive illustrations, notes, and a selective bibliography. Includes a detailed subject index.

VIII. Guides to Scholarship and General Literary Reference Materials

A. Guides to Scholarship

640 THORPE, JAMES, ed. *The Aims and Methods of Scholarship in Modern Languages and Literatures.* N. Y., 1963.

A collection of four essays by William G. Moulton, Fredson Bowers, Robert E. Spiller, and Northrop Frye on the aims, problems, methods, and purposes of modern scholarship in linguistics, textual criticism, literary history, and literary criticism.

641 THORPE, JAMES. *Literary Scholarship: A Handbook for Advanced Students of English and American Literature.* Boston, Mass., 1964.

A general guide to the principles of literary scholarship, with chapters on how to use reference works in the study of literature, how to document literary studies, etc. Includes an index to the principal topics and chief reference works discussed in the text.

642 ALTICK, RICHARD D. *The Art of Literary Research.* Rev. ed. N. Y., 1975.

A series of essays on various aspects of the art of literary research with extensive illustrations of the use (and misuse) of research tools. Some chapters – e. g. "Finding Materials" and "Libraries" – provide incisive comment on the research tools they discuss. Bibliography of writings on literary scholarship and extensive exercises in the use of research materials.

643 ALTICK, RICHARD D. *The Scholar Adventurers.* N. Y., 1950. Rptd.

An evocation of the excitement and human drama which can be part of research in literature.

644 BEAURLINE, LESTER A., ed. *A Mirror for Modern Scholars: Essays in Methods of Research in Literature.* N. Y., 1966.

A collection of representative scholarly studies in various fields of literary research: bibliography, textual studies, authorship and dating, biography, sources and analogues, style, historical periods, history of ideas, historical interpretation, form and convention. R B. McKerrow's essay, "Form and Matter in the Publication of Research" is provided in an appendix. Includes a list of suggested readings. A similar collection of essays may be found in Sheldon P. Zitner's *The Practice of Modern Literary Scholarship*, Glenview, Ill., 1966.

645 SANDERS, CHAUNCEY. *An Introduction to Research in English Literary History, With a Chapter on Research in Folklore by Stith Thompson.* N. Y., 1952.

A guide to materials and methods of research in English literary history. Includes chapters dealing with research problems and procedures in the areas of biography, source study, editing (this and some other parts are now outdated), authenticity and attribution, chronology, success and influence, interpretation, the history of ideas, and folklore. Extensive bibliographic references and illustrations of solutions and procedures for problems in literary history. Subject index.

646 FABIAN, BERNARD, hrsg. *Ein anglistischer Grundkurs zur Einführung in das Studium der Literaturwissenschaft.* Frankfurt a. M., 2. verbess. Aufl. 1973.

An introduction to literary scholarship in English literature, with essays on such topics as literary history, stylistic and metrical analysis, the linguistic analysis of texts, research materials, etc. Each chapter includes a bibliography. Appendixes provide reproductions of sample pages from some major reference works and an annotated guide to building a basic literary reference library. Title-subject index.

✻

646a Modern Language Association of America. *The MLA Style Sheet.* 2nd ed. N. Y., 1970.

A manual for the preparation of literary scholarship both for publication and for submission in unpublished form as thesis or course paper. Widely accepted in America by scholarly journals and presses, and by graduate and undergraduate departments of English. Includes a subject index. Two related pamphlets also published by the MLA are *On the Publication of Research* and *The Publication of Academic Writing;* these supply more detailed advice on writing research and arranging for its publication. All three pamphlets may be obtained from the Materials Center, Modern Language Association, 62 Fifth Ave., New York, N. Y., 10011.

646b *MHRA Style Book: Notes for Authors and Editors.* Ed. A. S. Maney and R. L. Smallwood. Cambridge, Modern Humanities Research Association, 1971.

Represents standard British practice.

B. General Literary Reference Materials

647 KENNEDY, ARTHUR G. and DONALD B. SANDS. *A Concise Bibliography For Students of English.* 5th ed., rev. by WILLIAM E. COLBURN. Stanford, Calif., 1972.

A selective but very comprehensive guide to research materials for literature in English produced in England, America, Canada, Australia, India, and other English speaking countries. Includes not only bibliographies, indexes, and other reference tools, but, also, studies on all aspects of language and literature except individual authors. Especially full treatment of all subjects, including such supplementary areas as handwriting, computers, author-audience relationship, censorship, theory and practice of scholarship, scholarly writing, translation, folklore, and linguistics. Indexes of periodicals, subjects, and persons.

648   BOND, DONALD. *A Reference Guide to English Studies.* 2nd ed. Chicago, 1971.

A selective but relatively full guide to research materials for English and American literature, with brief annotations. Especially useful is its extensive coverage of supplementary areas such as the literatures of Ireland, Scotland, Wales, the Commonwealth, France, Italy, Spain, Latin America, Germany, Scandinavia, and Russia, and of topics such as linguistics, history, journals, learned societies, genealogy and heraldry, education, music, paleography, philosophy, psychology, prohibited books, religion, science, social science, chapbooks, children's books, costume, courtesy books, dance, furniture, privately printed books, sport, travel, and unfinished books. Includes indexes of persons and subjects.

649   ALTICK, RICHARD D. and ANDREW WRIGHT. *Selective Bibliography for the Study of English and American Literature.* 5th ed. N. Y., 1975.

A highly selective guide to research materials for English and American literature. Includes an introductory essay on the use of scholarly tools, a brief list of "Some Books Every Student of Literature Should Read," a short glossary, and an author-title-subject index.

650   BELL, INGLIS and JENNIFER GALLUP. *A Reference Guide to English, American, and Canadian Literature: An Annotated Checklist of Bibliographical and Other Reference Materials.* Vancouver, B. C., 1971.

A highly selective annotated guide to general reference materials and to secondary bibliographies of individual authors. Special emphasis is given to Canadian literature. Author-editor-compiler-title index, and a separate index for subject authors. Intended for undergraduate students.

651   KOHL, NORBERT. *Bibliographie für das Studium der Anglistik.* Bad Homburg v. d. H., 1970– . Bd. I (1970): *Sprachwissenschaft, mit einem allgemeinen bibliographischen und lexikalischen Teil.* Bd. II (not yet publ.): *Literaturwissenschaft.* Bd. III, Teile 1 & 2 (1972–3): *Englische Fachdidaktik* (Norbert Kohl und Konrad Schröder). Bd. IV (not yet publ.): *Autoren- und Werkbibliographie.*

Vol. 1 includes an exceptionally full bibliography of materials supplementary to the study of English literature – general encyclopedias, biographical encyclopedias, special encyclopedias, bibliographies of bibliography, national bibliography, library catalogues, periodicals, reference materials in linguistics, etc.

652 MÜLLER-SCHWEFE, GERHARD. *Einführung in das Studium der Englischen Philologie.* 2. neubearb. Aufl. Tübingen, 1968.

An introduction to the study of English literature: essentially a selective bibliography with running commentary covering general materials, literary periods, genres and criticism, linguistics, etc. Includes separate name and subject indexes.

653 LUBBERS, KLAUS. *Einführung in das Studium der Amerikanistik.* Tübingen, 1970.

A guide in the form of a running commentary on materials for the study of American language and literature. Includes chapters on linguistics, literary scholarship, American English, American literature, and supplementary materials. Name and subject indexes.

654 ALTICK, RICHARD D. *Librarianship and the Pursuit of Truth.* New Brunswick, N. J., 1974.

Comments on the weaknesses and limitations of some frequently used literary reference tools.

655 THOMPSON, JAMES. *English Studies: A Guide for Librarians to the Sources and Their Organisation.* 2nd ed. rev. and enl. London, 1971.

Chapters 1–10 provide a critical survey of standard reference materials for the study of English, Commonwealth, and American literature. Intended primarily for librarians but useful for students of literature as well. Author-title-subject index.

656 CHANDLER, G. *How to Find Out About Literature.* Oxford, 1968.

A guide to literary study and a running commentary on literary reference materials. Arranged in chapters covering such topics as "How to Trace Novels and Prose," "How to Evaluate Literary Biographies," etc. Includes a subject index.

657 PATTERSON, MARGARET C. *Literary Research Guide.* Detroit, Mich., 1976.

A critically annotated guide to reference materials for the study of English and American literature. Arranged as a classified list with such headings as "Annual Bibliographies," "English Literature," "Indexing Services," etc.

658 *Literary Research Newsletter.* 1– (1976–).

A quarterly journal devoted to the publication of articles, notes, and reviews on new literary reference materials.

IX. Guides to General Reference Materials

660 WALFORD, ALBERT J. *Guide to Reference Material.* 3 vols. 2nd ed. London, 1966–70. 3rd ed. vol. 1: *Science and Technology.* London, 1973; vol. 2: *Social & Historical Sciences, Philosophy & Religion.* London, 1975.

A comprehensive, international, critically annotated guide to all kinds of reference materials on all subjects. Elaborately classified arrangement with very full author-title-subject index in each volume. Entries provide information on the scope, arrangement, and limitations of each reference work. The complete edition contains about 13,000 entries; vol. 3, which includes reference materials on literature, language, libraries, biography, bibliography, and the arts, has about 4,700 entries including some reference works on individual authors. Particularly strong on British and Commonwealth materials.

661 WINCHELL, CONSTANCE M. *Guide to Reference Books.* 8th ed. Chicago, 1967. *Supplement 1965–66,* 1969; *Supplement 1967–68,* 1970; *Supplement 1969–70,* 1972. [9th ed. announced for late 1976.]

A general annotated guide to all kinds of reference materials on all subjects. International scope, but particularly strong on American materials. Elaborately classified arrangement with author-subject index. Entries provide information on the scope, arrangement, and limitations of reference works including materials on literature, language, biography, bibliography, and the arts. The main volume has about 7,500 entries. The 1972 *Supplement* has a cumulated index.

662 MALCLÈS, L.-N. *Les sources du travail bibliographique.* 3 vols. in 4. Genève, 1950–58. Rptd., 1965.

A general guide to reference materials. Includes not only annotated lists of reference works but also introductions to each chapter which explain their uses. Now somewhat out of date, but still useful for its relatively full coverage of continental materials. Each volume has an author-title-subject index. See also L.-N. Malclès, *Manuel de bibliographie.* 2ᵉ éd. entièrement refondue et mise à jour. Paris, 1969.

663 TOTOK, WILHELM, *et al. Handbuch der Bibliographischen Nachschlagewerke.* 4., erweit., völlig neu bearb. Aufl. Frankfurt, 1972.

A general but highly selective guide to about 4000 reference works, primarily bibliographies and indexes, but including encyclopedias, biographical dictionaries, guides to pseudonyms, etc. Excludes such tools as language dictionaries, bibliographies on individuals or regions, atlases, etc. Includes sections on reference materials for language and literature. Main headings in the table of contents are in English and French as well as German. Annotations are brief. Includes an author-title-subject index.

664 IRELAND, NORMA O. *An Index to Indexes: A Subject Bibliography of Published Indexes.* Boston, Mass., 1942.

A guide to about 1,000 indexes to periodicals and books. Arranged alphabetically in some 280 subject headings with relevant indexes given beneath each heading. Does not include foreign indexes and is incomplete for American indexes. May be supplemented by the same author's *Local Indexes in American Libraries: A Union List of Unpublished Indexes,* Boston, Mass., 1947.

666 *American Reference Books Annual.* 1– (1970–).

An annual critically annotated guide to new reference material of all kinds which are published or distributed in the United States. Elaborately classified arrangement, including categories such as "General Reference," "Fine Arts," "Linguistics and Philology," "Literature," etc. Author-title-subject index. A cumulative index to the first five volumes is in progress.

667 *Reference Services Review.* 1– (1973–).

A quarterly survey of new reference materials on a wide variety of subjects including language and literature. Provides critically annotated lists and formal reviews of current reference books, reference services, and other reference materials. Each quarterly number includes an index to reviews of reference materials in about 80 journals, including *Aslib Booklist, British Book News, Choice, Journal of Documentation, New York Review of Books, Times Literary Supplement,* etc. Author-title index.

668 "Recent Foreign Reference Books." *American Notes and Queries,* 1– (1962–).

A monthly commentary on recently published foreign reference books and (since July, 1973) foreign bibliographic journals.

X. General Bibliographies of Bibliography

669 DOWNS, ROBERT B. and FRANCES B. JENKINS, eds. *Bibliography: Current State and Future Trends.* Urbana, Ill., 1967.

A collection of critical surveys in the form of running commentaries on the state of bibliography in different subject areas, including general bibliography, national bibliography, periodicals, newspapers, manuscripts and archives, incunabula, English and American literature, etc. Author-title-subject index.

670 BESTERMAN, THEODORE. *A World Bibliography of Bibliographies and of Bibliographical Catalogues, Calendars, Abstracts, Digests, Indexes, and the Like.* 4th ed. 5 vols. Lausanne, 1965–66.

An international bibliography of bibliographies on all subjects. Includes only bibliographies published separately – not as parts of books or serials. Contains about 117,000 entries arranged under some 16,000 subject categories (including authors as subjects) with elaborate cross-referencing. The number of items included in a bibliography is given in square brackets. Vol. 5 is an author-title-town-library index. Various parts of the *World Bibliography* have been published separately as individual subject bibliographies – including *Literature: English and American: A Bibliography of Bibliographies,* Totowa, N. J., 1971.

671 COLLISON, ROBERT L. *Bibliographies: Subject and National.* 3rd ed. rev. and enl. London, 1968.

A selective annotated guide to major subject, universal, and national bibliographies. The subject bibliographies treated include those for philosophy, psychology, religion, science, art, entertainment, sport, language and literature, geography, history, and biography. The section on national bibliographies is limited to Great Britain, the United States, France, and Germany. There is also a short guide to serial bibliographies and indexes. Includes an index of subjects and personal names.

672 COURTNEY, WILLIAM P. *A Register of National Bibliography: With a Selection of the Chief Bibliographical Books and Articles Printed in Other Countries.* 3 vols. London, 1905–1912. Rptd., N.Y., 1967.

A list of some 25,000 bibliographies printed separately or as parts of books or in serials. Vols 1–2 (bibliographies published up to 1905) are arranged alphabetically by subject with extensive cross-referencing; vol. 2 includes an appendix and an author-title-subject index. Vol. 3 (bibliographies published between 1905 and 1912) is a supplementary list arranged alphabetically by subject with an appendix and an author-title-subject index.

673 *Bibliographic Index: A Cumulative Bibliography of Bibliographies.* 1– (1938–).

A current bibliography of bibliographies on all subjects published three times a year with an annual cumulation. Includes bibliographies published separately, as parts of books and in periodicals; presently surveys about 2,200 periodicals. Arrangement is alphabetical by subject, with extensive cross-referencing. Coverage is primarily of bibliographies published in Germanic and Romance languages.

674 GRAY, RICHARD A. *Serial Bibliographies in the Humanities and Social Sciences.* Ann Arbor, Mich., 1969.

A very full bibliography of serial bibliographies arranged in Dewey Decimal classes and annotated by means of a number-letter code. Provides information about content, scope, arrangement, and frequency of serial bibliographies in all Dewey classes except pure science and technology. Indexes include titles, authors, and special characteristics of serial bibliographies. Subject index on pp. 287–340.

675 *Bulletin of Bibliography and Magazine Notes.* 1– (1897–).

Issues include enumerative bibliographies, checklists, studies in reference works, and lists of new, changed, and ceased periodicals. Many of the bibliographies and checklists published are on literary topics – individual author bibliographies, bibliographies on literary genres, and checklists and bibliographies on related literary subjects. There is an annual author-subject index.

XI. National Bibliography

A. General National Bibliography

680 CONOVER, HELEN F. *Current National Bibliographies.* Washington, D. C., 1955. Rptd. N. Y., 1968.

An extensively annotated bibliography of sources of information about book publishing in all countries of the world. Arranged by broad geographical areas and within these by country. Lists existing publishing records, periodical indexes, government publication, periodical directories, etc. Index of titles (and some authors), directory of publishers, and index to countries.

681 COLLISON, ROBERT L. *Bibliographical Services Throughout the World 1950–1959.* N. Y., 1961.

682 AVICENNE, PAUL. *Bibliographical Services Throughout the World 1960–1964.* N. Y., 1967. *Bibliographical Services Throughout the World 1965–1969.* N. Y., 1972.

683 UNESCO. *Bibliography, Documentation, Terminology.* Vol. 10– (1961–).

Published bi-monthly. Provides information about current national bibliographies of member nations of the U. N. Classified arrangement. See particularly the categories "National Activities," "National Bibliography," and "Bibliographic Services Throughout the World."

684 *International Literary Market Place 1975–1976.* N. Y., 1974.

A directory to the international book trade. Arranged alphabetically by country and under each country alphabetically by name of publishing firm. Entries give such information as address, telephone number, cable code, names of chief company officers, special subjects published, number of titles published in a recent year, etc.
See also **669–671**.

B. English National Bibliography

685 DUFF, EDWARD G. *Fifteenth Century English Books: A Bibliography of Books and Documents Printed in England and of Books for the English Market Printed Abroad.* London, 1917.

A descriptive bibliography of 431 books. Arranged as an author list (anonymous works by title). Entries give locations of copies in major British libraries. Chronological index.

NATIONAL BIBLIOGRAPHY: ENGLAND

A GRAPHIC OVERVIEW

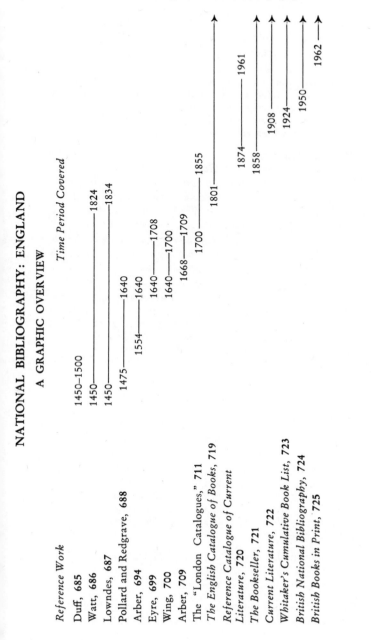

Reference Work	Time Period Covered
Duff, **685**	1450–1500
Watt, **686**	1450——1824
Lowndes, **687**	1450——1834
Pollard and Redgrave, **688**	1475——1640
Arber, **694**	1554——1640
Eyre, **699**	1640——1708
Wing, **700**	1640——1700
Arber, **709**	1668——1709
The "London Catalogues," **711**	1700——1855
The English Catalogue of Books, **719**	1801→
Reference Catalogue of Current Literature, **720**	1874——1961
The Bookseller, **721**	1858→
Current Literature, **722**	1908→
Whitaker's Cumulative Book List, **723**	1924→
British National Bibliography, **724**	1950→
British Books in Print, **725**	1962→

686 WATT, ROBERT. *Bibliotheca Britannica Or a General Index to British and Foreign Literature.* 4 vols. Edinburgh, 1824. Rptd. N. Y., 1965.

Attempts to list books published in England or related to England from the beginning of printing. Vols. 1–2 are arranged alphabetically by author (about 40,000 entries); each entry provides a very brief biographical note followed by a list of the author's works with indications of format, date of publication, and other bibliographic information. Vols. 3–4 provide an alphabetical subject and key-word index (about 150,000 items) to the entries in vols. 1–2; within each subject entry the arrangement is chronological.

687 LOWNDES, WILLIAM THOMAS. *The Bibliographer's Manual of English Literature Containing An Account of Rare, Curious, and Useful Books, Published in or Relating To Great Britain and Ireland, from the Invention of Printing; with Bibliographical and Critical Notices, Collations of the Rarer Articles, and the Prices at Which They Have Been Sold.* First ed., 4 vols., London, 1834. New ed., rev. and enl. by H. G. Bohn, 11 vols., London, 1857–64; reissued frequently in 6 vols between 1869–1914. Rptd. ed. (of the 6 vol. reissue) in 8 vols. with an essay on Lowndes by Francesco Cordasco, Detroit, Mich., 1967.

Attempts to list all books published in Great Britain and Ireland from the advent of printing to the first part of the 19th century. Arranged as a single-alphabet author list (about 55,000 authors); each author entry provides information on his printed works: details about editions, printings, and prices current in Lowndes' and Bohn's day, often with additional notes on contents, criticism, etc. Vol. 6 (vol. 8 in the 1967 rpt.) gives lists of the publications of learned societies, private presses, and publications in series, with an index to the entire volume.

688 POLLARD, A. W. and G. R. REDGRAVE. *A Short-Title Catalogue of Books Printed in England, Scotland & Ireland and of English Books Printed Abroad 1475–1640.* London, 1926. Rptd. New two-vol. ed. rev. K. F. Pantzer. Vol. II: I–Z announced by OUP for the Bibl. Soc. for 1976; vol. I: A–H for 1980.

Attempts to provide a list of all books printed in the British Isles and all English language books printed abroad up to 1640, copies of which are known to exist in at least one of 133 British and 15 American collections. The arrangement is essentially an author list of 26,143 consecutively numbered entries each giving bibliographic data followed by symbols identifying libraries which hold copies of the book.

689 WOODWARD, GERTRUDE L. *English Books and Books Printed in England Before 1641, in the Newberry Library. A Supplement to the Record in the Short Title Catalogue.* Chicago, 1939.

690 RAMAGE, DAVID, *et al. A Finding-List of English Books to 1640 in Libraries in the British Isles (Excluding the National Libraries and the*

Libraries of Oxford and Cambridge). Based on the Numbers in . . . STC 1475–1640. Durham, 1958.

691 Bishop, William W. *A Checklist of American Copies of "Short-Title Catalogue" Books.* 2nd ed. Ann Arbor, Mich., 1950. Rptd., N. Y., 1968.

692 Morrison, Paul. *Index of Printers, Publishers and Booksellers in A. W. Pollard and G. R. Redgrave A Short-Title Catalogue of Books . . . 1475–1640.* Charlottesville, Va., 1950. Rptd. 1961 with corrections and additions.

A single-alphabet list of names or initials of printers, publishers and booksellers appearing in the Pollard and Redgrave *STC*; each entry gives the date(s) and *STC* number(s) of entries in which the name or initial appears.

693 Duff, Edward G., *et al. Hand-Lists of Books Printed by London Printers, 1501–1556.* 4 vols. London, 1913.

Arranged by name of printer; provides for each printer a chronological list of titles, with locations of copies, followed by illustrations of the printer's devices. Chronological table and index to the printers.

694 Arber, Edward, ed. *A Transcript of the Registers of the Company of Stationers of London, 1554–1640 A. D.* 4 vols. London, 1875–77. Vol. 5, Birmingham, 1894. Rptd. N. Y., 1950; Gloucester, Mass., 1967.

A printed transcript, with some omissions and additions, of the records of the London Company of Stationers. The arrangement of vols. 1–4 is generally chronological, and the entries include records of books entered by members of the company and other records relating to receipts, apprentices, fines, etc., with supplementary illustrative documents, corrigenda, and addenda. Introductions to each volume give historical accounts of the company. Vol. 5 is an index volume.

695 Greg, Walter W. *A Companion to Arber.* Oxford, 1967.

A chronological calendar of all summaries of documents which Arber interpolated in his edition of the *Stationers' Register*, plus transcripts of supplementary documents relating to London publishing between 1550 and 1650. Extensive subject index.

696 Greg, Walter W. and Eleanore Boswell. *Records of the Court of the Stationers' Company, 1576 to 1602, From Register B.* London, 1930.

697 Maunsell, Andrew. *The First Part of the Catalogue of English Printed Books: Which concerneth such matters of Diuinitie, as haue bin either written in our owne Tongue, or translated out of anie other language . . .* London, 1595. *The Seconde Parte of the Catalogue of*

*English printed Bookes . . . which concerneth the Sciences Mathemati-
cal . . . and also, of Phisick and Surgerie . . . .* London, 1595. Both parts
rptd. in 1 vol., 1965

The *First Part* provides two single-alphabet author-title-subject lists, one on
Divinity and the other on secular books. Lists about 2900 items printed
between 1478 and 1595; deliberately omits books "written against the
present government" and by "fugitive Papists." The *Seconde Parte* provides
a single alphabet author-title-subject list with subject headings such as "Of
Bathes," "Of Earthquakes," "Of Musicke," etc. No index.

698 JACKSON, WILLIAM A. *Records of the Court of the Stationers' Company 1602–1640.* London, 1957.

699 EYRE, GEORGE E. B., ed. *A Transcript of the Registers of the Wor-
shipful Company of Stationers, From 1640 to 1708 A. D.* 3 vols. London, 1913–14. Rptd., N. Y., 1950, 1967.

A continuation of the Arber transcript, **694**; covers the years 1640–1708/9.
The arrangement is chronological and includes about 10,000 entries of books
and other printings. No supplementary materials and no index.

700 WING, DONALD. *Short-Title Catalogue of Books Printed in England,
Scotland, Ireland, Wales, and British America and of English Books
Printed in Other Countries, 1641–1700.* 3 vols. N. Y., 1945–51. 2nd ed.
rev. and enlgd., vol. 1–   (N. Y., 1972–   ).

Continues Pollard and Redgrave, **688**. Attempts to list all books printed
between 1641 and 1700, with location symbols provided for at least one
and no more than five copies. Contains about 50,000 entries for books which
are known to exist in at least one of 200 collections in England or America.
Arranged as a single-alphabet list by author, with anonymous works by
title; entries are numbered consecutively within each letter of the alphabet.
The term *Wing number* refers to this letter-number designation. The revised
edition (only vol. 1 has been published so far) will greatly increase the
number of books listed.

701 HISCOCK, WALTER G. *The Christ Church Supplement to Wing's Short-
Title Catalogue 1641–1700.* Oxford, 1956.

Includes a list of errata in Wing, **700**.

702 ALDEN, JOHN E. *Wing Addenda and Corrigenda. Some Notes on
Materials in the British Museum.* Charlottesville, Va., 1958.

703 WOLF, EDWIN. *A Check-List of the Books in the Library Company of
Philadelphia in and Supplementary to Wing's Short-Title Catalogue,
1641–1700.* Philadelphia, Pa., 1959.

704 FRY, M. ISABEL. "Supplement to the *Short-Title Catalogue, 1641–
1700.*" *Huntington Library Quarterly,* 16 (1953), 393–436.

705 "Additions and Corrections to the Second Edition of Donald Wing's Short-Title Catalogue." *Studies in Bibliography*, 29– (1976–).

Provides lists of corrigenda for the ongoing revision of Wing, 700.

706 MORRISON, PAUL G. *Index of Printers, Publishers and Booksellers in Donald Wing's Short-Title Catalogue . . 1641–1700*. Charlottesville, Va., 1955.

A single-alphabet list of the names or initials of printers, publishers, and booksellers appearing in Wing, 700. For each entry there is a list of references given by Wing number and arranged chronologically by years.

707 LONDON, WILLIAM. *Catalogue of the Most Vendible Books in England . . .* London, 1657. *Supplement . . . Till June the First 1658.* London, 1658. *A Catalogue of New Books By Way of Supplement . . . Till Easter-Term 1660.* London, 1660. Rptd., 1965.

Lists of books available for sale. Arranged in broad subject categories, and alphabetically by initial letter of title within the subject categories. Includes such categories as "Poems" and "Playes." Fiction is sometimes listed under "History." No index.

708 CLAVEL, ROBERT. *A Catalogue of Books Printed in England Since the Dreadful Fire of London in 1666 to the End of Michaelmas Term, 1672.* London, 1673. Followed by subsequent editions extending the coverage from 1666 to the end of Michaelmas term, 1695. Rptd., 4 vols., Farnborough, 1965.

Four lists of books available for sale in London at the time of publication of each list. Mostly arranged in broad subject categories (e. g., "Divinity in Octavo," "Poetry," "School Books," etc., and, within these categories, alphabetically by title. Novels are listed in the "History" categories. No index.

709 ARBER, EDWARD. *The Term Catalogues, 1668–1709. A Contemporary Bibliography of English Literature in the Reigns of Charles II, James II, William and Mary, and Queen Anne.* 3 vols. London, 1903–6. Rptd. N. Y., 1965.

An edition of trade lists of London publishers originally compiled by John Starkey and Robert Clavell between 1688 and 1711.

710 *Bibliotheca Annua: Or, The Annual Catalogue for the Year, 1699–1702.* 4 vols. London, 1700–1704. Rptd. in 2 vols., London, 1964.

Four annual lists of books published in England or imported from France. Deliberately intended to rival the *Term Catalogues*. Arranged under broad headings such as "Divinity," "History," "Plays," "Poetry," etc.

711 [*The London Catalogues*]

A series of contemporary booksellers' catalogues covering books published from 1700 to 1855. Titles and publishers vary. For details see Adolf Growoll's *Three Centuries of English Booktrade*. N. Y., 1903. Rptd. 1965.

712 LINTOT, BERNARD. *The Monthly Catalogue [1714–1717]: A Catalogue of All Books, Sermons, and Pamphlets, Publish'd in May 1714, and in Every Month to This Time*. 11 vols. London, 1714–1717. Rptd. in 1 vol., 1964.

Bimonthly lists of books newly published or reprinted and available in England. Arranged under the broad headings of "Books Published," "Books Reprinted," and "Books Appearing by Subscription."

713 WILFORD, JOHN. *The Monthly Catalogue [1723–30] Containing an Exact Register of All Books, Sermons, Plays, Poetry, and Miscellaneous Pamphlets, Printed and Published in London, or the Universities . . . With a Compleat Index to the Whole*. London, 1725–29. Rptd., 2 vols., 1964.

A reprinting of monthly lists of newly published books from March, 1723 to February, 1730. Each list is arranged under broad headings such as "New Pamphlets," "New Sermons," etc.

714 *A Register of Books, 1728–1732, Extracted from the Monthly Chronicle*. London, 1964.

Arrangement is under various subject headings – e. g., "Theological," "Law," "Plays," etc.

715 *Gentleman's Magazine, 1731–51: The Lists of Books Collected with Annual Indexes and the Index to the First Twenty Years Compiled by Edward Kimber*. London, 1966.

Arrangement of the lists varies but is primarily by broad subject categories such as "Divinity," "History," etc. The reprinting includes Edward Kimber's subject index (1753) to the lists.

716 *The Monthly Catalogues from The London Magazine, 1732–66, With the Index for 1732–58 Compiled by Edward Kimber*. London, 1966.

The arrangement of each list is by broad subject divisions such as "Law," "History," "Poetry," "Entertainment" [includes fiction], etc. The annual indexes to the lists and the title-catchword index published by Edward Kimber in 1760 are included in the reprinting of 1966.

717 *The Annual Catalogue: Or, a New and Compleat List of the New Books, New Editions of Books, Pamphlets, etc., Published in . . . Law, Poetry, Plays, Novels . . .* London, 1737. *The Annual Catalogue: (Numb. II.) Or, a New and Compleat List . . .* London, 1738. Rptd., 1 vol., 1965.

The 1737 volume covers the year 1736; the 1738 vol. covers the year 1737. Each vol. consists of a single-alphabet author-title list. Vol. 1 has separate lists of plays and lawbooks at the end; vol. 2 has an alphabetical list of booksellers mentioned in that volume.

718 *The Lists of Books From the British Magazine, 1746–50, Collected with Annual Indexes.* London, 1965.

The lists are arranged under broad subject headings such as "Poetry," "Divinity," etc. The original annual subject indexes to the lists are also included in the 1965 reprinting.

719 *The English Catalogue of Books.* London, vol. 1– (1864–). Vol. 1 published in 1864 for the years 1835–1863; succeeding vols. at intervals of 2 to 5 years. Now annually. An unnumbered vol. covering 1801–36 was published in London, 1914 and rptd. N. Y., 1963. Vols. for 1837–89 have a separate *Index,* 4 vols., London, 1858–93. Vols. for 1801–1959 have been rptd., N. Y., 1963.

Attempts a comprehensive listing of books issued in England and Ireland, but is relatively complete only for major publishing centers. The vols. for 1801–1960 provide author, title, and catchword title entries. Entries provide author, title, publisher, and price. Since 1960, each vol. has separate lists for paperback books, authors, titles and inverted catchword titles, maps and atlases, and publishers' names and addresses. The catchword title entries make the lists useful as subject indexes to books available in England and Ireland. Based upon the book lists appearing in *British Books.*

720 *Reference Catalogue of Current Literature: A National Inclusive Book-Reference Index of Books in Print and On Sale in the United Kingdom* . . . London, 1874–1961.

An index of books in print published during the period 1874–1932 about every four years as a bound collection of current publishers' catalogues arranged alphabetically by publishers' names. Thereafter published irregulary as an author-title index to books in print. Entries give publisher and price information. Succeeded by *British Books in Print,* **725.**

721 *The Bookseller.* 1– (1858–).

A weekly listing of books published in the United Kingdom. Arranged as a single-alphabet author-title-inverted title list. Now cumulated monthly in *Current Literature,* **722.**

722 *Current Literature.* 1– (1908–).

Each monthly issue contains a classified list of "Publications of the Month" which lists new books published in the United Kingdom; entries give information on publisher and price. Since December, 1969, this list serves as a monthly cumulation of the weekly lists appearing in *The Bookseller,* **721.** Arranged in broad subject classes.

723 *Whitaker's Cumulative Book List.* 1– (1924–).

A quarterly index of new books published in the United Kingdom. Cumulated annually and 5-yearly. Based on the weekly list of new books published in *The Bookseller* and cumulated monthly in *Current Literature.* Arranged as two lists: (1) a classified list arranged by broad subject headings – e.g., *aeronautics, fiction, mathematics, poetry & drama,* etc. – with entries providing full bibliographic information, and (2) an author-title list which serves as an index to the classified entries.

724 *British National Bibliography.* 1– (1950–).

A weekly subject index of new books, pamphlets, and periodicals published in the United Kingdom and Ireland. Quarterly and annual cumulations; cumulated indexes and subject catalogues published every five years. Based on (but not limited to) materials deposited at the British Museum Copyright Receipt Office. The weekly issues are lists arranged under Dewey Decimal subject headings with an author index; the last issue of each month provides a cumulated author-title-subject index. The annual cumulations provide a classified list arranged in Dewey classes with an author and title index, a subject index, a list of publishers' addresses, and a list of publisher prefixes. Entries give full bibliographic data and prices.

725 *British Books in Print: The Reference Catalogue of Current Literature.* 1– (1962–).

Annual index of British books in print. Arranged as two lists: (1) an author list and (2) a title and inverted-catchword title list. Entries give full bibliographic information, including prices.

726 *Paperbacks in Print.* 1– (1960–).

An annual catalogue of paperbound books on sale in Great Britain. Arranged as a classified list under some 50 broad headings. Entries give imprint and price. Author-title index. Includes a directory of publishers.

C. American National Bibliography

727 TANSELLE, G. THOMAS. *Guide to the Study of United States Imprints.* 2 vols. Cambridge, Mass., 1971.

A very full bibliographic guide to American publishing. Arranged as a classified bibliography with categories covering (1) basic imprint lists (regional, genre, and author), (2) related lists for copyright records, catalogues, and book trade directories, (3) lists of supplementary studies of individual printers etc. Author-title-subject index.

728 SABIN, JOSEPH, WILBERFORCE EAMES and R. W. G. VAIL. *A Dictionary of Books Relating to America, From Its Discovery to the Present Time.*

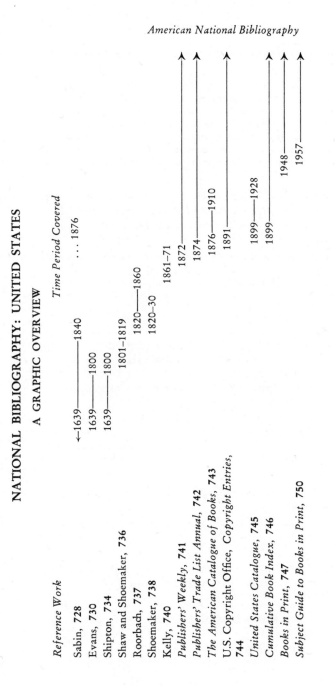

NATIONAL BIBLIOGRAPHY: UNITED STATES

A GRAPHIC OVERVIEW

Reference Work — *Time Period Covered*

Sabin, 728 — ←1639————1840 ...1876

Evans, 730 — 1639——1800

Shipton, 734 — 1639——1800

Shaw and Shoemaker, 736 — 1801–1819

Roorbach, 737 — 1820———1860

Shoemaker, 738 — 1820–30

Kelly, 740 — 1861–71

Publishers' Weekly, 741 — 1872↑

Publishers' Trade List Annual, 742 — 1874↑

The American Catalogue of Books, 743 — 1876——1910↑

U.S. Copyright Office, Copyright Entries, 744 — 1891↑

United States Catalogue, 745 — 1899———1928

Cumulative Book Index, 746 — 1899↑

Books in Print, 747 — 1948↑

Subject Guide to Books in Print, 750 — 1957↑

143

Half-title: *Bibliotheca Americana.* 29 vols. N. Y., 1868–1936. Rptd., Amsterdam, 1961.

A single-alphabet author list (anonymous works by title and, sometimes, under "the most obvious subject.") Attempts to include all books which had been written in the Western Hemisphere or written about it. The scope and *terminus ad quem* were changed in the course of publication: see vol. 29, pp. x-xi for details. The 106,413 entries give title, imprint, format, and number of pages. Some entries also include notes on content and other matters such as editions, review citations, and location of copies. Author-title index to Sabin comp. J. E. Molnar, Metuchen, N. J., 1975.

729 THOMPSON, LAWRENCE S. *The New Sabin: Books Described by Joseph Sabin and His Successors, Now Described Again on the Basis of Examination of Originals, and Fully Indexed by Title, Subject, Joint Authors, and Institutions and Agencies.* Vol. 1– . Troy, N. Y., 1974–

Not a revision of Sabin's *Bibliotheca Americana* but an entirely new work. Individual vols. are each arranged as a separate A–Z author list with accompanying separately published index. For an analysis of the weaknesses of this work see the review in *Choice*, 11 (October, 1974), 1114.

730 EVANS, CHARLES. *American Bibliography: A Chronological Dictionary of All Books, Pamphlets, and Periodical Publications Printed in the United States of America from the Genesis of Printing in 1639 Down to and Including the Year 1800 With Bibliographical and Biographical Notes.* 12 vols. Chicago, 1903–34. Vol. 13 ed. by CLIFFORD K. SHIPTON, Worcester, Mass., 1955. Vol. 14 ed. by ROGER P. BRISTOL, Worcester, Mass., 1959. Vols. 1–12 rptd., N. Y., 1941–42.

A list of 39,162 entries arranged chronologically year-by-year; within each year arranged as an author list with anonymous works by title. Entries include author's name with dates, title, imprint, number of pages, format, and library locations; additional notes supply biographical and bibliographical information.

731 BRISTOL, ROGER P. *Supplement to Charles Evans' "American Bibliography."* Charlottesville, Va., 1971.

Contains more than 11,200 additional entries arranged as in **730**. Provides a list of bibliographies cited, a key to library location symbols, and a list of addenda.

732 BRISTOL, ROGER P. *Index to Printers, Publishers and Booksellers Indicated by Charles Evans in His "American Bibliography."* Charlottesville, Va., 1961.

733 STARK, LEWIS M. and MAUD D. COLE. *Checklist of Additions to Evans' American Bibliography in the Rare Book Division of the New York Public Library.* N. Y., 1960.

734 SHIPTON, CLIFFORD K. and JAMES E. MOONEY. *National Index of American Imprints Through 1800: The Short Title Evans.* 2 vols. Barre, Mass., 1970.

A single-alphabet list of about 50,000 monographs printed in America up to and including 1800. Arrangement is by author with anonymous works by title and also by author if known. Intended as an index to the microprint edition of *Early American Imprints.* Includes many publications not in 730. Entries provide title, place of publication, date, number of pages, and the library location of the copy used in the microprint edition.

735 "A Check List of Americana in A Short-Title Catalogue of Books Printed in England, Scotland, & Ireland And of English Books Printed Abroad 1475–1640." *Early American Literature,* 9 (Supplement, Fall, 1974), 1–124.

A check list attempting to cite all books listed in Pollard and Redgrave, 688, which relate to America. Provides entries for over 1,300 items which mention America or any part of the new world by name or inference or that note uniquely American plants, animals, or diseases.

736 SHAW, RALPH R. and RICHARD H. SHOEMAKER. *American Bibliography: A Preliminary Checklist for [1801–1819].* [Title varies for vols. 20–22.] 22 vols. N. Y., 1958–66.

Intended as a continuation of 730 for books published in America 1801–1819. The lists are based entirely on secondary sources and the content of entries varies widely but can include publisher, place of publication, date, number of volumes, author's dates, and locations of copies.

737 ROORBACH, O. *Bibliotheca Americana: Catalogue of American Publications, Including Reprints and Original Works, from 1820 to 1852, Inclusive, Together with a List of Periodicals Published in the United States.* N. Y., 1852. Supplements, 1852–60, 3 vols., 1855–61. Rptd. in 2 vols., N. Y., 1939, and Metuchen, N. J., 1967.

A list of books published in the United States 1820–1860. Each volume is a single-alphabet author-title list; entries give publisher, format, price, and (sometimes) date.

738 SHOEMAKER, RICHARD H. *A Checklist of American Imprints for [date].* 10 vols. Vol. for 1820, N. Y., 1964; vols. for 1821–29, Metuchen, N. J., 1967–71.

Lists of American publications for the years 1820–1829; each vol. covers a single year. Arrangement is alphabetical by author, with anonymous works by title. Very much more complete than Roorbach for the years covered. There are two separately published indexes compiled by M. Frances Cooper, *A Checklist of American Imprints 1820–1829: Title Index,* Metuchen, N. J., 1972, and *A Checklist of American Imprints 1820–1829: Author Index, Corrections and Sources,* Metuchen, N. J., 1973.

739 COOPER, GAYLE. *A Checklist of American Imprints for [date].* Metuchen, N. J., 1972– .

Continues Richard H. Shoemaker's *A Checklist of American Imprints* for the year 1830 and after. Arrangement and entries follow the practice of Shoemaker.

740 KELLY, JAMES. *The American Catalogue of Books (Original and Reprints) Published in the United States … with Date of Publication, Size, Price, and Publisher's Name.* 2 vols. N. Y., 1866–71. Rptd., N. Y., 1938; rptd. in 1 vol., Metuchen, N. J., 1967.

A continuation of Roorbach's *Bibliotheca Americana* for the period Jan., 1861 to Jan., 1871. Arranged as a single-alphabet author-title list; entries provide information on date, format, price, and publisher. The first vol. supplies items omitted by Roorbach.

741 *Publishers' Weekly.* 1– (1872–).

A weekly journal of the American book trade, including lists of newly published books and announcements of forthcoming publications. Lists are usually arranged alphabetically by author. The weekly lists are now cumulated in *American Book Publishing Record,* 1– (1960–), in lists arranged by Dewey Decimal classes with an author-title index. The lists of forthcoming books are supplemented by *Forthcoming Books,* 1– (1966–) which is an author-title index and *Subject Guide to Forthcoming Books,* 1– (1967–) which provides a subject index; both are bi-monthly publications.

742 *Publishers' Trade List Annual.* 1– (1874–).

An annual collection of current publishers' catalogues bound together. There are usually several volumes for each year. Arrangement is alphabetical by publisher's name; an alphabetical list of publishers' names is usually given at the beginning of the first volume. Presently includes about 2500 publishers' catalogues. *Books in Print,* **747**, and *Subject Guide to Books in Print,* **749**, serve as indexes to *PTLA.*

743 *The American Catalogue of Books … Author and Title Entries of Books in Print and For Sale (Including Reprints and Importations) [1876–1910].* N. Y., 1880–1911. Rptd. 9 vols. in 13, N. Y., 1941.

A series of volumes attempting to list all books available in America for the years 1876–1910. Entries are based on the *Annual American Catalogue,* and give publisher, date of publication, format, and price information.

744 U.S. Copyright Office. *Catalog of Copyright Entries.* New Series, 1891–1946. Series 3, 1947– . Washington, D. C., 1891– .

Records of books deposited for copyright with the U. S. Copyright Office. The Copyright Office publishes lists of all materials copyrighted, with separate lists for books, pamphlets, periodicals, works of art, music, etc. For a very useful and full discussion of U. S. Copyright records, see G.

Thomas Tanselle's "Copyright Records and the Bibliographer," *Studies in Bibliography*, 22 (1969), 77–124.

745 *United States Catalog*. 1st. ed. 1900; 2nd ed. 1903; 3rd ed. 1912; 4th ed. 1928.

Lists of books in print. The first ed. cited books in print for 1899 and was arranged in two lists: (1) author-title and (2) subjects. The 4th ed. is arranged as a single-alphabet author-title-subject list. Entries give publisher and price information. Continued by the *Cumulative Book Index.*

746 *The Cumulative Book Index: A World List of Books in the English Language*. N. Y., 1898– . Title and frequency have varied; now published monthly (except August), with tri-monthly and annual cumulations. From 1928 to 1968 appeared also in 2-, 4-, and 5-yr. cumulations.

The annual volumes provide a single-alphabet author-title-subject list which attempts to include all books written in English and published anywhere in the world, excepting only limited editions, local publications, government documents, pamphlets, cheap reprints, and "propaganda." Main entries are under author's name and include full name (pseudonyms are identified), complete title, series, edition, number of pages, imprint, ISBN code, LC card number, and price. Provides a directory of publishers.

747 *Books in Print [year]*. N. Y., 1948– .

An annual author-title index of books currently available from publishers and distributors in the United States. Provides separate author and title lists, a key to abbreviations for publishers and distributors cited, and a very full directory of U. S. publishers with ISBN codes. Entries give author, title, editor, series, number of vols., edition, LC card number, type of binding, imprint, ISBN, publishers' order number, and price. Based on but not limited to the *Publishers' Trade List Annual*, **742**, for which it serves as an index. Supplemented by *Forthcoming Books*: bi-monthly author and title indexes of recently published books, plus forecasts of books to be published in next few months, and by *Subject Guide to Forthcoming Books*, which provides a bi-monthly subject index.

748 *Books in Print Supplement: Authors, Titles, Subjects*. N. Y., 1972– .

Published annually six months after *Books In Print*; supplies a six-month cumulated supplementary author-title-subject index. Entries provide the same kinds of information as given in *Books In Print*.

749 *Subject Guide to Books in Print*. N. Y., 1957– .

An annual subject index to *Books in Print*. Arranged in subject classes that generally follow the Library of Congress subject headings. Entries include the same kinds of information found in *Books in Print*.

750 *Paperbound Books in Print.* N. Y., 1955–   .

Annual volume (frequency has varied) providing separate author, title, and subject indexes to books currently available in paperbound form, many of which are not listed in *Books in Print.* Entries give imprint, ISBN code, and price.

XII. Microforms and Reprints: Guides and Bibliographies

753 Philadelphia Bibliographical Center and Union Library Catalogue. *Union List of Microfilms*. Rev. ed. Ann Arbor, Mich., 1951. *Cumulation 1949–1959*. 2 vols. Ann Arbor, Mich., 1961.

> A list of all kinds of magazines, journals, and other titles on microfilm, excluding newspapers listed in *Newspapers in Microform*, 889. Arrangement is alphabetical by author, with title entries for serial and anonymous works. The main volume lists 25,000 microfilms owned by 197 institutions; the 1949–1959 cumulation adds 52,000 entries representing microfilm accessions reported by 215 libraries.

754 TILTON, EVA MAUDE. *A Union List of Publications in Opaque Microforms*. 2nd ed. N. Y., 1964.

> A single-alphabet author, genealogical subject, and series title list, comprising 7,640 numbered entries citing works available on micro-card and microfiche from 26 European and American publishers. Author-subject index.

755 *Guide to Microforms in Print*. 1961– .

> An annual bibliography of books, journals, and other materials currently available in microform from United States publishers. Arranged as a single-alphabet list.

756 *Subject Guide to Microforms in Print*. 1962– .

> A biennial classified list of microforms in print. Arranged in about 135 subject classes; an index to these classes is given in the front matter.

757 U.S. Library of Congress. *National Register of Microform Masters*. 1965– .

> An annual non-cumulating register of microform masters – i.e., microforms retained solely for the purpose of making other copies – of books, pamphlets, serials, and doctoral dissertations, except U.S. dissertations. The register issues report accessions of microform masters in more than 200 commercial and non-profit repositories in Europe and America. The arrangement of the first issues was by Library of Congress card number; since 1970 arrangement is a single-alphabet list by author, with serials and anonymous works by title. Entries locate microform masters and, when possible, give the Library of Congress card number.

758 *Microform Review*. 1– (1971–).

> A quarterly journal providing news, notes, articles, etc. on microform publishers. Includes bibliographies of recent microform publications and bib-

liographies of microform projects recently completed by libraries, with indications of the libraries' borrowing rules.

759 *Guide to Reprints [year].* Washington, D. C., 1967– .

An annual index to available materials which have gone out of print and have been reprinted in full size (not in microtext) by any kind of reproduction process other than by recomposing the text. Arranged alphabetically by author (journals and sets by title). Entries include original date of publication, reprint, publisher, and price; for journals the entries give the volume numbers and years of the issues reprinted.

760 *Catalog of Reprints in Series.* 20th ed. N. Y. & London, 1965.

761 *Reprint Bulletin.* 1– (1965–).

762 *Announced Reprints.* 1– (1969–).

XIII. Media: Guides, Bibliographies, and Indexes

A. General Guides

765 CHISHOLM, MARGARET E. *Media Indexes and Review Sources.* College Park, Maryland, 1972.

A brief annotated guide to indexes and reviews of media – film, television, and recordings. Includes a list of more than 100 sources. Index to subjects and to media types.

766 *Media Review Digest [date]. Part I: Films and Filmstrips. Part II: Records and Tapes.* Ann Arbor, Michigan, 1974– . Published with semiannual supplements to each part, cumulating annually. Separately published indexes to each part.

Intended to be an annual index to and a digest of reviews, evaluations, and descriptions of all forms of non-book media, particularly those prepared for educational use. Indexes about 200 periodicals. Each part is arranged alphabetically by title or, in the case of recordings, sometimes by artist. Entries provide information about producer, technical details, a brief description, symbols indicating review ratings, brief extracts from reviews, and symbols indicating the educational level for which the material is useful. Separately published indexes of subjects and producers/directors.

B. Recordings

767 ROACH, HELEN. *Spoken Records.* 3rd ed. Metuchen, N. J., 1970.

An annotated bibliography of spoken recordings. Arranged as a classified list with major headings such as "Authors' Readings," "Readings by Other Than Authors," "Plays," etc., with sub-classes within these main classifications. The annotations are in the form of a running commentary on the recordings in each category, followed by a list of the recordings discussed. The appendixes include a list of record publishers, producers, and distributors. Author-title-reader index.

768 National Council of Teachers of English. *An Annotated List of Recordings in the Language Arts.* Champaign, Ill., 1964.

An annotated list arranged by 3 instructional levels – elementary, secondary, and college – and within these categories by classes such as "Anthologies," "Poetry, American," "Prose, English," "Drama and Shakespeare," etc. Title and author indexes.

769 U.S. Library of Congress. *Literary Recordings: A Checklist of the Archive of Recorded Poetry and Literature in the Library of Congress.* Washington, D. C., 1966.

770 CHICOREL, MARIETTA. *Chicorel Theatre Index to Plays in Anthologies, Periodicals, Discs and Tapes. 3 vols.* [Title of vol. 3: *Chicorel Theatre Index to Plays in Collections, Anthologies, Periodicals and Discs in England.*] N. Y., 1970–1972.

An index to plays, playwrights, editions, and recordings. Entries give information on the location of each play, publishing data, and price. Author, play, editor, and subject indexes. Vol. 3 provides an additional list of Shakespeare's plays.

771 CHICOREL, MARIETTA. *Chicorel Index to Poetry in Collections in Print, on Discs and Tapes.* N. Y., 1972. [Vol. 4 of *Chicorel Index.*]

An index to recorded poetry. Arranged as a single-alphabet index of titles, first lines, poets, readers, and directors. Main entries are by title and give full publishing information and analyze the contents of the disc, tape, or cassette. An appendix provides names, addresses, and telephone numbers of producers and distributors of discs and tapes, and a brief glossary of technical terms.

772 CHICOREL, MARIETTA. *Chicorel Index to the Spoken Arts on Discs, Tapes, and Cassettes.* 2 vols. N. Y., 1973. [Vols. 7 and 7 A of *Chicorel Index.*]

Indexes plays, short stories, poems, essays, novels, and speeches in over 1200 recorded media. Each volume is arranged as a single-alphabet index of titles, authors, actor-performers, and directors. Appendix provides names and addresses of producers and distributors of discs and tapes.

773 The Gramophone. *Spoken Word and Miscellaneous Catalogue.* London, 1965– .

An annual index to titles, authors, and performers on spoken records available in England.

774 *Schwann Record and Tape Guide.* 1– (1949–).

Semi-annual supplements to the monthly Schwann catalogues provide lists of records and tapes of plays, poetry, prose, and speeches available in America.

775 *Polyglotte: Poesie und Drama auf Schallplatten, Ausgabe 1975–76.* Düsseldorf, [1975].

Annual classified index to available records, tapes, and cassettes of poetry, drama, and (in spite of its title) prose of all major languages. Entries sometimes provide fuller information than the Schwann or Gramophone catalogue. Index of authors recorded.

C. Film

1. Primary Materials

776 GIFFORD, DENIS. *The British Film Catalogue 1895–1970.* London, 1973.

Intended to be a complete list of all films produced in Britain since the invention of cinema. Arranged chronologically. Entries give title, director, studio, release date, distributor, cast, running time, indications of any awards won, and a brief summary. Lists about 15,000 films. Index to titles cited. Illustrated.

777 *The British National Film Catalogue.* 1– (1963–).

A bi-monthly record (with annual cumulation) of films, exclusive of feature films, produced in Great Britain. Arranged as two lists: (1) a classified list of subject headings (following the Universal Decimal Classification system) with appropriate non-fiction films listed beneath each heading, and (2) a list of films on fictional topics arranged alphabetically by title. Entries give information on running time, distributor, whether color or black-and-white, whether sound or silent, cost, etc. Appendixes give lists of distributors and producers. Subject-title index.

778 British Film Institute. *Monthly Film Bulletin.* London, 1934– .

A monthly report on British films and films appearing in Britain. Entries give title, date, distributor, producer, cast, running time, etc., and, in the case of feature films, include extensive reviews. A title index is published annually. Can be used as supplementary to **777**, which does not cover feature films.

779 U.S. Library of Congress. *Catalog of Copyright Entries: Cumulative Series: Motion Pictures.* 4 vols. covering the years 1894–1959. Washington, D. C., 1951–60.

Each volume provides an alphabetical title list of films registered for copyright during the period covered by that volume. Entries can include author, producer, distributor, cast, director, number of reels, etc.; some entries also provide a summary. The volume for 1894–1912 includes an index of claimants; subsequent volumes include indexes of persons and organizations cited in the entries (the indexes are not exhaustive) and a list of the series titles given in the entries. For a more detailed descriptive catalogue of early holdings see Kemp Niver's *Motion Pictures From the Library of Congress Paper Print Collection 1894–1912*, Berkeley, Calif., 1967.

780 U.S. Library of Congress. *Library of Congress Catalog: Motion Pictures and Filmstrips.* 5 vols. covering the years 1953–1967. Ann Arbor, Mich., 1958–69.

Consists of three lists (covering the periods 1953–57, 1958–62, and 1963–67) of reproductions of Library of Congress cards for films. Each list is arranged alphabetically by title. Entries give information on producer, director, author, etc., and provide summaries of the film. There is a subject index for each of the three periods covered. Continued by: *Library of Congress Catalog: Motion Pictures and Filmstrips.* Ann Arbor, Mich., 1968– .

781 *The American Film Institute Catalog of Motion Pictures Produced in the United States.* N. Y., 1971– .

A projected 18 vol. catalogue of motion pictures, including short films and newsreels, which were produced between 1893 and 1970 in the United States. One part, *Feature Films 1921–1930*, has been published. Entries give director, producer, cast, source of the screenplay, and short summary.

782 LIMBACHER, JAMES L. *Feature Films on 8 mm and 16 mm.* 3rd ed. N. Y., 1971.

A directory of more than 10,000 feature films (i.e., films running 45 minutes or more) that are available for rental, sale, or lease from American distributors. Arranged alphabetically by title of film. Entries give information on country of origin, studio, running time, size, whether sound or not, color or not, name of director, name of distributor, cast, etc. Entries include information on whether the film is available for rental, sale, or lease. Appendixes give a list of addresses of film companies and distributors and a brief bibliography of film reference works. Index to directors and their films.

783 McCARTY, CLIFFORD. *Published Screenplays: A Checklist.* Kent, Ohio, 1971.

A list of published screenplays written in English for all types of films. Arranged alphabetically by title of screenplay. Entries give production company and date, director, author of screenplay, source (when the screenplay was based on a novel, play, etc.) and a bibliographic citation to the book or periodical in which the screenplay was published. Name-title index.

784 ENSER, A. G. S. *Filmed Books and Plays: A List of Books and Plays From Which Films Have Been Made, 1928–1974.* Rev. ed. London, 1975.

A list of films (nearly all British or American) made since 1928 which were based upon a book or play. Arranged alphabetically by title of film; entries in parallel columns give the source of the film, including the original title (when different), the author, publisher, date, etc.

785 MANVELL, ROGER. *Shakespeare & the Film.* London, 1971.

Examines the principal films which have been adapted from Shakespeare's plays during the period of the sound-film since 1929. At the end of the book there is a Filmography, a Selected Bibliography and an Index. See also "Shakespeare on Film, with an Index of Films: 1929–1971," *Films in Review,* 24:3 (1973), 132–63.

For other bibliographies and indexes of primary film materials see entries **361** and **389**.

2. Secondary Materials

a. General Reference Works

786 BESSY, MAURICE et JEAN-LOUIS CHARDANS. *Dictionnaire du Cinema et de la Télévision.* 4 vols. Paris, 1975.

A general, illustrated dictionary of film and television of all countries. Arranged as a single-alphabet list of articles on actors, directors, technical terms, etc. Bibliography under the entry *bibliographie.* No index.

786a MANVELL, ROGER, ed. *The International Encyclopedia of Film.* London, 1972.

An international encyclopedia of film history and the film industry, containing more than 1000 alphabetically arranged articles and some 1000 illustrations. Entries include persons (actors, directors, etc.), national film histories, technical terms (but not for the highly technical aspects of film production, sound recording, etc.), and general topics. Includes a chronological outline of film history, a select bibliography on film, an index of film titles, and an index of names.

786b BAWDEN, LIZZ-ANNE. *The Oxford Companion to Film.* London, 1976.

Covers aspects of film as art form, technology, industry, political weapon, mass entertainment, etc. The 3,000 entries are concerned, among other subjects, with artists, critics, genres, movements, and some 700 films. Illustrated.

787 GOTTESMAN, RONALD and HARRY M. GEDULD. *Guidebook to Film: An Eleven-In-One Reference.* N. Y., 1972.

A comprehensive reference guide to film study, divided into 11 categories: (1) annotated bibliography of books and periodicals on film, (2) theses and dissertations, (3) museums and archives, (4) film courses and schools, (5) film terminology, (6) equipment and supplies, (7) distributors, (8) film organizations and services, (9) festivals and contests, (10) film awards, (11) bookstores, publishers, and sources for stills. Some categories (e.g., the annotated list of books and periodicals) are elaborately subclassified, but there is no index.

788 SADOUL, GEORGES. *Dictionary of Films.* Trans. and rev. by PETER MORRIS. Berkeley, Calif., 1972.

A selective guide to some 1,300 films made from the beginning of motion pictures through the 1960's. Arranged alphabetically by film title, with cross-references to alternate titles. Entries range from a few lines to 1½ pages and can include a list of credits, running time, a plot summary, and

155

a brief critical commentary on special film techniques used, the relation of the film to its literary sources, etc. No index.

789 SADOUL, GEORGES. *Dictionary of Film Makers.* Trans. and rev. by PETER MORRIS. Berkeley, Calif., 1972.

A dictionary list of over 1,000 entries providing information on film directors, scriptwriters, cinematographers, art directors, composers, producers and inventors in the film industry. Does *not* include entries for individual actors.

790 DAISNE, JOHAN. *Dictionnaire Filmographique de la Littérature Mondiale.* Ghent, 1971.

Arranged in 3 parts: (1) a list of films arranged alphabetically by author of the works upon which the films were based – e.g., under the name *Hemingway, Ernest* are listed 13 films based on his writings; (2) a selection of pictures of scenes taken from films, also arranged by author, as for (1); and (3) a title index. The author entries in (1) give title of film, country of production, name of director, and cast.

791 LEVITAN, ELI L. *An Alphabetical Guide to Motion Picture, Television, and Videotape Production.* N.Y., 1970.

An encyclopedic guide to all technical aspects of film and videotape production. Includes many diagrams and illustrations. Arranged as a single-alphabet list of topics with a subject index.

792 DIMMITT, RICHARD B. *A Title Guide to the Talkies.* N.Y., 1965.

A comprehensive listing of about 16,000 feature-length films produced from 1927 to 1963. Arranged alphabetically by title of the film. Entries give date of release, producer, etc., and cite the source of the film when it is based on a published novel, play, short story, or poem. The name index includes the names of the authors of the sources cited.

793 HALLIWELL, LESLIE. *The Filmgoer's Companion.* 3rd ed. rev. and enl. N.Y., 1970.

An encyclopedia of film arranged as a single-alphabet list of more than 6,000 entries on all aspects of film, with particular emphasis on British and American cinema, actors, directors, and producers.

794 BAER, D. RICHARD. *The Film Buff's Bible of Motion Pictures (1915–1972).* Hollywood, Calif., 1972.

A guide to about 13,000 films, including silents, short features, and films made for television. Arranged in chart form, alphabetically by film title. Entries give information on alternate titles, year of release, distributor, running time, and critical ratings. Index to alternate titles.

795 MICHAEL, PAUL. *The American Movies Reference Book: The Sound Era.* Englewood Cliffs, N.J., 1969.

Arranged in 6 parts: a brief history of American movies followed by lists of players (each with brief biography and list of films), of films (casts, credits, running time, studio, date of release), of directors (with list of films directed), of producers (with list of films produced), and of awards. Brief bibliography and indexes to actors, directors, and producers.

b. Bibliographies, Indexes, and Research Guides

796 REHRAUER, GEORGE. *Cinema Booklist.* Metuchen, N. J., 1972. *Supplement One*, 1974.

Both the original volume and the supplement are annotated bibliographies of currently available books on all aspects of the cinema. Arrangement is alphabetical by title. Entries give full bibliographic citation followed by a descriptive (and sometimes critical) annotation. An appendix provides a list of film periodicals. Separate subject and author indexes.

797 JINKS, WILLIAM. *The Celluloid Literature: Film in the Humanities.* 2nd ed. Beverly Hills, Calif., 1974.

Includes a "Selected Bibliography" on pp. 202–212; classified arrangement includes such categories as film history, general reference works, film theory, film scripts, etc., plus a list of film periodicals and a directory of major film distributors.

798 GERLACH, JOHN C. and LANA GERLACH. *The Critical Index: A Bibliography of Articles on Film in English, 1946–1973, Arranged by Names and Topics.* N. Y., 1974.

An index to about 5,000 articles on cinema in 22 British and American periodicals for the period 1946–1973. Arranged in two parts: (1) an index by names of directors, producers, actors, critics, and screenwriters and (2) an index arranged by topics such as "Economics," "History," "Britain," "Theory," "Criticism," "Archives," etc. Indexes to authors and to film titles.

799 MANCHEL, FRANK. *Film Study: A Resource Guide.* Cranbury, N. J., 1973.

A selective, elaborately annotated bibliographic guide to film study. Arranged as a series of essays followed by annotated lists of writings on film; the topics treated include subjects such as "Film Literature," "Stereotyping in Film," "A Thematic Approach," "Approaching the History of the Film," etc. Includes a glossary and appendixes on such topics as film distributors, the American Motion Picture Code, dissertations on film, etc. Provides 7 indexes: article titles, authors-articles, authors-books, book titles, film personalities, film titles, and subjects.

800 DANIEL, WENDELL. "A Researcher's Guide and Selected Checklist to Film as Literature and Language." *Journal of Modern Literature*, 3 (April, 1973), 323–350.

An annotated bibliography of writings on the topic "film and literature." Divided into seven parts: (1) research guides, (2) bibliographies and filmographies, (3) periodical bibliographies, (4) periodical indexes, (5) theoretical studies, (6) brief guide to film and language, and (7) a "selected chronology" of major writings on film as art and literature arranged by year.

801 BUKALSKI, PETER J. *Film Research: A Critical Bibliography With Annotations and Essay.* Boston, Mass., 1972.

A classified bibliography using categories such as "Essential Works," "Film Rental," "Film Periodicals," and a category "The Major Bibliography" which is sub-divided into categories such as "Film History," "Society and Economics of Film," "Film Scripts," "Bibliographies, Guides, and Indexes," etc. No index.

802 *The Film Index: A Bibliography.* Vol. 1. *Film as Art.* N.Y., 1941. [No further volumes are forthcoming.]

An annotated bibliography of about 8,600 entries – about 700 entries for books wholly or in part devoted to motion pictures; about 3,000 entries for magazine articles; and about 4,000 entries for film reviews. Mentions about 4,300 films, of which some 3,200 are described. Entries are arranged as a classified list with categories such as "Criticism and Aesthetics," "History," "Technique," "Fictional Film," etc., each elaborately sub-classified. Name and title index.

803 *The New York Times Film Reviews 1913–1968.* 6 vols. N.Y., 1970.

Vols. 1–5 provide the reviews themselves reproduced by photo-offset from the New York *Times.* Arrangement is chronological. Vol. 6 provides corrections, various addenda, and separate indexes to film titles, persons, and corporations.

804 SCHUSTER, MEL. *Motion Picture Performers: A Bibliography of Magazine and Periodical Articles 1900–1969.* Metuchen, N. J., 1971.

Arranged alphabetically by name of actor, with citations to relevant articles for each name. Includes a list of actors for whom no citations were given. No index.

805 SCHUSTER, MEL. *Motion Picture Directors: A Bibliography of Magazine and Periodical Articles 1900–1972.* Metuchen, N. J., 1973.

Arranged alphabetically by name of director, with citations to relevant articles for each name. Includes over 300 directors and indexes more than 300 journals.

806 POWERS, ANNE. *Blacks in American Movies: A Selected Bibliography.* Metuchen, N. J., 1974.

807 *Film Literature Index.* 1– (1973–).

A quarterly index to periodical literature on the film, with annual cumulations. Indexes about 300 periodicals of all countries. Arranged as a single-alphabet author-subject index with more than 1,000 subject headings.

808 *International Index to Film Periodicals [year].* 1– (1973–).

A projected series of annual indexes to the literature on film in periodicals. The volume for 1972 has about 7,000 entries providing citations to reviews and articles in about 60 journals published throughout the world. Arrangement is classified, with main categories such as "Society and Cinema," "Aesthetics, Theory, Criticism," "History of Cinema," etc. Detailed subject index.

808a MacCann, Richard Dryer and Edward S. Perry. *The New Film Index: A Bibliography of Magazine Articles in English 1930–1970.* N. Y., 1975.

An index of over 12,000 annotated citations to articles on film in about 40 English language periodicals. Arranged in 278 subject categories, with personal name index.

c. Dictionaries and Encyclopedias of Terms and Technical Matters

809 *The Focal Encyclopedia of Film & Television Techniques.* N. Y., 1969.

A comprehensive encyclopedia covering the technical elements in British and American film and television production. Arranged as an alphabetical list of signed articles prepared by specialists. One of two symbols to the left of each article enables a reader to tell at a glance whether the article concerns primarily film or television. Includes many illustrations and diagrams. Detailed subject index.

810 Clason, W. E. *Elsevier's Dictionary of Cinema, Sound, and Music.* Amsterdam, 1956.

A dictionary of 3213 numbered entries providing in tabular arrangement the Dutch, French, German, Italian, and Spanish equivalents for specialized English terms in the fields of cinema, recording, and music; arranged as a dictionary list of English terms and definitions, with foreign terms given in parallel columns. Appendixes include alphabetical lists of terms in the foreign languages cross-referenced to the English term.

811 Skilbeck, Oswald. *ABC of Film and TV Working Terms.* London, 1960.

A brief dictionary of technical terms used in film and television production – e.g., terms such as *aerial, dub, logo, jump cut, explode, 'T' stops,* etc.

For other references to secondary materials on film see entries **257, 372a, 376, 379, 383, 383a,** and **396.**

XIV. Dissertations: Bibliographies, Indexes, and Abstracts

816 Association of Special Libraries and Information Bureaux. *Index to Theses Accepted for Higher Degrees in the Universities of Great Britain and Ireland.* 1– (1953–).

An annual list of doctoral dissertations accepted in institutions of higher learning in England and Ireland and their overseas branches. Arranged by broad subject classes, with extensive sub-classification and elaborate cross-referencing. Within subject categories the arrangement is by name of the university accepting the dissertation. Index of subject headings and author index.

817 U. S. Library of Congress. *List of American Doctoral Dissertations Printed.* 27 vols. Washington, D. C., 1913–1940. Rptd., N. Y., 1965.

Annual lists of American doctoral dissertations for the years 1912–1938. These lists record only those dissertations printed (either separately or in another publication) which were received by the Library of Congress. Because the requirement for printing dissertations varies widely among American universities, the lists are in no sense a complete record of dissertations actually finished and accepted during the years covered. Each annual volume is in 4 main parts: (1) an author list, (2) a classified list arranged in broad subject categories following the Library of Congress classification system, (3) a subject index, and (4) a list of dissertation authors arranged by degree granting institutions.

818 *Doctoral Dissertations Accepted by American Universities.* 22 vols. N. Y., 1934–56. Rptd., N. Y., 1964.

Annual lists of published and unpublished doctoral dissertations accepted by institutions of higher learning in the United States and Canada during the period 1933/34–1954/55. Arranged as classified lists with broad subject headings such as "Philosophy," "Literature and Art," etc., with subdivisions such as "General Literature," "English Literature," etc. Alphabetical subject index in the front matter and author index.

819 *Index to American Doctoral Dissertations [year].* 1– (1957–).

An annual listing of doctoral dissertations accepted by American and Canadian universities; compiled from the commencement programs issued by the universities. Arranged in broad subject categories such as "Language and Literature," with sub-categories such as "Classical" and "Modern." Within these categories arrangement is by granting institution. Current volumes include lists of those university serial publications which abstract dissertations, statistical tables (including dissertation loan and publication practice᷊ of the universities), and an author index.

820 *Dissertation Abstracts International.* 1–   (1938–   ). [Formerly titled *Microfilm Abstracts* (1938–1951) and *Dissertation Abstracts* (1952–1968).]

A monthly publication of abstracts of dissertations submitted to Xerox University Microfilms, Ann Arbor, Michigan. The number of contributing institutions has greatly increased since publication of the *Abstracts* began in 1938; now more than 345 cooperating universities in the United States and Canada regularly submit copies of accepted dissertations to be made available on microfilm or Xerox copy. Abstracts are also published of dissertations completed in earlier years whenever these are added to the file of dissertations available on microfilm or Xerox.

Since 1966 the *Abstracts* has been published in two sections (A-Humanities and B-Sciences). Current issues include an author index in each issue plus cumulated author and key-word subject indexes for each volume. Xerox University Microfilms has also published a *Retrospective Index* (9 vols., Ann Arbor, Mich., 1970) which is an 8 vol. key-word-out-of-context subject index and a 1 vol. author index to vols. 1–29 (1938–1969) of *Dissertation Abstracts International.* For comment on the errors, limitations, and weaknesses of that index, see *Wilson Library Bulletin* for Sept., 1971, pp. 73–77. A section C, covering European dissertations, is planned for 1976.

821 *Comprehensive Dissertation Index, 1861–1972.* 37 vols. Ann Arbor, Mich., 1973.

A computer generated key-word-out-of-context index to some 417,000 doctoral dissertations accepted by over 380 institutions of higher learning in the United States and "some foreign universities." Compiled from the entries for *Dissertation Abstracts International* and from other lists of dissertations accepted published by the granting institutions. Arranged alphabetically by subject keywords (drawn from the titles of the dissertations indexed); under each keyword dissertations are listed chronologically. For an important analysis of the limitations and weaknesses of this index, see *RQ*, 14 (fall, 1974), pp. 61–62.

822 The *Datrix II* Service. 1974–   .

Datrix II is a service of Xerox University Microfilms, 300 North Zeeb Road, Ann Arbor, Michigan, 48106. It is a computerized information retrieval system which conducts a progammed search of a computer data bank to identify doctoral dissertations whose titles contain a selected key word or words. The service provides a computer printout for each selected dissertation; printout citations include the title, author, degree, date, granting institution, and a reference to *Dissertation Abstracts International* if the dissertation has been abstracted there. The *Datrix II* data base now includes information on over 430,000 dissertations – virtually all accepted by universities in the United States since 1861, plus many accepted in Canada.

More than 300,000 of these dissertations are available on microfilm or Xerox. Instructions for using the *Datrix II* system are available on order forms supplied by Xerox University Microfilms.

823 *Masters Abstracts: Abstracts of Selected Masters Theses on Microfilm.* 1– (1962–).

Now a quarterly index to masters' theses accepted by about 25 institutions of higher education in the United States. In each quarterly number entries are arranged under headings such as "Language and Literature," "Speech-Theatre," etc.; within these categories entries are arranged alphabetically by author and give title, date, granting institution, abstract, and an order number for requesting microfilm copy.

824 "Dissertations in Progress: Sources in the Social Sciences and Humanities." *RQ*, 14 (fall, 1974), 37–41.

A survey of currently published lists of dissertations in progress, including those in English and American literature, theatre arts, etc.

825 REYNOLDS, MICHAEL M. *A Guide to Theses and Dissertations: An Annotated, International Bibliography of Bibliographies.* Detroit, Mich., 1975.

A descriptively annotated guide to bibliographies of dissertations and theses on all subjects and from all countries. Arrangement is by subject classes such as "Communication," "Fine Arts," "Language and Literature," etc. Includes a short supplement, an index of institutions, a name-title index, and a subject index.

For information on which serial bibliographies include dissertations and theses, see the heading "Dissertations and Theses" in the Characteristics Index of RICHARD A. GRAY, 674. For other bibliographies and indexes of dissertations see entries 18, 19, 20, 21, 114, 260–262, 396, and 949.

XV. Serial Directories, Indexes, and Union Lists

A. Periodicals

1. Guides and Directories to Periodicals

830 VESENYI, PAUL E. *An Introduction to Periodical Bibliography.* Ann Arbor, Mich., 1974.

An annotated guide to periodical indexes, abstracts, union lists, directories, and miscellaneous bibliographies. Arranged in two main parts: (1) a series of chapters providing running commentaries on such topics as periodical indexes, periodical abstracts, etc., and (2) a selected, annotated list of periodical bibliographies with special emphasis on the humanities and social sciences, arranged alphabetically by title. Appendixes include a list of references for part 1, a subject-title-author index to part 1, and a subject guide to part 2.

831 *Ulrich's International Periodicals Directory: A Classified Guide to Current Periodicals, Foreign and Domestic.* 2 vols. 15th ed. N.Y., 1973–74.

A directory to about 55,000 periodicals currently being published throughout the world. Divided into a main list of periodical entries, a separate index to new periodicals appearing in the period 1971–73, a separate list of periodicals that have ceased publication, and a title-subject index. The main list of periodical entries is classified, with headings such as "Education," "Linguistics," "Literature," etc., with relevant periodicals listed alphabetically by title under each heading. Entries give full title, language of text, year first published, frequency, editor, address, subscription rates, special features – e.g., reviews, bibliographies – the Dewey Decimal number, country of publication, and ISSN.

832 *Irregular Serials and Annuals: An International Directory; A Classified Guide to Current Foreign and Domestic Serials, Excepting Periodicals Issued More Frequently Than Once a Year.* 3rd ed. N.Y., 1974.

An international directory to about 20,000 publications in the "twilight area" between books and periodicals – irregular periodicals, proceedings, transactions, annual reviews, handbooks, periodical supplements, conference proceedings, etc. Arranged as a classified list under subject headings such as "History," "Linguistics," "Literature," etc., with a cross-index of subjects provided before the main list and a title-subject index given after. Entries give subtitle, date publication began, frequency, price, editor, address, where indexed, Dewey Decimal number, country of publication, and ISSN.

833 *Bowker Serials Bibliography Supplement 1974.* N. Y., 1974.

A supplement to **831** and **832**. Includes entries for about 4,500 regular periodicals and 2,700 irregular periodicals and annuals. Entries are arranged as a classified list with subject headings such as "Education," "Literature," etc., and provide the same kinds of entry information as *Ulrich's.* Includes four indexes: (1) index to new serial publications, (2) key title index, (3) ISSN index, and (4) title index.

834 WOODWORTH, DAVID. *Guide to Current British Journals.* 2nd ed. 2 vols. London, 1973.

A directory of 4,705 currently published British periodicals. Vol. 1 is arranged as a classified list by the subject headings of the Universal Decimal Classification system. Entries give title, publisher's name, address, subscription price, frequency of publication, circulation figures, and other details not found in *Ulrich's.* Vol. 2 is arranged by publisher. Index to titles and three appendixes: journals publishing abstracts, discontinued titles, and sponsoring societies.

835 WOODWORTH, DAVID. *Directory of Publishers of British Journals.* London, 1971.

An alphabetical listing of publishers of current British journals. Entries give publisher's name, address, and titles of journals published. Index of journal titles.

836 *Commonwealth Directory of Periodicals.* London, 1973.

A classified list of 1970 journals "published in the developing countries of the Commonwealth." Includes annuals as well as more frequently published serials. Arrangement follows the classification system used in *Ulrich's,* **831.** Index to titles.

837 *Standard Periodicals Directory.* N. Y., 1964–   .

A biennial directory to about 53,000 periodicals currently published in the United States and Canada. Includes all kinds of periodicals but not newspapers. Arranged as a classified list by subject – e.g., "Literature and Linguistics," "Art and Sculpture," etc. – and within these categories alphabetically by title. Entries give name and address of publisher, subscription rates, circulation figures, and other information not included in *Ulrich's,* **831.** Cross-index of subjects before the main list of entries and index of periodical titles after.

838 *Serials Review.* 1–   (1975–   ).

A quarterly review of new serials and information sources about serials such as indexes, abstracts, bibliographies, etc. Quarterly issues include indexes to reviews of serials in other journals and in books.

839 *Victorian Periodicals Newsletter.* 1–   (1968–   ).

Issues include bibliographic articles and notes on periodicals published in the Victorian period.

839a MADDEN, LIONEL and DIANA DIXON. *The Nineteenth-Century Periodical Press in Britain: A Bibliography of Modern Studies 1901–1971.* Toronto, 1975. Published as a supplement to *Victorian Periodicals Newsletter,* 7 (Sept., 1975).

An annotated list of 2632 books, articles, and theses on the British periodical press in the nineteenth century. Organized in 4 parts: bibliographies arranged chronologically; general history of periodicals arranged chronologically; studies of individual periodicals and newspapers arranged alphabetically under the title of the serial; and studies and memoirs of proprietors, editors, journalists, and contributors to serials. Includes an author index.

840 HOFFMANN, FREDERICK J., *et al. The Little Magazine: A History and a Bibliography.* Princeton, N. J., 1946. Rptd., N. Y., 1967.

An historical study of "little magazines" which includes on pp. 231–403 an annotated bibliography of little magazines up to 1946, and a title index. May be supplemented by C. F. Ulrich and E. Patterson's "Little Magazines," *Bulletin of the New York Public Library* (1947) and L. Fulton's "Anima Rising: Little Magazines in the Sixties," *American Libraries* (1971).

840a BRYER, JACKSON R. *The Little Magazine in America and England: A Guide to Information Sources.*

A selective annotated guide announced for publication by Gale Research Co. of Detroit, Mich.

841 *International Guide to Literary and Art Periodicals.* London, 1960–   . [Title has varied.]

An annual international index to little magazines. Arranged geographically by country. Entries give editor, address, subscription price and information for potential contributors. Includes press directory and title index. Supplementary material was provided three times yearly in *Trace: A Chronicle of Living Literature, Comprising Annual Directories of (English Language) Poetry and Small Literary Magazines Appearing Throughout the World,* 1952–1970.

842 *International Directory of Little Magazines and Small Presses.* [Title has varied.] 1–   (1965–   ).

An annual directory of "little magazines" mostly published in the United States, Canada, Australia, and England. Arranged alphabetically by title. Entries give publisher, address, frequency, subscription rates, and information for potential contributors. Includes an index to members of the Committee of Small Magazine Editors and Publishers (COSMEP). Supplemented by

Directory: Small Magazine and Press Editors and Publishers and *Small Press Record of Books.* The 10th edition of the *International Directory* is also supplemented by *The Whole Cosmep Catalog,* Paradise, Calif., 1974.

843 LEVI, DORIS J. and NERISSA L. MILTON, eds. *Directory of Black Literary Magazines.* Washington, D. C., 1970.

844 *Small Press Review.* 1–   (1967–   ).

Frequency of publication has varied; now bimonthly. A review of small presses and their publications; often includes comment and information on personalities connected with small presses.

845 *Margins.* 1–   (1972–   ).

A bimonthly review of little magazines. Includes bibliographic articles.

846 *Scholar's Market: An International Directory of Periodicals Publishing Literary Scholarship.* Columbus, Ohio, 1974.

An international directory to more than 800 periodicals, including annuals, printed totally or in part in English, which publish scholarly (not merely creative) writing on literature. Arranged as a classified list under broad headings such as "Single and Multiple Author Periodicals," "Genre," "Film," etc., which are in turn subdivided into other subject headings such as "American," "Popular Culture," "Theatre," etc. Entries for each journal give title, editor, addresses, publishing and circulation information, manuscript requirements, payment, copyright policy, time needed for editorial decision, time between acceptance and publication, etc. Author and journal title indexes.

847 GERSTENBERGER, DONNA and GEORGE HENDRICK. *Fourth Directory of Periodicals Publishing Articles on English and American Literature and Language.* Chicago, 1974.

An international directory listing more than 600 journals (mostly scholarly) which publish articles on English and American literature. Arranged as a single-alphabet list by journal title. Entries give journal address, date of founding, information on special fields of interest, form for manuscript submission, payment and copyright policies, and information on other features – e.g., whether the journal regularly publishes a bibliographical issue, whether it restricts publication to subscribers, whether it carries non-scholarly material, etc. Includes a subject index which lists journals under subject headings which indicate their special field of interest – e.g., "Aesthetics and Theory," "Byron," etc.

848 MESEROLE, HARRISON T. and CAROLYN J. BISHOP. *Directory of Journals and Series in the Humanities: A Data List of the Periodical Sources on the Master List of the MLA International Bibliography.* N. Y., 1970.

A directory (not complete) of journals on the master list of the MLA International Bibliography. Arranged alphabetically by title. Entries give sub-title, MLA acronym, date publication began, editor's name, address, frequency of publication, cost of subscription, and an indication of whether the journal does or does not review books. No index.

2. Indexes to Periodicals

849 KUJOTH, JEAN S. *Subject Guide to Periodical Indexes and Review Indexes.* Metuchen, N. J., 1969.

A subject guide to periodical indexes arranged in three parts: (1) an alphabetical list of subject headings with relevant periodical indexes listed beneath each heading and annotated as to the kind of information each index supplies; (2) a list of indexes arranged alphabetically by title, with annotations providing information on content, subjects covered, and type of information given; and (3) a list of index titles with brief indication of the scope and kinds of information supplied. Covers about 2000 indexes.

850 CHICOREL, MARIETTA. *Chicorel Index to Abstracting and Indexing Services: Periodicals in Humanities and the Social Sciences.* 2 vols. (Vols. 2 and 2a of the Chicorel index series.) N.Y., 1974.

An index to about 33,000 indexes and abstracts of periodicals in the humanities and social sciences. Entries are arranged alphabetically by title of periodical and cite for each periodical the relevant indexing and abstracting services. Vol. 2a includes a directory of abstracting and indexing services.

851 MARCONI, JOSEPH V. *Indexed Periodicals,* Pierian Press, Ann Arbor, Mich. Announced for publication.

852 POOLE, WILLIAM F. and WILLIAM I. FLETCHER. *Index to Periodical Literature, 1802–1881.* 2 vols. Rev. ed., Boston, 1882. *Supplements 1882–1907.* 5 vols. 1888–1908. Rptd., N.Y., 1958.

A subject index to 479 English and American periodicals. Arranged as a single-alphabet list of subject headings with citations to relevant periodical articles beneath. Fiction and poetry are indexed under title; authors' names are given as subjects (e.g., when the author is the subject of a review), but very brief reviews are not included. Entries give article title (sometimes altered), author (sometimes wrongly attributed), periodical title (or the "best known" title if the title changed), volume number (but with continuous numbering, ignoring any changes to "new series," etc.), and page numbers of the article. Corrections of various errors have been published in the *Bulletin of Bibliography*, vols. 1–4. The eccentric treatment of volume numbering and titles in Poole's *Index* has prompted the publication of supplementary aids:

BELL, MARION V. and JEAN C. BACON. *Poole's Index, Date and Volume Key.* Chicago, 1957.

DEARING, VINTON. *Transfer Vectors for Poole's Index to Periodical*

Literature. No. 1. Titles, Volumes, and Dates. Los Angeles, Calif., 1967.

An index to authors' names appearing in Poole's *Index* is provided in Edward C. Wall's *Cumulative Author Index to Poole's Index to Periodical Literature,* Ann Arbor, Mich., 1971; note, however, that Poole's *Index* generally does not attempt to identify the authorship of anonymous writings it indexes.

853 COTGREAVE, ALFRED. *A Contents-Subject Index to General and Periodical Literature.* London, 1900. Rptd. Detroit, Mich., 1971.

A subject index to nineteenth-century monographs, chapters in monographs, anthologies, and periodicals. Supplementary to *Poole's Index,* 852.

854 *Nineteenth Century Readers' Guide to Periodical Literature, 1890–1899. With Supplement Indexing 1900–1922.* 2 Vols. N.Y., 1944.

Intended to be an extensive index of subjects, authors, and illustrators in 19th century periodicals, but the project was abandoned after the first two volumes. The extant volumes cover some 50 periodicals. Arranged as a single-alphabet list with main entries under author and cross-referencing under subject headings. Book reviews are listed under the name of the author of the book reviewed. Poems are listed under the heading "Poems" and cross-indexed by subject. Identifies authors of anonymous articles.

855 *The Wellesley Index to Victorian Periodicals, 1824–1900.* Ed. WALTER E. HOUGHTON. Toronto, 1966– .

The Wellesley Index is intended to be an extensive subject, author, and book review index to Victorian periodicals. Now in progress; the editors have chosen to begin by publishing the author index. The two volumes published so far provide author indexes to 20 Victorian periodicals. The arrangement of each of these volumes is alphabetical by journal indexed, and, for each journal, chronological by issue. For each issue indexed, a table of contents is provided (but excluding poetry) and the name of the author of each contribution listed is given; in cases of anonymous or doubtful authorship, citations are given to the sources of evidence upon which attributions of authorship are based. Each volume also includes a list of the authors cited, with bibliographies of their writings.

856 CAMERON, KENNETH W., ed. *Research Keys to the American Renaissance: Scarce Indexes of the Christian Examiner, The North American Review, and the New Jerusalem Magazine for Students of American Literature, Culture, History, and New England Transcendentalism.* Hartford, Conn., 1967.

Provides reprints of indexes.

857 TYE, J. R., comp. *Periodicals of the Nineties: A Checklist of Literary Periodicals Published in the British Isles at Longer than Fortnightly Intervals, 1890–1899.* Oxford, 1974.

A checklist of literary periodicals of the 1890's arranged in four parts: (1) a list of periodicals arranged alphabetically by title and giving place of publication, date, frequency, average number of pages, price, publisher, printer, editor, number of copies printed or circulated, and location of copy examined; (2) a list of periodical publishers with addresses and the dates they published periodicals; (3) a list of printers of periodicals with their addresses, and (4) a list of editors of periodicals with the dates of their editorship.

858 *British Humanities Index.* 1– (1962–). Continues the *Subject Index to Periodicals* (1916–1961) and the *Athenaeum Subject Index* (1915).

Scope and arrangement has varied. *The Subject Index to Periodicals* attempted international coverage and indexed as many as 500 periodicals, but during World War II indexing was confined to British periodicals and after the 1946 volume no international coverage was attempted. The *British Humanities Index* is now published quarterly with annual cumulation and analyzes about 300 British journals in the humanities and social sciences including journals such as *Critical Quarterly, Modern Language Review, Notes and Queries, Thomas Hardy Yearbook*, etc. Arranged as a subject index followed by an author index.

859 *Readers' Guide to Periodical Literature: An Author-Subject Index to Selected General Interest Periodicals of Reference Value in Libraries.* 1– (1901–). [Title has varied.]

A semimonthly index with annual and larger cumulations. Arranged as a single-alphabet author-subject index. Arrangement and coverage have varied; early issues also indexed composite books, and since 1953 some scientific periodicals have been included. Now indexes some 150 general periodicals such as *Saturday Review World, Poetry, English Journal, The Writer*, etc. Reviews of fiction and drama are indexed under the subject author's name, with title cross-referenced; reviews of film are indexed under the heading "Moving Pictures."

860 *Humanities Index.* 1– (1974–). Continues the *Social Sciences and Humanities Index*, 1965–1973, which continued the *International Index to Periodicals*, 1907–1965. Published quarterly with annual cumulation.

Arranged in two parts: (1) an author-subject index to periodicals publishing articles in the humanities, and (2) a list of book reviews published in those periodicals and arranged alphabetically under the names of the authors of the books reviewed. Includes literary authors' names as subjects, and other subject categories such as "folk lore," "language and literature," "literary and political criticism," etc.

861 *Internationale Bibliographie der Zeitschriftenliteratur mit Einschluß von Sammelwerken und Zeitungen.* Begründet von FELIX DIETRICH, fortgeführt von REINHARD DIETRICH. Abt. A. B. Leipzig (ab 1948, Osnabrück), 1897–1964.

Abt. A: *Bibliographie der deutschen Zeitschriftenliieratur mit Einschluß von Sammelwerken.* Bde. 1–128, 1897–1964.

An index to periodicals and annuals published in German. Coverage varies from less than 300 periodicals in the early volumes to over 4000 in the later. Main entries are arranged under alphabetically organized subject headings; each semiannual volume includes an author index. There is no cumulative index to the series.

Abt. B: *Bibliographie der fremdsprachigen Zeitschriftenliteratur. Répertoire bibliographique international des revues. International index to periodicals.* Bde. 1–22, 1911–1921/25. N. F. Bde. 1–51, 1925–64.

An international subject index to periodicals which complements the index to German periodicals published in Abt. A. Of special value for French and other European periodicals. Coverage has varied; later volumes index nearly 3500 periodicals. Main entries are arranged under subject headings; after 1925 the semiannual volumes included an author index. There is no cumulative index to the series.

Internationale Bibliographie der Zeitschriftenliteratur aus allen Gebieten des Wissens. International Bibliography of Periodical Literature Covering All Fields of Knowledge. Bibliographie internationale de littérature périodique dans tous les domaines de la connaissance. Halbbde. 1– . Osnabrück, 1965– .

An international subject index to some 8000 periodicals and annuals published in English, French, German, and other languages. Main entries are arranged under German subject headings, with English and French subject headings cross-referenced. The semiannual volumes include an author index.

862 *Index to Little Magazines.* 1–   (1949–   ).

A comprehensive biennial index to articles and reviews published in American little magazines. Arranged as a single-alphabet author-title list. For a similar indexing of little magazines published during the period 1900–1950, see the following: *Index to Little Magazines 1943–1947*, Denver, Colo., 1965; *Index to Little Magazines 1940–1942*. Troy, N. Y., 1967; *Index to American Little Magazines 1920–1939*. Troy, N. Y., 1969; *Index to American Little Magazines, 1900–1919, to Which Is Added a Selected List of British and Continental Titles from the Years 1900–1950, Together with Addenda and Corrigenda to Previous Indexes.* 4 vols., Troy, N. Y., 1974. Marion Sader's *Comprehensive Index to English-Language Little Magazines, 1890–1970*, 9 vols. Millwood, N. Y., 1976, includes indexing of book and film reviews.

863 *Popular Periodical Index.* 1–   (1973–   ).

A biannual subject index to popular American periodicals such as *Psychology Today, Intellectual Digest, Ms., Playboy*, etc.

864 *Alternative Press Index: An Index to the Publications Which Amplify the Cry for Social Change and Social Justice.* 1– (1969–).

A quarterly index to leftist and politically or culturally radical serial publications.

865 *Index to Periodical Articles By and About Negroes.* 1– (1960–). *Cumulation*, 1960–1970.

An annual subject-author-title index analyzing about 50 journals currently.

3. Periodical Union Lists

866 FREITAG, RUTH S. *Union Lists of Serials: A Bibliography.* Washington, D. C., 1964.

An annotated bibliography of over 1,200 union lists of serials including periodicals, newspapers, government publications, proceedings, etc. Index of names of authors, compilers, and editors of the union lists cited and a separate index of subjects of the union lists.

867 STEWART, JAMES D. *et al. British Union Catalogue of Periodicals: A Record of the Periodicals of the World, from the Seventeenth Century to the Present Day, in British Libraries.* 4 vols. London, 1955–58. *Supplement to 1960.* 1962. Rptd., Hamden, Conn., 1968.

A union list of about 140,000 periodicals (excluding newspapers) in more than 400 British libraries. Arranged as a single-alphabet title list. Entries give earliest and subsequent titles, issuing bodies, dates of publication, and symbols of British libraries holding runs of the journal with information on the holdings of each library, and on facilities for loan and for copying.

868 *British Union Catalogue of Periodicals Incorporating World List of Scientific Periodicals: New Periodical Titles.* 1964– .

A quarterly union list of new periodicals in British libraries; annual cumulations. Intended to continuously update the *British Union Catalogue of Periodicals* (1955–1962), **867**.

869 TITUS, EDNA B. ed. *Union List of Serials in Libraries of the United States and Canada.* 3rd ed. 5 vols. N. Y., 1965.

A union list of more than 150,000 serials in 956 libraries in the United States and Canada. Arranged as a title list. Entries give subtitle, date and place of publication, and symbols for libraries holding runs of the periodical, with information about their holdings. Explanations of the symbol system used are given at the beginning of each volume. Does not cover library holdings of American newspapers, English newspapers published after 1820, and certain other classes of serials such as government and U.N. publications. The library symbols in the front matter are followed by letters indicating whether the library will lend, photocopy, or microfilm its periodicals.

870 *New Serial Titles: A Union List of Serials Commencing Publication After December 31, 1949.* 1953– .

Intended as a continuing supplement to the *Union List of Serials*, 3rd ed. Since 1955 *New Serial Titles* has been published also in a supplementary form arranged by Dewey Decimal classes, *New Serial Titles: Classed Subject Arrangement*; publication of this classed list is monthly, with no annual cumulation, but a fifteen-year cumulation has been published: *Subject Index to New Serial Titles, 1950–1965*, Ann Arbor, Mich., 1968.

870a *Gesamtverzeichnis ausländischer Zeitschriften und Serien 1939–1958.* Bearb. und hrsg. v. d. Staatsbibliothek der Stiftung Preußischer Kulturbesitz, 5 Teile, Wiesbaden, 1963–68.

A list of the holdings of non-German periodicals in West German and West Berlin libraries. Supplemented and continued as *Gesamtverzeichnis ausländischer Zeitschriften und Serien. Nachträge.* Lfg. 1–   Lfg. 1– . Marburg, 1966– .

871 *Union List of Little Magazines: Showing Holdings of 1,037 Little Magazines in the Libraries of Indiana University, Northwestern University, Ohio State University, State University of Iowa, University of Chicago, and the University of Illinois.* Chicago, 1956.

872 DANKY, JAMES P. *Undergrounds: A Union List of Alternative Periodicals in Libraries of the United States and Canada.* Madison, Wis., 1974.

B. Newspapers

1. Guides and Directories to Newspapers

873 *Willing's Press Guide [year].* London, 1871– .
[Title has varied.]

An annual directory, index, and handbook for the serial press of the United Kingdom and the Commonwealth. Now lists about 1,500 newspapers, 4,700 magazines, and 1,500 annuals. Arranged as an alphabetical list of newspaper and periodical titles. Current entries give date of first issue, frequency of publication, address, telephone number, subscription rates, and an indication of political orientation.

874 *Newspaper Press Directory.* London, 1846– .

Provides information similar to that found in *Willing's Press Guide*.

875 *Ayer Directory of Publications.* Philadelphia, Pa., 1880– . [Title has varied.]

A directory and gazetteer of American newspapers and periodicals, including those published in Canada. Arrangement is (in the case of the U.S.A.) geographical by state, and within each state by city or town. Entries give editor, address, date of foundation, information on technical matters of printing, subscription rates, circulation figures, and publication frequency for more than 25,000 titles. Subject index and other appendices.

2. Indexes to Newspapers

876 *Palmer's Index to the Times Newspaper.* London, 1868–1943. Rptd. Nendeln, Liechtenstein, 1956–66.

A subject index to the London *Times* covering the years 1790–1941.

877 *The Times Index.* London, 1906–   . Rptd. Nendeln, Liechtenstein. [Title has varied.]

A bi-monthly (monthly to 1914, quarterly 1914–1956) subject index to the *London Times*, the *Times Literary Supplement*, the *Times Educational Supplement*, and the *Times Higher Education Supplement*. Arranged as a single-alphabet list of subject headings and descriptive phrases (including proper names, places, titles, etc.) with citations to relevant issue, page, and column. Citations to plays and books reviewed are given under their authors' names.

878 *New York Times Index.* 1913–   . [A 15 vol. compilation of earlier existing indexes and original indexes (for the years when the *Times* kept no index) has been published with the sub-heading, "Prior Series," N.Y., 1967–74. It covers the period 1851–1912.]

Now a semi-monthly subject-person-organization index with annual cumulations. Entries give date, page, column of relevant news items, cross-references, and provide a concise summary of the material indexed. Book reviews, deaths, and news of art and entertainment are only indexed under subject headings. Frequency and arrangement of the index in earlier periods has varied.

3. Bibliographies and Union Lists of Newspapers

a. British

879 *Tercentenary Handlist of English and Welsh Newspapers, Magazines, and Reviews.* London, 1920. Rptd., 1966.

A chronological list of English serials from 1620 to 1919. Arranged in two main geographical lists, one for London and environs, the other for the rest of England and Wales. Corrections were published in *Notes and Queries* issues for 1921–2.

880 WEED, KATHERINE K. and RICHMOND P. BOND. *Studies of British Newspapers and Periodicals From Their Beginning to 1800: A Bibliography.* Chapel Hill, N.C., 1946.

A bibliography of about 21,000 books and articles written about British newspapers and periodicals which were published before 1800. Arranged as a classified list of subjects including individual publications and general categories such as "Editors," "Freedom of the Press," etc. Author index.

881 CRANE, RONALD S. and FREDERICK B. KAYE. *A Census of British Newspapers and Periodicals, 1620–1800.* Chapel Hill, N.C., 1927. Rptd. N.Y., 1963, and London, 1966.

Arranged in two major parts: (1) A union list, arranged by title, of 981 British newspapers and periodicals published during the period 1620–1800 and available in at least one of 62 American libraries; (2) a list of 1445 newspapers and periodicals *not* held in the 62 libraries surveyed. Separate chronological and geographical indexes.

882 WILES, ROY. *Freshest Advices: Early Provincial Newspapers in England.* Columbus, Ohio, 1965.

A history of early provincial English newspapers including appendixes providing: (1) a chronological chart in graph form of the publication spans of each provincial newspaper believed to have been published in England from 1701 to 1760; (2) a register of those newspapers, arranged geographically by place of publication and giving subsequent titles, date of 1st issue, the serial number of the earliest issue seen, terminal date, day of publication, number of pages and columns, imprint or colophon, holdings in libraries in the United Kingdom in order of proximity to the place of publication, and holdings in the United States and Canada; (3) a bibliography; and (4) an author-title-subject index.

883 WARD, WILLIAM S. *Index and Finding List of Serials Published in the British Isles, 1789–1832.* Lexington, Ky., 1953.

A union list of about 5000 newspapers and periodicals in more than 350 repositories in England, the United States, and Canada. Entries are arranged by serial title and provide information on place of publication, frequency, dates published, etc., with citations to repositories having runs of the serial.

884 WARD, WILLIAM S. *British Periodicals and Newspapers, 1789–1832: A Bibliography of Secondary Sources.* Lexington, Ky., [1972].

Intended to supplement Ward's *Index and Finding List.* A bibliography of 2991 books and articles written about the newspapers and periodicals in the *Index,* with some annotation. Separate indexes of authors, subjects, and library catalogues/union lists.

885 MILFORD, ROBERT T. and DONALD M. SUTHERLAND. *A Catalogue of English Newspapers and Periodicals in the Bodleian Library, 1622–1800.* Oxford, 1936.

A catalogue of English, Scottish, Welsh, and Irish newspapers arranged alphabetically by title. Includes an index to editors, authors, and contributors.

b. American

886 BRIGHAM, CLARENCE S. *History and Bibliography of American Newspapers, 1690–1820.* 2 vols. Worcester, Mass., 1947. *Supplement*, 1961.

A bibliography of 2120 newspapers published in America in the period 1690–1820, including 194 newspapers no copy of which has been found. Arranged geographically by states, and within each state by city, with the newspapers of each city listed alphabetically by title. Each entry also provides a list of repositories with information on the holdings of the newspaper. Includes lists of libraries and private owners cited, and separate indexes of titles and printers. Corrections were published in *Proceedings of the American Antiquarian Society*, 71 (1961), 15–62.

887 LATHEM, EDWARD CONNERY. *Chronological Tables of American Newspapers, 1690–1820: Being a Tabular Guide to the Holdings of Newspapers Published in America Through the Year 1820.* Barre, Mass., 1972.

A supplement to Brigham, **886**. Arranged as a series of chronological tables which display year-by-year what American newspapers were being published in which geographic locations.

888 GREGORY, WINIFRED, ed. *American Newspapers, 1821–1936: A Union List of Files Available in the United States and Canada.* N.Y., 1937. Rptd., 1967.

A union list of more than 35,000 newspapers in more than 5,600 repositories in the United States and Canada. Information about what libraries have runs of the newspaper and what the nature of these holdings is.

889 Library of Congress. *Newspapers in Microform, United States, 1948–1972.* 7th ed. Washington, D.C., 1973.

A bibliography of some 34,200 titles of newspapers published in 7,457 locations, with more than 2,300 cross-references. Title index.

XVI. Review Indexes

892 GRAY, RICHARD A. *A Guide to Book Review Citations: A Bibliography of Sources.* Columbus, Ohio, 1968.

A comprehensive annotated guide to indexes and bibliographies containing book review references – such as book review indexes, periodical indexes, serial and monographic bibliographies, and the like. Arranged as a classified list with entries for specific indexes and bibliographies listed under broad headings such as "General," "Religion," "Modern Languages, Philology, and Literature," etc., with sub-categories such as "Comparative Literature," "English," "Author Bibliographies, 1660–1800," etc. Within each such section sources that cite reviews are listed and annotated. Includes sources of reviews for English and American literature generally and for specific periods, types, authors, etc. Provides a brief glossary of foreign words and abbreviations and 5 indexes: (1) subject, (2) title, (3) personal name, (4) chronological, and (5) country.

892a *Current Book Review Citations.* 1– (1976–).

A monthly index to reviews published in over 1000 journals.

893 *An Index to Book Reviews in the Humanities.* 1– (1960–).

An annual index (published quarterly until 1963) of reviews of books in the humanities published in about 400 scholarly and general periodicals. Coverage includes such journals as *Anglia, Archiv, The Browning Newsletter, Criticism, Drama & Theatre, Philological Quarterly, Victorian Poetry, Victorian Studies,* and *Yale Review.* Arranged as a single-alphabet list by author of the book reviewed.

894 *Book Review Index.* 1– (1965–).

Until 1969 a monthly index with quarterly and annual cumulations; suspended publication at the end of 1968 and began publication again as a bimonthly index with annual cumulations in 1972. Retrospective vols. have been prepared for 1969–71. The 1974 cumulation provides 76,400 citations to reviews of about 35,400 books in 228 periodicals; current indexing covers such journals as *American Literature, Criticism, JEGP, Modern Language Review, Modern Philology, Film Quarterly, The Library, Quarterly Journal of Speech,* and *Speculum.* Arranged as a single-alphabet list by author of book reviewed.

895 *Book Review Digest.* 1– (1905–).

An index and digest of reviews of books published in about 80 journals, mostly general, but including such journals as *American Literature, Commen-*

tary, *Journal of Aesthetics and Art Criticism, Modern Philology, New York Review of Books,* and the *Times Literary Supplement.* Published 10 times yearly with annual indexed cumulations and 5-year cumulations with cumulative index. Arranged as a single-alphabet list by author of book reviewed. Entries include identification of pseudonyms, citations to non-critical reviews, and extended quotations from critical reviews. Indexing practice has varied; currently there is a subject-title index with elaborate sub-classifications of headings such as "biography" and "fiction." A cumulative author-title index for 1904–74 has been published in 5 vols., N. Y., 1976.

896 *The New York Times Book Review Index 1896–1970.* 5 vols. N. Y., 1973.

An index to the first 124 vols. of the weekly *New York Times Book Review* (1896–ᅠ), but not to other reviews published in the *New York Times.* Divided into 5 indexes, each in its own volume: (1) authors, including editors, translators, authors of letters, etc., (2) titles, (3) byline – i.e., reviewers, (4) subjects, largely limited to general articles, letters, and non-fiction works reviewed, and (5) categories such as *anthologies, criticism, drama, short stories,* etc.

897 *Internationale Bibliographie der Zeitschriftenliteratur mit Einschluß von Sammelwerken und Zeitungen.* Begründet von FELIX DIETRICH, fortgeführt von REINHARD DIETRICH. Abt. C: *Bibliographie der Rezensionen und Referate.* 1–77, Leipzig, 1901–44. Rptd.

An annual (semiannual 1911–1914) index to book reviews, covering only reviews in German during 1901–10, and, thereafter, reviews in about 5000 German and foreign periodicals, including English, with issues alternately giving German and foreign reviews. Each volume is arranged as an author list of books reviewed, with review citations given beneath each title. No index.

898 DIETRICH Abt. C, **897**, continued as:
Internationale Bibliographie der Rezensionen wissenschaftlicher Literatur. Hrsg. OTTO ZELLER. 1–ᅠ. Osnabrück, 1971–ᅠ.

A semiannual review index intended to continue Part C of the *Internationale Bibliographie der Zeitschriftenliteratur* which was discontinued in 1944. Retrospective volumes are being prepared for the intervening years. Covers reviews of books and book series. Arranged in three indexes--to subjects, to books reviewed, and to reviewers. Very broad coverage of German and foreign reviews.

For other bibliographies and indexes of reviews see entries **109, 110, 383–385,** and **803.**

899 *Cumulative Book Review Index 1905–1974.* Princeton, N. J., 1975.

Provides an author-title index to all reviews in the *Book Review Digest, Library Journal, Choice,* and *The Saturday Review* for the period 1905–1974.

XVII. Indexes to Books, Collections of Essays, and Other Composite Works

900 PEDDIE, ROBERT A. *Subject Index of Books Published Before 1880.* London, 1933. *Subject Index of Books Published Up To and Including 1880.* Second series. London, 1935. *Subject Index ... Third Series.* London, 1939. *Subject Index ... New Series.* London, 1948.

A four vol. subject guide to books published before the period covered by the B. M. *Subject Index*, 1179. Each of the 4 vols. is arranged as a separate A–Z subject index, and each has a separate A–Z supplementary index appended. The subject categories used are relatively narrow. The 3rd vol. entries provide cross-referencing to the subject headings of the 1st and 2nd vols. The 4 vols. include entries for about 200,000 books.

901 *The A. L. A. Index: An Index to General Literature, Biographical, Historical, and Literary Essays and Sketches, Reports, etc.* 2nd ed. Boston, Mass., 1901. *Supplement, 1900–1910.* Chicago, Ill., 1914. Rptd., Ann Arbor, Mich., 2 vols., 1970–71.

An index to books in English which treat of more than one subject-–e.g., collections of essays in the fields of literature, history, and biography; books of travel dealing with different geographical areas; reports of literary and historical societies, etc. Arrangement is alphabetical by catchword subject and includes authors' names as subject headings. Both the original index and the supplement include lists of the books indexed. See also C. Edward Wall's *ALA Index to General Literature: Cumulative Author Index* (Ann Arbor, Mich., 1972) which provides a single-alphabet author index of some 80,000 citations.

902 *Essay and General Literature Index, 1900–1933: An Index to about 40,000 Essays and Articles in 2,144 Volumes of Collections of Essays and Miscellaneous Works.* N.Y., 1934. *Supplements.* 1934–   .

An index to books treating of more than one subject--e.g., collections of essays on literature, or history, or collective biographies, etc. Arranged as a single-alphabet subject-author index which includes some titles. The supplements are cumulated about every 6 years. The supplementary issues published from 1934 to June, 1974, provide citations to 168,898 essays and articles in 8,944 volumes. Presently the index is published semi-annually with annual cumulations. Since 1946 the analysis of collective biography is done by *Biography Index*, **950**. Each issue of the *Essay and General Literature Index* includes a list of the books analyzed. There is a cumulative index for the issues through 1969: *Essay and General Literature Index: Works Indexed 1900–1969*, 7 vols., N.Y., 1972.

903 *Index to the Contemporary Scene.* 1–   (1973–   ).

An annual subject index to about 300 popular current new books. Supplementary to **902**.

904 *Vertical File Index.* [Title has varied.] 1–   (1935–   ).

A monthly index to selected free or inexpensive pamphlet materials. Annual cumulations. Arranged alphabetically by subject, including such categories as "Books," "Authorship," "Libraries," etc. Entries include information on how to obtain the materials. Title index.

905 COMBS, RICHARD E. *Authors: Critical and Biographical References.* Metuchen, N. J., 1971.

An index to nearly 500 books written in English and dealing with more than one author. Supplies 4,700 citations to critical and biographical references to more than 1,400 English, American, and other authors. Arranged in three parts: (1) an alphabetical list of authors' names with citations to relevant parts of books given beneath each name; (2) a key to the symbols used; and (3) an author index to the books analyzed.

See also **853**.

XVIII. Rare and Used Book Trade: Guides, Catalogues, Directories and Glossaries

908 *Book-Auction Records: A Priced and Annotated Annual Record of International Book Auctions.* 1902– . [Title has varied.]

An annual list of books sold in major auction centers throughout the world – London, Edinburgh, Glasgow, New York, Montreal, and Melbourne. Coverage has varied; New York auctions were not included until 1939. Entries are derived from auction catalogues and are arranged alphabetically by author of the book auctioned; entries include bibliographic information about the book sold, where sold, the price, and name of buyer when known. Seven cumulative indexes have been published, covering the years 1902–1963.

909 *American Book Prices Current [year].* 1– (1895–). [Title has varied.]

A guide to auction prices of books sold in major auction centers throughout the world. Coverage and scope have varied; now includes auction houses in France, England, and Canada as well as in the United States, and can include over 29,000 entries from more than 170 sales. Currently arranged in 2 main parts: (1) books, including broadsides, maps, charts, and uncorrected proofs, and (2) autographs and manuscripts. Entries in each part are arranged alphabetically by author (anonymous works by title) and give title, imprint, edition, information on book condition, size, binding, auction house, date of sale, price, and purchaser when known. Indexes covering periods from 5 to 7 years have been published for the years 1916–1970.

910 *Jahrbuch der Bücherpreise: Ergebnisse der Versteigerungen in Deutschland, Österreich, Holland, der Schweiz, Skandinavien, der Tschechoslowakei, Ungarn.* Jg. 1–34. Leipzig, 1907–40.

CONTINUED AS:

Jahrbuch der Auktionspreise für Bücher und Autographen (ab 1953: *Handschriften und Autographen). Ergebnisse der Auktionen in Deutschland, Holland, Österreich und der Schweiz.* Jg. 1– . Heidelberg, 1951– .

911 British Museum. *List of Catalogues of English Book Sales 1676–1900 Now In the British Museum.* London, 1915.

912 McKay, George L. *American Book Auction Catalogues 1713–1934: A Union List.* N.Y., 1937. Rptd., "Including the Supplements of 1946 and 1948," Detroit, Mich., 1967.

A list of about 10,000 U.S. auction catalogues of books, pamphlets, broadsides, newspapers, manuscripts, autographs, and bookplates. Titles of catalogues are arranged chronologically by opening date of auction. Entries include, if known, the owner(s) of the auctioned property, number of pages of the catalogue, and number of lots auctioned. Copies of practically all 19th and 20th-century catalogues are located, but only 19 out of 473 18th-century catalogues. Includes an index of owners; the supplementary lists are not indexed. Additions were published in *Bulletin of the New York Public Library*, 50 (1946), 177–84, and 52 (1948), 401–12.

913 AMORY, HUGH, ed. *Sales Catalogues of Libraries of Eminent Persons.* Vol. 8. *Poets and Men of Letters.* London, 1974.

914 MANDEVILLE, MILDRED S. *The Used Book Price Guide.* 2 vols. Kenmore, Washington, 1972–73.

A guide to ascertaining the current American booksellers' price for rare, scarce, used, and out-of-print books of all kinds. Arranged alphabetically by author, with anonymous works by title and sometimes by subject. Entries give in a highly abbreviated form (a key to abbreviations is in vol. 1, p. 367) the title, place of publication, date, size, kind of binding, other identifying points, condition of book, price in dollars, and identification of the dealer's catalogue from which the price was taken. Covers catalogues issued from May, 1968 to May, 1973. An appendix gives dealer catalogue code identifications and dealer addresses.

915 *Bookman's Guide to Americana.* 6th ed. Metuchen, N. J., 1971.

A guide to current prices for Americana. Arranged as a single-alphabet author list (anonymous works by title). Entries are derived from booksellers' catalogues issued between 1969 and 1970.

916 *Bookman's Price Index: An Annual Guide to the Values of Rare and Other Out-of-Print Books* [the title of vol. 1 continues with the words *and Sets of Periodicals*]. 1– (1965–).

Arrangement is a single-alphabet author list with anonymous works and conventionally titled works (e.g., *bible*) by title. Entries are based on descriptions of books offered for sale in recent (i.e., within the last 3 or 4 years) catalogues of leading book dealers.

917 *AB Bookman's Yearbook.* 1949– .

An international annual guide to the antiquarian book trade. Includes a subject directory of specialist and antiquarian book dealers, a book-trade services directory, and other information relevant to the antiquarian book trade.

918 *Directory of Dealers in Secondhand and Antiquarian Books in the British Isles.* 1951– .

919 *Book Dealers in North America: A Directory of Dealers in Second-hand Antiquarian Books in Canada and the United States of America.* 1954– .

920 PETERS, JEAN. *The Bookman's Glossary.* 5th ed., rev. N.Y., 1974.

A dictionary list of terms, abbreviations, and names connected with antiquarian and modern book trade. Two appendixes: proofreader's marks and a brief reading list. The 4th ed. includes an appendix on foreign book-trade terms deleted from this ed.

XIX. Sources of Biographical Information

A. General Biography, Autobiography, Diaries, Genealogy, and Heraldry

1. Histories

925 ALTICK, RICHARD D. *Lives and Letters: A History of Literary Biography in England and America.* N. Y., 1965.

Includes an author-title-subject index and extensive bibliographical notes.

926 JOHNSON, EDGAR. *One Mighty Torrent: The Drama of Biography.* N. Y., 1936. Rptd., 1955.

A history of English biography with occasional attention to biography in other countries. Includes an author-title-subject index.

927 STAUFFER, DONALD A. *English Biography Before 1700.* Cambridge, Mass., 1930. Rptd., N .Y., 1964.

Includes chapters on autobiography and on the critical study of biography. Pp. 389–372 provide an extensive bibliography with some annotation. Index of names cited.

928 DELANY, PAUL. *British Autobiography in the Seventeenth Century.* London, 1969.

Includes an index of names, with a few subject and title entries. The bibliography on pp. 175–90 is divided into two parts: (1) a check-list of seventeenth-century autobiographies and (2) a brief list of secondary works.

929 STAUFFER, DONALD A. *The Art of Biography in Eighteenth Century England.* Princeton, N. J., 1941. *Bibliographical Supplement,* 1941. Rptd. 2 vols., N. Y., 1970.

The *Bibliographical Supplement* contains an annotated bibliography in two parts: (1) an author list (anonymous works by title) of biographies and autobiographies written or translated in England, 1700–1800; entries give place and date of publication, brief annotations, and an indication if the work is discussed in the main volume; and (2) a very short annotated list of secondary materials.

930 REED, JOSEPH W. *English Biography in the Early Nineteenth Century 1801–1838.* Yale Studies in English, vol. 160. New Haven, Conn., 1966.

Includes a brief bibliography on pp. 167–170 and an author-title-subject index.

931 O'NEILL, EDWARD H. *A History of American Biography 1800–1935.* Philadelphia, Pa., 1935. Rptd., N. Y., 1961.

Pp. 369–417 provide a bibliography of primary and secondary materials: primary materials are arranged first, alphabetically by name of the biographical subject, followed by a brief list of secondary books and articles. Includes an index of names.

2. Bibliographies

932 SLOCUM, ROBERT B. *Biographical Dictionaries and Related Works.* Detroit, Mich., 1967. *First Supplement,* 1972.

An international bibliography of more than 4800 collections of biographies, bio-bibliographies, collections of epitaphs, selected genealogical works, dictionaries of anonyms and pseudonyms, historical and specialized dictionaries, biographical materials in government manuals, bibliographies of biography, biographical indexes, and selected portrait catalogues. Arranged in three main categories: (1) universal biography, (2) national or area biography, subdivided into headings such as "Africa," "Great Britain," etc., and (3) biography by vocation, subdivided by headings such as "Arts," "Language and Literature," etc. Within these categories entries are arranged alphabetically by author (anonymous works by title) and give full available bibliographic information including notes and editions, illustrations, etc., and some descriptive annotation. The *Supplement* is similarly arranged and contains about 3400 new entries. Both the original volume and the supplement have separate author-title-subject indexes.

933 KLINE, JANE. *Biographical Sources for the United States.* Washington, D. C., 1961.

An annotated bibliography of 163 sources of current biographical information about living Americans, with emphasis on materials published between 1945–1960. Arranged in three main lists: (1) general U. S. biographical sources, (2) regions and states, and (3) special and professional groups – e.g., "Artists," "Authors," "Education," etc. Author-title-subject index.

934 O'NEILL, EDWARD HAYES. *Biography by Americans 1658–1936.* Philadelphia Pa., 1939.

Arranged in two parts. Part I is a bibliography of biographies written by Americans 1658–1936; it attempts to be exhaustive for all but biographies written on particularly famous men. Part I is arranged alphabetically by name of biographee; entries include locations of copies. Part II is a list of 707 collective biographies compiled by Americans and arranged by compilers' names; contents are analyzed except when the collection includes more than 20 biographies. No index.

935 MATTHEWS, WILLIAM. *British Autobiographies: An Annotated Bibliography of British Autobiographies Published or Written Before 1951.* Berkeley, Calif., 1955. Rptd., Hamden, Conn., 1968.

An annotated bibliography of more than 6500 autobiographies written by native or naturalized Englishmen. Arranged alphabetically by author (anonymous works by title). Entries give title, date, and a brief descriptive annotation. Includes a subject index to occupations, geographical locations, historical events, etc.

936 KAPLAN, LOUIS, *et al. A Bibliography of American Autobiography.* Madison, Wis., 1961.

A bibliography of more than 6000 autobiographies of Americans. Arrangement is alphabetical by author of the biography (anonymous works by title). Includes an extensive index to biographees and to various subjects such as occupations, area of country, etc.

937 LILLARD, RICHARD G. *American Life in Autobiography: A Descriptive Guide.* Stanford, Calif., 1956.

An annotated bibliography of autobiographies by Americans published after 1900. Arranged in classes such as "Actors and Show People," "Writers and Critics," etc., and, within these classes, alphabetically by author. Entries provide authors' dates, title, imprint, and a brief summary of the autobiography. Highly selective. Includes an index of authors and special lists of writers of autobiographies in four minority categories – immigrants, American Indians, Jews, and Negroes.

938 BRIGANO, RUSSELL C. *Black Americans in Autobiography.* Durham, N. C., 1974.

An annotated bibliography of 459 autobiographies of black Americans written from the end of the Civil War to early 1973, with a checklist of autobiographical writings before 1865. Arranged in two main parts – autobiographies and autobiographical writings – and alphabetically by author in each part. The annotations identify the author, provide a summary of the work, and list locations of libraries having copies of the work.

939 MATTHEWS, WILLIAM. *British Diaries: An Annotated Bibliography of British Diaries Written Between 1442 and 1942.* Berkeley, Calif., 1950. Rptd., Gloucester, Mass., 1967.

An annotated bibliography of published and unpublished diaries written by citizens of the United Kingdom living either at home or abroad, and including, also, diaries in English by other nationals when these have been published in England. Arrangement is chronological. Entries include a brief descriptive annotation and, in the case of unpublished diaries, the location. Author index.

939a BATTS, JOHN STUART. *British Manuscript Diaries of the Nineteenth Century: An Annotated Listing.* Totowa, N. J., 1976.

Supplements Matthews, **939**. Provides an annotated list of over 3000 diaries
arranged chronologically by year of beginning. Entries provide notes on the
writer, the contents of the diary, and its present location. Author and subject
indexes.

940 PONSONBY, ARTHUR. *English Diaries: A Review of English Diaries
from the Sixteenth to the Twentieth Century With an Introduction
on Diary Writing.* London, 1923. Rptd., Ann Arbor, Mich., 1971.

941 PONSONBY, ARTHUR. *More English Diaries: Further Reviews of Diaries from the Sixteenth to the Nineteenth Century With an Introduction on Diary Reading.* London, 1927.

942 MATTHEWS, WILLIAM. *American Diaries: An Annotated Bibliography
of American Diaries Written Prior to the Year 1861.* Berkeley, Calif.
1945. Rptd., Boston, 1959.

An annotated bibliography of published diaries written in English in America
between 1629 and 1861. Arranged chronologically. Entries identify authors by
name, dates, and occupation; the annotations describe briefly the contents of
the diary.

943 MATTHEWS, WILLIAM. *American Diaries in Manuscript, 1580–1954:
A Descriptive Bibliography.* Athens, Ga., 1974.

An annotated bibliography of 5022 unpublished American diaries written
during the period 1580–1954. Arranged chronologically. Entries give author,
time span of the diary, a description of the contents, and location of the diary
and of any copies. Index to authors.

944 FILBY, WILLIAM P. *American and British Genealogy and Heraldry.*
Chicago, 1970.

A selective but relatively full critically annotated bibliography of about 1800
sources of information on genealogy and heraldry. Arranged in broad classes:
(1) the United States, general works, (2) individual states, (3) Canada, (4)
United Kingdom, and (5) heraldry. The annotations provide information on
the contents, arrangement, and use of each item and also make critical
comparative analyses – e.g., of the relative merits of Burke's, Debrett's, and
Lodge's *Peerages.* Author-title-subject index.

3. Indexes

945 HYAMSON, ALBERT M. *A Dictionary of Universal Biography of All
Ages and All Peoples.* 2nd ed. London, 1951.

An index to more than 100,000 biographies appearing in 23 major collective
biographies of all countries.

946 RICHES, PHYLLIS. *Analytical Bibliography of Universal Collected Biography Comprising Books Published in the English Tongue in Great Britain and Ireland, America, and the British Dominions.* London, 1934.

Attempts to provide an index to all collective biographies written in English up to 1934. Arranged in the following parts: (1) an index of biographees arranged alphabetically by name, giving dates, brief biographical note, and reference to the more than 3000 volumes of collective biography analyzed; (2) an annotated bibliography of the biographical works indexed; (3) two indexes to the more than 50,000 biographees, one arranged chronologically, the other by occupation; and (4) a list of collective biographies arranged by subject.

947 CHICOREL, MARIETTA. *Chicorel Index to Biographies.* 2 vols. Vols. 15 and 15 A of the Chicorel Index series. N. Y., 1974.

An index to more than 21,000 published biographies. Arranged as a classified list by occupation of biographees. Entries give author, imprint, number of pages, cost, LC number, etc. Vol. 15a includes an alphabetical index to biographees by name and a subject index.

948 HEFLING, HELEN and EVA RICHARDS. *Index to Contemporary Biography and Criticism.* 2nd ed., rev. and enl. Boston, 1934.

An index to more than 400 collections of biographical and critical material on persons born after 1850. Arranged as a single-alphabet list of names and titles; entries give references to the collections analyzed. Attempts to exclude from analysis the most common biographical reference works such as *Who's Who.*

949 REEL, JEROME V., Jr. *Index to Biographies of Englishmen, 1000–1485, Found in Dissertations and Theses.* Westport, Conn., 1975.

An index to more than 150 theses containing biographies of Englishmen who lived between 1000 and 1485. Entries are arranged alphabetically by name of biographee and include a brief biographical sketch and a reference to the thesis which includes fuller biographical information. Provides indexes to biographees by chronology, by occupation, and by geographical area.

950 *Biography Index: A Cumulative Index to Biographical Material in Books and Magazines.* 1–   (1946–   ).

A quarterly index, cumulating annually, to about 1,700 periodicals, plus works of collective biography and separately published biographies, autobiographies, and incidental biographical material. The index also covers obituaries, diaries, memoirs.

951 *The New York Times Obituaries Index, 1858–1968.* N. Y., 1970.

A single-alphabet index of over 353,000 names, including all names listed under the heading "Deaths" in the issues of the *New York Times Index* from

September 1958 to December 1968, augmented by entries for the years 1907–12 and by other entries for the period 1913–25 not listed in the published indexes. Does not include obituaries which were paid notices rather than news stories.

4. Collections of Biographies

952 *Chambers's Biographical Dictionary.* Ed. J. O. THORNE. Rev. ed. London, 1969.

A biographical dictionary containing more than 15,000 short biographies of persons of all countries. Arranged alphabetically by name of biographee; entries can include pronunciation of name and/or references to biographical sources. Contains an extensive subject index to biographees with categories for literature, art, nicknames, etc.; the index category "Literature and Drama" gives titles of works arranged alphabetically with author identifications.

953 *Webster's Biographical Dictionary.* Springfield, Mass., 1972.

A frequently revised biographical dictionary of living and dead persons of all countries; the 1972 edition contains upwards of 40,000 brief biographies. Arranged alphabetically by name of biographee; entries give pronunciation of name, dates, citizenship, profession, and summary of career.

954 KAY, ERNEST, ed. *Directory of International Biography.* London, 1965– .

An annually published biographical directory. The 1974 edition, in 4 vols., lists 19,000 biographees and includes a cumulative index to about 100,000 names appearing in the first 10 vols. Entries are arranged alphabetically by biographee's name, provide brief biographical information, and cite other biographical sources in which further information may be found.

955 *International Who's Who.* London, 1935– .

An annual compilation of very brief biographies of persons currently of international prominence. Arranged alphabetically by biographee and based on information usually supplied by the biographee.

956 *Current Biography.* N. Y., 1940– .

Collections of short biographical articles on currently newsworthy persons of all nations. Published monthly, with annual and 10-year cumulations. The issues through 1970 are also covered by the separately published *Current Biography: Cumulative Index, 1940–1970*, N. Y., 1973.

957 *Dictionary of National Biography.* Ed. LESLIE STEPHEN and SIDNEY LEE. 63 vols. London, 1885–1900. *Supplement*, 3 vols., 1901. *Errata*, 1904. The original 63 vols. plus the 3 vol. supplement rptd. in 22 vols., London, 1921. 'Compact Edition' (with reading glass), 2 vols., 1975.

Subsequent decennial supplements cover the period 1901–1960; further supplements are planned.

A selective but very extensive and scholarly collection of biographies of deceased noteworthy residents of Great Britain and the colonies from the beginning of history to the present. Arranged alphabetically by biographees' names. Entries are relatively full (some extend to more than 100 pages) and can include all the kinds of information found in full-length biographies. Bibliographies of sources used in preparing the biography are provided at the end of each article. Indexing varies. The original 66 vols. are not indexed. The first 21 vols. of the 1921 reprint each contain an index that supplies references to vol. 22 which is a reprint of the original 3 vol. supplement of 1901. The supplementary vols. covering the period 1901–1960 have cumulating indexes; thus, the most recent supplement (for the years 1951–60) includes an index to all the supplements for 1901–1960. *The Concise Dictionary of National Biography*, 2 vols. (1903, 1961) is an epitome of the *DNB* and its supplements, in which entries are reduced to about 1/14 of the original.

958 *Dictionary of National Biography: Corrections and Additions, Cumulated From the Bulletin of the Institute of Historical Research, University of London, Covering the Years 1923–1963.* Boston, 1966.

A list of the 1,300 corrections and additions to the *DNB* recorded in the *Bulletin of the Institute for Historical Research* during the period 1923–63. Arranged in alphabetical order by name of biographee. An incomplete but indispensable supplement to the *DNB*.

959 BOASE, FREDERICK. *Modern English Biography Containing Many Thousand Concise Memoirs of Persons Who Have Died Since the Year 1850, With an Index of the Most Interesting Matter.* 6 vols. Truro, 1892–1921. Rptd., London, 1964; N.Y., 1965.

Supplementary to the *DNB*, *957*, for the period 1850 onwards. Vol. 3 includes a subject index to pseudonyms, facts, etc. The last three vols. are supplementary to the first three.

960 *Who's Who.* London, 1849– .

An annual biographical dictionary of prominent Englishmen. Arranged alphabetically by name of biographee. Entries are compiled from information supplied by the biographee and include such details as full name, address, occupation, degrees and education, honors, family background, etc.

961 *Who Was Who.* London, 1920– .

A continuing biographical dictionary of deceased prominent Englishmen who have previously been included in *Who's Who*. Six volumes have been published to date covering the years 1897–1970; other volumes covering future 10-year periods are planned. Arrangement is alphabetical by name of biographee; entries include the same kinds of information found in *Who's Who entries*, with final details and date of death added.

962 *Dictionary of American Biography.* Ed. ALLEN JOHNSON and DUMAS
MALONE. 20 vols. plus *Index.* N. Y. and London, 1928–37. *Supplement
One* (to Dec. 31, 1935), 1944. Rptd. in 22 vols. with corrigenda in vol.
1, 1946. *Supplement Two* (to Dec. 31, 1940), 1958. *Supplement Three*
(to Dec. 31, 1945), 1973.

A selective but very extensive and scholarly collection of biographies of prominent deceased Americans who lived from colonial times to the present.
The 23 volumes published so far contain 14,443 biographical articles. Articles
are relatively long and can include all of the kinds of information found in
full-length biographies. Bibliographies of sources used in preparing the biography are provided at the end of each article. Arrangement is alphabetical
by name of biographee. The Index for the original 20 vols. consists of 6 separate lists: (1) biographees, alphabetically by name, (2) contributors, alphabetically by name, (3) biographees, by state (or country) and city of birth,
(4) biographees, by schools and colleges attended, (5) biographees, by occupation or activity (e.g., *abolitionist, writer*), and (6) topics and subjects,
including titles of literary works. *Supplement Three* includes a name index to
the three supplement volumes. *The Concise Dictionary of American Biography* (N. Y., 1964) is an epitome of the *DAB* and its first two supplements;
it provides 14,870 biographical articles averaging about 1/14 the length of
the originals.

963 *The National Cyclopaedia of American Biography.* N. Y., 1892– .
Index. N. Y., 1971.

Published in two series whose total volumes now include over 55,000 entries.
The "Permanent" series vols. are numbered (54 was published in 1973); these
provide biographies of deceased Americans from colonial times to the present. Entries are arranged in rough chronological order, and each vol. includes
an alphabetical index of biographee's names. Articles are shorter and less
scholarly than those in the *DAB*, but greater inclusiveness makes it a useful
supplement to that work. The "Current" series vols. are lettered (*L* was
published in 1972); these provide biographies of living Americans much
fuller than those in *Who's Who in America* and, therefore, useful as a
supplement to it. The *Index* (1971) is a comprehensive name and subject index
to vols. 1–52 of the "Permanent" series and vols. A–K of the "Current"
series; the subject headings include such terms as "Poetry," "Drama," etc.
The "Current" series vols. are not arranged in any systematic way, but each
vol. includes an alphabetical index of biographees' names.

963a GARRATY, JOHN A. and JEROME L. STERNSTEIN, eds. *Encyclopedia of
American Biography.* N. Y., 1974.

A collection of biographies of more than 1000 living and dead Americans.
Each biography is divided into two parts: a brief factual narrative followed
by a signed interpretative essay. Each essay ends with a citation to one
source providing further biographical information. No index.

964 *Who's Who in America.* Chicago, 1899– .

A biennial biographical dictionary of Americans and some persons from other countries who are "of current reference inquiry because of meritorious achievement." Arranged alphabetically by name of biographee.

965 *Who Was Who in America.* Chicago, 1942– .

A continuing biographical dictionary of deceased notable Americans who have previously been included in *Who's Who in America.* Five vols. have been published to date, covering the years 1897–1973.

Many reference works – e.g., literary histories, general encyclopedias, and general histories – include biographical information; for some other sources which include biographies see entries **92, 151, 170–182, 205–210, 213, 214, 304, 311–315, 324–326, 390–392a, 437–442,** and **446–450.**

5. Identification of Anonymous and Pseudonymous Writings

966 HALKETT, SAMUEL and JOHN LAING. *Dictionary of Anonymous and Pseudonymous English Literature.* 9 vols. New ed. by JAMES KENNEDY *et al.* Edinburgh, 1926–62.

An extensive dictionary (some 72,000 entries) of anonymous and pseudonymous English literature. Vols. 1–6 provide an alphabetical list of titles with identifications of authorship. Entries give relatively full information: title, format, imprint, number of pages, editions, illustrations, etc. Sources for the authority of attributions are frequently given. Vol. 7 includes (1) an index of authors, (2) an index of initials and pseudonyms, and (3) a short alphabetical supplement to vols. 1–6. Vols. 8 and 9 provide additional alphabetical lists. A revision is in progress.

967 SHARP, HAROLD S. *Handbook of Pseudonyms and Personal Nicknames.* 2 vols. Metuchen, N. J., 1972.

A single-alphabet list of some 15,000 real names cross-referenced to about 25,000 pseudonyms and nicknames. The term "nickname" is interpreted very broadly and includes many variants of names of literary characters.

968 TAYLOR, ARCHER and FREDRICK J. MOSHER. *The Bibliographical History of Anonyma and Pseudonyma.* Chicago, 1951.

An extensively documented history of primary and secondary materials of anonyma and pseudonyma. Includes an annotated bibliography on pp. 207–279.

6. Portraits and Photographs

969 National Portrait Gallery. *Concise Catalogue 1856–1969.* Ed. MAU-
REEN HILL. London, 1970.

An alphabetical index arranged by name of sitter. There is an appendix:
Groups and Collections. Index of Artists. The NPG is publishing a series of
full catalogues (*catalogues raisonnés*), each dealing with a special period. The
existence of a full catalogue entry is indicated at the end of the *Concise
Catalogue* entry.
The Trustees of the British Museum, London, have published a *Catalogue
of the Engraved British Portraits Preserved in the Department of Prints
and Drawings*, 6 vols., London, 1908–25.

970 *A. L. A. Portrait Index: Index to Portraits Contained in Printed Books
and Periodicals.* Ed. WILLIAM C. LANE and NINA E. BROWNE. Washington, 1906. Rptd. 3 vols. N. Y., 1964.

Locates well over 120,000 portraits. Brief entries give name, dates, profession,
source, name of artist, engraver, etc. Photographic reproductions are asterisked.

971 SINGER, HANS W. *Allgemeiner Bildniskatalog.* 14 Bde. Leipzig, 1930–
36. Repr. Stuttgart, 1967. [and] *Neuer Bildniskatalog. 5 Bde. Leipzig*
1936–37. Rptd. Stuttgart, 1967.

The main work records more than 100,00 engraved portraits of all times
and countries in 20 German collections. The supplementary *Neuer Bildniskatalog* lists portrait paintings, sculpture and photographs.

Other sources for portraits and photographs are given in entries **172,
173, 174, 177, 214, 304, 325, 391, 446,** and **932**.

B. Biographies and Directories of Scholars

974 *The World of Learning 1974–5.* 2 vols. 25th ed. London, 1974.

Selective lists of officers and members of faculties of colleges and universites
throughout the world. Arranged alphabetically by name of country. Vol. 2
includes an index of institutional names.

975 *International Handbook of Universities and Other Institutions of
Higher Education.* Published triennially. Paris, 1959–   .

976 *The Academic Who's Who 1973–1974.* London, 1973.

A biographical dictionary of university teachers in the British Isles; attempts
to include "those, in all disciplines except the sciences, whose first university
appointment was more than five years ago." Arranged alphabetically by
name of biographee. No index.

977 *Directory of American Scholars: A Biographical Directory.* 4 vols. 6th ed. N. Y. and London, 1974. First published in 1942.

Provides brief biographies of more than 38,000 American scholars in the humanities and law. Vol. II covers scholars in English, speech, and drama; Vol. III includes scholars in foreign languages, linguistics, and philology.

978 *The National Faculty Directory.* Detroit, Mich., 1970– .

An annual index to about 400,000 American and Canadian faculty members of institutions of higher learning. Arranged as a single-alphabet list by faculty member's name; entries give academic address. No index.

979 "Directory." *PMLA,* 1– (1884–).

A directory of the officers and members of the Modern Language Association of America. Title and method of publication have varied; now issued separately as no. 4 of the current annual *PMLA.* Entries give member's name, rank, and current academic address. Additional separate lists are provided for chairmen of English and foreign language departments, whether members of the MLA or not.

XX. Sources of Information on Religion, Myth, Folklore and Popular Custom

A. General Mythology, Classical Mythology, and the Classics

985 GRAY, LOUIS H., ed. *The Mythology of All Races.* 13 vols. Boston, Mass., 1916–32. Rptd., 1964.

Individual volumes deal with the mythology of particular peoples--e.g., Greek and Roman, Celtic, Semitic, etc. Each volume includes an extensive bibliography. Vol. 13 is a very extensive index of subjects and persons treated in the first 12 vols.

986 *New Larousse Encyclopedia of Mythology.* Trans. by R. ALDINGTON and D. AMES. Illustrated. Rev. ed. London, 1968.

A one-volume encyclopedia of mythology of all countries. Arranged by cultures – e.g., Greek, Indian, Black African, etc. – with articles on various topics within these categories. Subject-name index.

987 *The Oxford Classical Dictionary.* Ed. N. G. L. HAMMOND and H. H. SCULLARD. 2nd ed. Oxford, 1970.

A scholarly dictionary of relatively brief articles on Greek and Roman life and thought, including mythology and literature. The articles are initialed and include brief bibliographies. General bibliography and index of names.

988 ROSCHER, WILHELM HEINRICH. *Ausführliches Lexikon der griechischen und römischen Mythologie.* 6 Bde. u. 4 Suppl.bde. Leipzig, 1884–1937. Rptd. Hildesheim, 1965.

The most comprehensive scholarly work of its kind. Signed articles with bibliographies (sources, secondary material) and many illustrations.

989 *Paulys Realencyclopädie der Classischen Altertumswissenschaft.* Neue Bearb. v. GEORG WISSOWA. Hrsg. v. Konrat Ziegler *et al.* Reihe 1: 24 Bde., Reihe 2: 10 Bde. (= 68 Teile); 15 Supplbde. Stuttgart, 1894–1976.

A comprehensive classical encyclopedia providing signed articles on all aspects of classical literature, history, geography, archaeology, and civilization, with extensive bibliographies of sources and secondary material. Columns are numbered in tens for easy cross-referencing. There is a thoroughly revised concise edition: *Der kleine Pauly. Lexikon der Antike.* Auf der Grundlage von Pauly's Realencyclopädie ... bearb. u. hrsg. v. K. Ziegler *et al.*, 5 Bde. Stuttgart, 1964–75.

Another scholarly encyclopedia is the one-vol. *Lexikon der Alten Welt*, hrsg. Carl Andresen *et al.*, Zürich, 1965.

990 GRIMAL, PIERRE. *Dictionnaire de la mythologie grecque et romaine.* 4. éd. corr. Paris, 1969.

A dictionary of widely known myths and legends. Greek and Latin names are entered in their French forms, with the original forms given after each French entry word. References to sources are provided in footnotes. Includes genealogical tables, an index of mythological, historical, and geographical proper names, and a subject index.

991 HUNGER, HERBERT. *Lexikon der Griechischen und Römischen Mythologie mit Hinweisen auf das Fortwirken antiker Stoffe und Motive in der bildenden Kunst. Literatur und Musik des Abendlandes bis zur Gegenwart.* 6. Aufl. Wien, 1969.

A dictionary of Greek and Roman mythology. Entries are arranged to follow three main divisions indicated in the margin by *M, R,* and *N*. The *M* section provides information on the myth itself; the *R* section deals with the religious origins of the myth, and the *N* section provides a detailed account of the uses of the myth as subject or motif in literature, opera, music, mosaic, sculpture, painting, etc. Entries are documented and primary sources cited. Bibliographies.

992 HIGHET, GILBERT. *The Classical Tradition: Greek and Roman Influences on Western Literature.* London, 1949. Rptd. with corrections, 1953.

A comprehensive survey of the "ways in which Greek and Latin influence has moulded the literatures of western Europe and America." Annotated bibliography, extensive bibliographic notes, and a very full author-title-subject index.

993 LAW, HELEN H. *Bibliography of Greek Myth in English Poetry.* Oxford, Ohio, 1955; rptd. Folcroft, Pa., 1969.

A bibliography arranged as an alphabetical list of topics in Greek mythology – e.g., Achilles, Endymion, Muses, Zeus, etc. – and underneath each topic arranged chronologically. Entries give poet, title of poetic work, and date.

994 BUSH, DOUGLAS. *Pagan Myth and Christian Tradition in English Poetry.* Philadelphia, Pa., 1968.

A survey of pagan and Christian elements in English literature from the Renaissance to 1967, with some attention to American writing. Extensively documented and includes a bibliography. Index to authors, subjects, and bibliographical references.

995 BUSH, DOUGLAS. *Mythology and the Renaissance Tradition in English Poetry.* Minneapolis, 1932. Rev. ed. N. Y., 1963.

An extensive and fully documented study of mythology in English poetry from the middle ages to 1680. An appendix supplies an annotated chronological conspectus of mythological poems. Includes a bibliography arranged according to the chapters in the book, and a subject-author index.

996 BUSH, DOUGLAS. *Mythology and the Romantic Tradition in English Poetry.* Cambridge, Mass., 1937. Rptd. (with new preface), 1969.

A sequel to Bush's *Mythology and the Renaissance Tradition,* providing a fully documented study of mythology in English poetry from 1680 to 1935. Includes a chapter on American poetry. An appendix supplies an annotated chronological register of mythological poems. Includes a bibliography arranged according to the chapters in the book, and a subject-author index.

For other sources of information on mythology see entries **544** and **1007**.

B. Religion

997 BARROW, JOHN G. *A Bibliography of Bibliographies in Religion.* Ann Arbor, Mich., 1955.

A comprehensive annotated bibliography of bibliographies on all aspects of religion. Includes an author-title-subject index.

998 ADAMS, CHARLES J. *A Reader's Guide to the Great Religions.* N.Y., 1965.

A critically annotated bibliography of writings on all aspects of world religion. Arranged as a series of bibliographic essays on topics such as "Hinduism," "Christianity," etc. Separate author and subject indexes.

999 FRAZER, Sir JAMES G. *The Golden Bough: A Study in Magic and Religion.* 3rd. ed. rev. and enl. 12 vols. London, 1911–15. Supplement titled *Aftermath,* 1936.

A very broad study of primitive religious beliefs. Arranged under topics such as "The Dying God," "Adonis, Attis, Osiris," "The Scapegoat," etc. Vol. 12 contains an extensive bibliography and a general index.

1000 ROBBINS, ROSSELL HOPE. *The Encyclopedia of Witchcraft and Demonology.* N.Y., 1959.

Compendium of fact, history and legend about witchcraft and demonology from its origins in the Middle Ages to modern times. Illustrated from rare books, contemporary prints and old manuscripts. There is a bibliographical, appendix: "Classified Subject Bibliographies" and "Select Bibliography" comprising 1140 titles.

1001 *Oxford Dictionary of the Christian Church.* Ed. F. L. CROSS. 2nd ed. ed. by F. L. Cross and E. A. Livingstone. London, 1974.

Aims to provide factual information on every aspect of Christianity, esp. in its historical development and to be of interest to the educated public as a whole. It contains well over 6000 entries, more than two thirds of which have bibliographies.

1002 HERBERT, A. S. *Historical Catalogue of Printed Editions of the English Bible 1525–1961.* London, 1968.

A descriptive bibliography with extensive annotation. Locates copies in 6 libraries in the United Kingdom and 5 in the United States. Includes 4 indexes: (1) translators, revisors, and editors, (2) printers and publishers, (3) places of printing and publishing, and (4) general index.

1003 STRONG, JAMES. *Exhaustive Concordance of the Bible.* London, 1894. Often rptd.

An exceptionally full concordance of about 400,000 entries for the King James version of the Bible. Appendixes include references to 47 common words not included in the main concordance, a comparative concordance of the Authorized and Revised versions, and Hebrew and Greek glossaries.

1004 YOUNG, ROBERT. *Analytical Concordance to the Bible on an Entirely New Plan* ... Rev. ed. by W. B. Stevenson. London, 1902. Frequently rptd. in England and America.

A very full alphabetical index to words in the Bible; provides about 311,000 entries "subdivided under the Hebrew and Greek originals, with the literal meaning and pronunciation of each." Includes supplementary indexes and a list of biblical names.

1005 CRUDEN, ALEXANDER. *Cruden's Complete Concordance to the Old and New Testaments.* London, 1737. Frequently rev. and rptd. in England and America.

An extensive alphabetical index to words in the "Authorized Version" of the Bible (i. e., the "King James's Version" of 1611). The more than 220,000 entries are supplemented by an appendix of proper names seldom mentioned in the Bible and not included in the body of the concordance.

1006 MIGNE, JACQUES P. *Patrologiae Cursus Completus ... Series Latina ... a Tertulliano ad Innocentium III.* 221 vols. Paris, 1844–80. *Supplementum,* 3 vols., 1958–63. *Series Graeca,* 166 vols., 1857–66. *Indices Digessit Ferdinandus Cavallera,* 1912. *Index Locupletissimus,* 1928–1945.

The most extensive compilation of the writings of the Fathers of the Christian Church. Vols. 218–221 of the *Series Latina* provide an exceptionally full alphabetical index which analyzes the contents of the *Series* writings and includes key topics and words. Less complete to date, but providing much better critical texts: *Corpus Christianorum,* 1954– .

For other sources of information on religion see **1007, 1150** and **1151.**

C. Folklore, Popular Custom, and Ballad

1007 DIEHL, KATHERINE S. *Religion, Mythologies, Folklore: An Annotated Bibliography.* 2nd ed. N. Y., 1962.

An extensively annotated bibliography of 2,388 books and periodicals dealing with religion, mythology, and/or folklore. Classified arrangement with broad subject headings such as "Fine Arts," "Folklore," etc. Includes an author-title index.

1007a ZIEGLER, ELSIE B. *Folklore: An Annotated Bibliography and Index to Single Editions.* Westwood, Mass., 1973.

An annotated title bibliography followed by a subject index, a motif index, a country index, a type of folklore index and and an illustrator index.

1008 BONSER, WILFRED. *A Bibliography of Folklore: As Contained in the First Eighty Years of the Publications of the Folklore Society.* London, 1961.

An annotated bibliography which serves as an index to the publications of the Folklore Society. Arrangement is classified, with categories such as "Folklore of the British Isles," "Folklore in Literature and Art," etc. Separate indexes of authors, topography of the British Isles, foreign cultures, and subjects.

1009 HAYWOOD, CHARLES. *A Bibliography of North American Folklore and Folksong.* 2nd ed., rev. and enl. 2 vols. N. Y., 1961.

An extensive annotated bibliography of primary and secondary materials on the folklore of Americans, and American Indians, north of Mexico and including Canada. Arrangement is elaborately classified by types, areas, etc. Vol. 2 includes a comprehensive author-title-subject index for both vols.

1010 Cleveland Public Library. *Catalog of Folklore and Folk Songs.* 2 vols. Boston, 1964.

A reproduction by photo-lithography of the more than 24,000 catalogue entries of the John G. White folklore collection in the Cleveland Public Library. This extensive collection includes material on the folk lore, folk tales, folk sayings, and folk songs of all countries.

1011 *Internationale Volkskundliche Bibliographie. International Folklore and Folklife Bibliography. Bibliographie Internationale des Arts et Traditions Populaires 1939/41–* . Basel [later Bonn], 1949– . [Title has varied.]

Continuation of *Volkskundliche Bibliographie,* 1–13 (1917-36), Berlin, 1919–41. Universal coverage. Systematically arranged under such headings as ... folk-literature in general, popular poetry, music and dance, folk-tales, myths, legends, folk drama, other literature, popular speech, names. Contains list of periodicals, index of authors' names, subject index.

1012 "Folklore Bibliography [year]." *Southern Folklore Quarterly.* 1–
(1938–).

An annual international bibliography of folklore studies. Arrangement is classified, with headings such as "Drama," "Ritual," etc.

1013 *Abstracts of Folklore Studies.* 1– (1963–).

Published quarterly. Abstracts in each issue are arranged under the titles of the periodicals abstracted. Annual volumes include a name-subject-title index. A list of journals abstracted was published in vol. 4 (1968), no. 4, pp. 71–85. Vols. 2 and 3 each include an annual bibliography thereafter discontinued. An "Annual Bibliography of Folklore [1887–1963]" was published in *Journal of American Folklore,* 1888–1964.

1014 *Funk and Wagnalls' Standard Dictionary of Folklore, Mythology, and Legend.* Ed. by Maria Leach. 2 vols. N. Y., 1949–50. Rptd. 1 vol., 1972.

A comprehensive encyclopedic dictionary covering all aspects of folklore, mythology, and legend of all countries and times. The initialled articles are usually short and include summaries of folk tales and ballads, descriptions of beliefs, definitions, etc. There are, however, some much more extensive articles on different national mythologies and on broad topics such as the fairy tale, the ballad, phallism, ritual drama, etc; some of these include bibliographies. The 1972 one-volume ed. includes a place and culture index.

1015 Jobes, Gertrude. *Dictionary of Mythology Folklore and Symbols.* 3 vols. N. Y., 1961.

A very full dictionary of terms relating to myth, folklore, folk-sayings, and symbols of all countries and times. Includes a bibliography. No index, but extensive cross-referencing. No illustrations.

1016 Briggs, Katherine M., ed. *A Dictionary of British Folk-Tales in the English Language Incorporating the F. J. Norton Collection.* 4 vols. Bloomington, Ind., 1970–71.

A collection of folk tales and legends, some reproduced full-length, some summarized, with citations to the sources given for each. Arranged in two parts. *Part A* (vols. 1–2) provides about 850 folk tales arranged in broad classes; the front matter of vol. 1 includes a bibliography, an index by tale types, and an index of story titles. *Part B* (vols. 3–4) has a similar arrangement and covers some 1,200 folk legends.

1017 Brand, John. *The Popular Antiquities of Great Britain.* Rev. by W. Carew Hazlitt. 2 vols. London, 1905. Rptd., 1967. Rptd. as *Faiths and Folklore of the British Isles,* N. Y., 1965.

A dictionary of English popular customs and lore. Entries provide descriptions, cite examples, and give sources and locales. Covers such subjects as "James's Day," "Mab, Queen," "Skimmington," etc.

1018 THOMPSON, STITH. *Motif-Index of Folk-Literature: A Classification of Narrative Elements in Folktales, Ballads, Myths, Fables, Medieval Romances, Exempla, Fabliaux, Jest-Books and Local Legends.* Rev. and enl. ed. 6 vols. Bloomington, Ind., 1955–58.

A comprehensive index to themes and motifs in folk literature. Vols. 1–5 provide a classified list of citations to folk literature of all times and places; arrangement is by broad categories such as "Animals," "Tests," "Reversal of Fortune," etc., each main category being elaborately sub-divided. Entries give a brief summary statement of the motif (e.g., "Bird rescues man from sea," "Origin of clouds," etc.), citations to relevant sources of folk literature, and cross-references. Vol. 6 is a very full subject index.

1019 AARNE, ANTTI. *The Types of Folk-Tale: A Classification and Bibliography.* Rev. and trans. by STITH THOMPSON. Helsinki, 1961; rptd. N.Y., 1971.

A classified bibliography of thousands of oral folktales of Europe, Asia, and India, exclusive of local legends and tales not oral in origin. Arranged in categories such as "Animal Tales," with sub-classes. Each tale entry is numbered and identified by a descriptive phrase such as "Supposed Chest of Gold Induces Children to Care for Aged Father." Entries provide bibliographic source references, geographical locations, and sometimes include references to constituent motifs and cross-referencing to Thompson's *Motif-Index.* There is an alphabetical index to tale types.

1020 BAUGHMAN, ERNEST W. *Type and Motif Index of the Folklore of England and North America.* The Hague, 1966.

1021 BREWER, J. MASON. *American Negro Folklore.* N.Y., 1974.

1022 CHILD, FRANCIS JAMES, ed. *The English and Scottish Popular Ballads.* 5 vols. Boston, Mass., 1882–1898. Rptd., 3 vols., 1956.

An anthology containing the texts of 305 ballads in all their extant versions, with historical and bibliographical introductions to each ballad. Volume 5 contains a glossary, sources of the texts, an index of published airs, an index of titles (including titles of collections), an index of matter, and an extensive bibliography. Supplemented by Bertrand Harris Bronson's *The Traditional Tunes of the Child Ballads, with Their Texts According to the Extant Records of Great Britain and America,* 4 vols., Princeton, N.J., 1959–72, which deals extensively with the musical tradition of the ballads, publishes the scores of all known tunes associated with the Child ballads, and includes every known variation of the Child texts.

For other sources of information on folklore see entries **38, 257,** and **542.**

XXI. History

A. World History

1030 HEPWORTH, PHILIP. *How to Find Out in History: A Guide to Sources of Information for All.* Oxford, N. Y., Braunschweig, 1966.

A survey of select sources of information on history and biography. Arranged in chapters covering general works; general history; Europe, including Britain and the Commonwealth; individual countries arranged by continent; etc. Index.

1030a HOWE, GEORGE FREDERICK *et al.*, eds. *The American Historical Association's Guide to Historical Literature.* N. Y., 1961.

An annotated guide to selected materials for the study of world history. Arranged by geographical areas and by some topical divisions such as "General Reference Resources," "History of Religion," etc. Author-subject index.

1031 *The Cambridge Ancient History.* 12 vols. and 5 vols. of plates. Cambridge, 1924–39. Rev. ed. 1961– . *The Cambridge Medieval History.* Ed. H. M. GWATKIN *et al.* 8 vols. and portfolios of maps. Cambridge, 1911–36. 2nd ed., ed. JOSEPH ROBSON TANNER *et al.* Cambridge, 1966– . *The New Cambridge Modern History.* 13 out of 14 vols. publ. Cambridge, 1957–1970. [vol. 13, period after 1945, not yet published; vol. 14 *Atlas*] See also J. ROACH, ed., *A Bibliography of Modern History*, Cambridge, 1968, closely related to the NCMH and largely the work of its contributors.

Taken together, the 39 published volumes of the Cambridge ancient, medieval, and modern histories comprise an exceptionally full account of world history. All include notes and analytical indexes; bibliographies are included in the *Ancient History* and *Medieval History* volumes.

1032 STOREY, R. L. *Chronology of the Medieval World, 800 to 1491.* London, 1973.
WILLIAMS, NEVILLE. *Chronology of the Expanding World, 1492 to 1762.* London, 1969.
WILLIAMS, NEVILLE. *Chronology of the Modern World, 1763 to the Present Time.* London, 1968.

Extensive chronologies of world history arranged as a series of parallel columns taking up both the recto and verso of each opening. On the left dates are given by year, month, and, sometimes, day; historical events in different areas – e.g., economics, politics, science, the arts, etc. – are arrayed on the right. Each volume provides an analytical index to persons, places, subjects, titles, and works of art.

1033 PLÖTZ, KARL. *Auszug aus der Geschichte.* 27. Aufl. Würzburg, 1967. A new English version of Plötz's work is W. L. LANGER'S *An Encyclopaedia of World History, Ancient, Medieval and Modern, Chronologically Arranged.* 5th ed., rev. and enl. Boston, 1972. A summary of world history arranged chronologically by major periods, and within each period by country or area. Both Plötz and Langer treat social, economic and cultural as well as political history, and both provide very full indexes.

B. British History

A series of bibliographies for the study of different periods of English history has been published by Cambridge University Press. These are highly selective (limited to about 2000 items) and contain some annotation. They are arranged as classified lists under headings such as "General Surveys," "Political History," "Social History," "Economic History." "Science and Technology," "Intellectual History," etc., and include indexes of authors, editors, and translators. They include the following:

1034 ALTSCHUL, MICHAEL. *Anglo-Norman England, 1066–1154.* Cambridge, 1969.

1035 LEVINE, MORTIMER. *Tudor England, 1485–1603.* Cambridge, 1968.

1036 SACHSE, WILLIAM L. *Restoration England, 1660–1689.* Cambridge, 1971.

1037 ALTHOLZ, JOSEF L. *Victorian England, 1837–1901.* Cambridge, 1970.

These selective bibliographical handbooks may be supplemented by another series of period bibliographies published by Oxford University Press:

1037a GRAVES, EDGAR B. *A Bibliography of British History to 1485.* Oxford, 1975.

1038 READ, CONYERS. *Bibliography of British History: Tudor Period, 1485–1603.* 2nd ed. Oxford, 1959.

1039 DAVIES, GODFREY. *Bibliography of British History: Stuart Period, 1603–1714.* 2nd ed. rev. by MARY FREER KELLER. Oxford, 1970.

1040 PARGELLIS, STANLEY and D. J. MEDLEY. *Bibliography of British History: The Eighteenth Century, 1714–1789.* Oxford, 1951.

1041 BONSER, WILFRID. *An Anglo-Saxon and Celtic Bibliography, 450–1087.* 2 vols. Berkeley, 1957.

1042 STEINBERG, S. H. and I. H. EVANS, eds. *Steinberg's Dictionary of British History.* 2nd ed. London, 1970.

A dictionary handbook of British history, providing brief signed articles by a dozen contributors. Covers all aspects of British and British colonial history, but generally excludes biographies of individuals.

1043 *The Oxford History of England.* Gen. ed. G. N. CLARK. 15 vols. Oxford, 1934–65. [Some of the vols. in 2nd or 3rd edition].

The most comprehensive history of England. Individual volumes provide historical surveys for particular periods from the Roman invasions (vol. 1) to the period 1914–1945 (vol. 15). The volumes include valuable annotated bibliographies and are fully indexed.

1044 TREVELYAN, GEORGE MACAULAY. *[Illustrated] English Social History.* 4 vols. London, 1949–52. Rptd.

Provides a detailed account of the daily life of English people from the Middle Ages through the Victorian Period, with descriptions of their work, food, homes, clothes, customs, beliefs, and pastimes. Includes some 600 illustrations derived, so far as possible, from contemporary sources.

1045 TRAILL, H. DUFF, ed. *Social England: A Record of the Progress of the People in Religion, Laws, Learning, Arts, Industry, Commerce, Science, Literature, and Manners, from the Earliest Times to the Present Day.* Illustrated ed. 6 vols. London, 1901–4. Rptd., 1909.

An older social history of England but still useful as a supplement to Trevelyan's *Illustrated English Social History.* Each volume includes a list of authorities consulted and a general index.

1045a BLAIR, PETER HUNTER. *An Introduction to Anglo-Saxon England.* Cambridge, 1956.

A 2nd ed. is in preparation.

1046 POOLE, AUSTIN LANE, ed. *Medieval England.* 2nd ed. 2 vols. Oxford, 1958.

A series of essays on all aspects of the social history of medieval England, including such topics as architecture, shipping, communications, trade, costume, coinage, religious life, art, education, handwriting, the book trade, libraries, science, and recreation. Essays are written by specialists and include lists of reference works. Indexed. May be supplemented by G. G. Coulton's *Medieval Panorama*, Cambridge, 1938.

1047 [ONIONS, C. T., *et al.*, eds.] *Shakespeare's England: An Account of the Life and Manners of His Age.* 2 vols. Oxford, 1916. Rptd.

A series of essays on all aspects of the social history of Shakespeare's England, including such topics as religion, the court, scholarship, law, handwriting, gardening, the sciences, the fine arts, heraldry, costume, town life, the book trade, theatre, sports and pastimes, language, etc. Bibliographies are appended to each chapter. Includes indexes to passages cited from Shakespeare's works, proper names, and subjects and technical terms.

1048 LOVEJOY, ARTUHR O. *The Great Chain of Being.* Cambridge, Mass., 1936. Rptd.

A study of the history of a complex of ideas which Lovejoy calls "the great chain of being" – ideas about god, ultimate value, and the order of the universe – from their beginnings in Greek philosophy to the Romantic Movement. Includes bibliographic notes and a name-subject index.

1049 TURBERVILLE, A. S., ed. *Johnson's England: An Account of the Life and Manners of his Age.* 2 vols. Oxford, 1933.

A series of 27 essays on all aspects of the age of Johnson, including such topics as the church, the army, town-life, sports and games, costume, painting and engraving, music, drama, authors and booksellers, the press, etc. Indexed. Each chapter includes bibliographic notes.

1050 BECKER CARL. *The Heavenly City of the Eighteenth Century Philosophers.* New Haven, Conn., 1932. Rptd.

Four lectures on the characteristic intellectual point of view of 18th century thinkers. No index.

1051 GAY, PETER. *The Enlightenment: An Interpretation.* 2 vols. N. Y., 1966–69.

A comprehensive interpretation of the intellectual life of the enlightenment, with special emphasis on the struggle between pagan and Christian thought. Each volume includes extensive bibliographic notes and a subject index.

1052 HALÉVIE, ÉLIE. *History of the English People in the Nineteenth Century.* Trans. from the French *Histoire du peuple anglais au XIXᵉ siècle* (1913–46) by E. I. WATKIN and D. A. BARKER. 6 vols. London, 1949–52. Rptd.

A comprehensive treatment of all aspects of British history in the nineteenth century, starting with *England in 1815*, a survey of English society at the beginning of the Victorian period, and concluding with *The Rule of Democracy (1905–1914)*. Particularly full treatment of the years up to 1852; includes political, social, and cultural history. Individual volumes provide extensive bibliographic notes and subject indexes.

1053 HOUGHTON, WALTER E. *The Victorian Frame of Mind.* New Haven, Conn., 1957. Rptd.

A survey of English thought in the 19th century, with extensive illustrative quotation, most often from literary sources. Arranged in chapters covering such topics as "Optimism," "Anxiety," "The Commercial Spirit," "Love," etc., all fully documented. Includes a bibliography and a name-subject index. A parallel work is John R. Reed's *Victorian Conventions*, Athens, Ohio, 1975, which has chapters on such topics as "Women," "Coincidence," "Deathbeds," "Inheritance," etc., and includes extensive notes, a "Bibliographical Essay," and a name-title-subject index.

1054 [YOUNG, G. M., ed.] *Early Victorian England, 1830–65.* 2 vols. Oxford, 1934.

A series of essays on all aspects of the social history of the Victorian period – working conditions, home life, life in London, the army and navy, the merchant marine, music and drama, architecture, emigration, etc. See also Young's *Victorian England: Portrait of an Age*, which is an expansion of his final chapter in *Early Victorian England*. Both may be supplemented, particularly for the period after 1865, by Richard D. Altick's *Victorian People and Ideas: A Companion for the Modern Reader of Victorian Literature.* N. Y., 1973.

1055 NOWELL-SMITH, SIMON. *Edwardian England 1901–1914.* London, 1964.

A series of 15 essays on aspects of Edwardian England, including such topics as politics, domestic life, science, theatre, music, sport, popular reading, etc. No bibliographies. Indexed.

1056 WILLIAMS, RAYMOND. *Culture and Society 1780–1950.* London, 1958.

A study emphasizing social and cultural criticism in England from Burke and Coleridge onwards. Includes particularly valuable analyses of nineteenth-century prose fiction and non-fiction.

C. American History

1057 FREIDEL, FRANK and RICHARD K. SHOWMAN, eds. *Harvard Guide to American History.* Rev. ed. 2 vols. Cambridge, Mass., 1974.

A classified, selective bibliography of research materials in American history. Entries in volume 1 are arranged under topics such as "Care and Editing of Manuscripts," "Materials of History," "Literature," "The Arts," etc. Entries in volume 2 are arranged by chronological periods in American history, each period elaborately sub-classified. Includes separate name and subject indexes.

1058 ADAMS, JAMES TRUSLOW and R. V. COLEMAN. *Dictionary of American History.* 2nd ed. rev. 5 vols. and *Index.* N. Y., 1942–63. *Supplement 1, 1940–1960.* 1961. *Index* [for orig. vols. and supp.] 1963.

An encyclopedic dictionary of American history, including some 7000 entries, mostly with bibliographies. Conceived as a companion work to the *DAB*, 962, and does not, therefore, include biographical articles. For illustrations, may be supplemented by Adams' *Album of American History*, 5 vols. and *Index*, 1944–61.

1059 *Concise Dictionary of American History.* Ed. WAYNE ANDREWS. N. Y., 1962. Rptd.

Despite its title, a relatively large (1156 pp.) dictionary of American history. Provides some 7000 entries, including lengthy articles on broad topics such as "Labor," "Negro in America," etc. and short articles. A one volume epitome of Adams, **1058**.

1060 *The Oxford Companion to American History.* Ed. THOMAS H. JOHNSON and H. WISH. N. Y., 1966.

A handbook providing more than 4,500 entries, Arranged alphabetically with extensive cross-referencing. Entries include many biographies and also articles covering topics in literature and the arts, business, education, law, entertainment, etc.

1061 SCHLESINGER, ARTHUR M. and DIXON R. FOX, eds. *A History of American Life.* 13 vols. N. Y., 1927–48.

A comprehensive multi-volume history of America from the beginnings to 1941. Each volume is written by a specialist and includes an annotated bibliography (titled "Critical Essay on Authorities") and a subject index.

1062 LERNER, MAX. *America as a Civilization.* 2 vols. N. Y., 1957. Rptd.

An interpretation of contemporary American civilization. Divided into 12 chapters devoted to such topics as "The Culture of Science and the Machine," "Class and Status," "The Arts and Popular Culture," etc. Selected "Notes for Further Reading" (pp. 955–98) and author-title-subject index.

1063 FURNAS, J. C. *The Americans: A Social History of the United States 1587–1914.* N. Y., 1969.

A history of the United States which focuses on cultural and social matters rather than political events. Arranged in 8 chapters, each dealing with one epoch in American cultural history. Includes notes, a list of references, and a name-title-subject index.

1064 PARRINGTON, VERNON LOUIS. *Main Currents in American Thought: An Interpretation of American Literature from the Beginnings to 1920.* Vol. I, *1620–1800: The Colonial Mind;* Vol. II, *1800–1860: The Romantic Revolution in America;* Vol. III, *1860–1920: The Beginning of Critical Realism in America.* 3 vols. N. Y., 1927. Often rptd. in 1 and 3 vol. formats.

An account of the genesis and development of certain key ideas in American literature. Arranged as a narrative history, with chapters on topics such as "The Rise of Liberalism," "New England in Decay," "Sinclair Lewis," etc. Each volume includes a selective bibliography and an author-title index.

1065 CURTI, MERLE E. *The Growth of American Thought.* 3rd ed. N. Y., 1964.

A study of the intellectual history of America, with particular emphasis on the cultural context of American thought. Selective bibliography on pp. 797–900, and subject index.

1066 CARGILL, OSCAR. *Intellectual America: Ideas on the March.* N. Y., 1941. Rptd., 1968.

A study of the impact of various ideologies in American life from 1890 to 1940. Treats such topics as "The Naturalists," "The Decadents," "The Primitivists," etc., with frequent reference to American literary works. Index to fundamental definitions and important persons.

1067 MILLER, PERRY. *The New England Mind: The Seventeenth Century.* Cambridge, Mass., 1939. Rptd., 1954.

An extensive study of the intellectual history of 17th century New England, with particular emphasis on religious and philosophical thought. Subject-name index. See also Miller's *Orthodoxy in Massachusetts*, Cambridge, Mass., 1933.

1068 MILLER, PERRY. *The New England Mind: From Colony to Province.* Cambridge, Mass., 1953.

A continuation of Miller's *The New England Mind: The Seventeenth Century* and *Orthodoxy in Massachusetts..* Arranged under chapter headings such as "The Protestant Ethic," "Propaganda," "The Failure of Centralization," etc. Appendix of bibliographical notes and author-subject index.

1069 COMMAGER, HENRY STEELE. *The American Mind: An Interpretation of American Thought and Character Since the 1880's.* New Haven, Conn., 1950.

A commentary on American thought from 1880 to 1940. Arranged as a series of chapters on topics such as "Transition Years in Literature and Journalism," "Determinism in Literature," "The Literature of Revolt," etc. Selective annotated bibliography on pp. 445–467 and author-title-subject index.

XXII. Dictionaries

A. Guides to Dictionaries

1075 COLLISON, ROBERT L. *Dictionaries of English and Foreign Languages.* 2nd ed. N. Y., 1971.

A bibliographic guide to both general and technical dictionaries for all languages. Classified arrangement employs some geographical (e.g., "Scandinavian," "African") and some linguistic (e.g., "German, Dutch, and Afrikaans") categories. Entries give full bibliographic citations and often include comment on the history, contents, and uses of particular dictionaries. There are two chapters on English dictionaries, one covering dictionaries published in the period up to 1753, the other dictionaries published after that date. Three appendices: (1) a list of technical dictionaries, (2) a list of specialized dictionaries, and (3) a general bibliography of books on dictionaries. Single-alphabet index of compilers, editors, principal contributors, titles, languages, areas and regions, etc.

1076 MATHEWS, M. M. *A Survey of English Dictionaries.* London, 1933.

A history of English dictionaries from the beginnings of English dictionary making to the 19th century. Includes discussions of methodology in lexicography and a study of the characteristics of modern dictionaries.

B. Historical Dictionaries and Supplementary Works

1077 *The Oxford English Dictionary: Being a Corrected Re-Issue With an Introduction, Supplement, and Bibliography of A New English Dictionary on Historical Principles.* Ed. JAMES A. H. MURRAY, et al. 13 vols. Oxford, 1933. Rptd., London, 1961. Reissued as the 'Compact Edition,' 2 vols. and magnifying glass, 1971. In progress is *A Supplement to the Oxford English Dictionary,* 4 vols., 1972–   .

The most comprehensive dictionary of British English. Intended to "furnish an adequate account of the meaning, origin, and history of English words now in general use or known to be in use at any time during the last seven hundred years." The original work (published 1884–1928) and the 1933 supplement contain together some 450,000 entries arranged alphabetically under the "modern" or "most usual" British spelling; other British spellings are listed alphabetically and cross-referenced to the main entry. Main entries give the modern British spelling; the standard pronunciation; the part of speech; the status of the word (e.g., *obsolete, Americanism*); variant spelling forms; inflected forms; the etymology and subsequent form-history of the word, including phonetic changes, contractions, etc.; the various meanings of the word arranged in historical order, with obsolete senses identified; and dated, identified quotations, arranged chronologically, to illustrate the history of changing meanings of the word. The 1933 supplement contains some 26,000 entries. The new 4 vol. *Supplement* now in progress will incorporate and supersede the original 1933 supplement and will provide information on changes in vocabulary which took place between 1884, when the first fascicle of the original dictionary was published, to about 1970.

1078 *The Shorter Oxford English Dictionary on Historical Principles.* 3rd ed., rev. by C. T. ONIONS. Oxford, 1944. [Later reprints have revised *addenda*].

An abridged single volume version of the *OED*, about 1/6th the length of the original and containing about 65 % of its vocabulary. Entries are highly abbreviated but retain many of the dated illustrative quotations of the original. Includes new words not recorded in the *OED*.

1078a BARNHART, CLARENCE *et al. Dictionary of New English.* Bronxville, N. Y., and Berlin, 1973.

Lists 6,000 new words first recorded in 1963–72.

1078b CRAIGIE, SIR WILLIAM A. *A Dictionary of the Older Scottish Tongue From the Twelfth Century to the End of the Seventeenth.* Part 1– . Chicago, 1931– . In progress; volume IV (*M-N*) was published in 1971, and additional fascicles of volume V have appeared.

A comprehensive historical dictionary of Scottish from the 12th century through the 16th, and for 17th century Scottish "so far as it does not coincide with the ordinary English usage." Entries give variant spellings, part of speech, etymology, definition(s), and dated quotations illustrating meaning(s).

1078c *The Scottish National Dictionary Designed Partly on Regional Lines and Partly on Historical Principles, and Containing All the Scottish Words Known to Be in Use or to Have Been in Use Since c. 1700.* Ed. WILLIAM GRANT. Vol. 1– . Edinburgh, 1931– . In progress; vol. 7 (*pace-ryve*) was published in 1966.

A comprehensive regional and historical dictionary of Scottish from 1700 onwards. Entries give variant spellings, part of speech, pronunciation (an adaptation of the IPA is used), status, inflections, origin, definition(s), and dated identified quotations illustrating the use of the word. The front matter of volume I includes an extensive analysis of Scottish phonetics and Scottish dialects.

1079 SHIPLEY, JOSEPH T. *Dictionary of Early English Words.* N. Y., 1955.

Entries include words from 700 to 1800 drawn from English authors; useful for students of literature and general readers for the lively and informative discussions Shipley provides.

1080 DOBSON, E. *English Pronunciation 1500–1700.* 2nd ed. Cambridge, 1968.

1081 *A Dictionary of American English on Historical Principles.* Ed. SIR WILLIAM CRAIGIE, *et al.* 4 vols. Chicago, 1936–44. Rptd.

A dictionary which attempts to list all words which either have originated in America, have an American meaning different from British English, or have some special significance in the cultural life of America. Entries include words from the colonial period to 1900; dated, identified quotations are used to illustrate changes in meaning. Entries also give variant spellings but not pronunciation, and only rarely etymologies (e.g., if the word is of American origin). No slang words are included which appeared in the language after 1875. Vol. 4 includes a bibliography of sources from which illustrative quotations are taken.

1082 MATHEWS, MITFORD M. *A Dictionary of Americanisms on Historical Principles.* Chicago, 1951.

A dictionary of terms either originating in the United States or having senses first given them in American usage. Rejects many words recorded in the *DAE* and adds others not recorded there; includes 20th century American words. The main entries give definitions followed by dated, identified illustrative quotations; etymologies and pronunciations are provided only for words which originated in the United States.

1083 WALL, EDWARD C. and EDWARD PRZEBIENDA. *Words and Phrases Index.* 4 vols. Ann Arbor, Mich., 1969–70.

An index of about 176,000 entries to published information on antedatings, new words, new compounds, and new meanings supplementary to the *OED*, the *DAE*, the *Dictionary of Americanisms*, and other major dictionaries of the English language. Indexes such information published in *American Notes and Queries*, *American Speech*, *Publication of the American Dialect Society*, *Notes and Queries*, and similar journals. Each volume provides an A–Z list of key words followed by bibliographic citations to articles dealing with each word; information on the journals indexed in each volume is provided in the front matter.

C. Dictionaries of Modern English

1084 *Chambers Twentieth Century Dictionary.* Ed. A. M. MACDONALD. "New Edition." Edinburgh, 1972; rev. and rptd. 1973; N. Y., 1974.

A relatively full single-volume dictionary of modern British English, with some attention to American spellings and pronunciations. Includes more than

150,000 definitions. Entries provide the British spelling, pronunciation, and syllabification; part of speech; status label; definition; and etymology. A special feature of this dictionary is its inclusion of "literary words" from the 16th century onward. Appendixes are provided for foreign phrases, abbreviations and symbols, English personal names, Greek and Russian alphabets, notes on American English, Roman numerals, mathematical symbols, and conversion tables.

1085 *Webster's New International Dictionary of the English Language.* Ed. W. A. NEILSON. 2nd ed. unabridged. Springfield, Mass., 1934. Rptd. (with corrections).

A comprehensive unabridged dictionary of modern English; includes words current in English from 1500 onwards, and major varieties of English – e.g., American, British, lowland Scottish, etc. Includes more than 550,000 words. Main entries provide (1) common spelling, American first, then alternate spellings, (2) pronunciation, "based upon the cultivated usage of all parts of the English speaking world," (3) part of speech, (4) inflections, (5) special area of usage – e.g., *physics, minerology,* (6) etymology, (7) definitions, arranged with older meanings first, (8) status labels – e.g., *dialectical, colloquial, illiterate,* and (9) other notes and cross-references. Includes many rare and obsolete words, often given in special lists at the bottom of the page. Provides extensive lists of synonyms and antonyms, with cross-referencing to them. Appendixes include (1) common abbreviations, (2) arbitrary signs and symbols, (3) a pronouncing gazetteer, and (4) a pronouncing biographical dictionary.

1086 *Webster's Third International Dictionary of the English Language Unabridged.* Ed. PHILIP B. GOVE. Springfield, Mass., 1961.

An extensive unabridged dictionary of modern English, covering words mostly in use after 1775 and excluding proper names of persons and places. Lists about 450,000 words. A detailed explanation of the entry form and conventions for entries is given on pp. 15a–20a. Entries provide (1) American spelling and syllabification (British spellings are given in alphabetical order and cross-referenced to the American term), (2) American pronunciation, (3) part of speech, (4) inflections, (5) capitalization, (6) etymology, (7) status (*archaic, slang,* etc. but the term *colloquial* is not used, and the other terms are used more sparingly than in *Webster's New International*), (8) definitions, arranged with older meanings first, (9) cross-references, (10) run-on entries, and (11) synonymies.

1087 *Funk & Wagnalls Standard Dictionary of the English Language.* N.Y., 1913. Frequently reprinted with revisions. Most recently reprinted as *Funk & Wagnalls Comprehensive Standard International Dictionary,* Bicentennial Edition, Chicago, 1974.

A comprehensive international dictionary emphasizing modern English but including archaic and obsolete words from 1500 on. Entries provide the

American spelling (British spellings are listed in alphabetical order and cross-referenced); capitalization and syllabification; pronunciation (only American pronunciation is given); part of speech; inflections; usage labels; definitions, arranged with the current meanings first, then older meanings; etymology; synonyms and antonyms; cross references; and run-on entries.

1088 *Random House Dictionary of the English Language.* Unabridged ed. Ed. JESS STEIN and LAURENCE URDANG. N. Y., 1966.

A comprehensive dictionary of American English, treating more than 250,000 words. Entries include American spelling, syllabification, capitalization, and pronunciation; part of speech; inflected forms; definitions (arranged with current meanings first, then specialized senses, then archaic and obsolete meanings); status labels (including identifications of British usage); cross-references and variants (including variant British spellings); etymology; run-on entries; synonyms and antonyms; and usage notes. Provides some 33 appendixes including separate concise dictionaries of French, Spanish, Italian, and German, a dictionary of signs and symbols, a directory of colleges and universities, a basic manual of style, and a world atlas and gazetteer. Abbreviated (but still very comprehensive) as *The Random House College Dictionary*, ed. L. Urdang and S. B. Flexner, N.Y., 1968. Rptd.

*

The following are some useful desk dictionaries of modern English:

British dictionaries:

1089 *The Concise Oxford Dictionary of Current English.* Ed. W. H. FOWLER and F. G. FOWLER. 5th ed. rev. by E. McINTOSH. Oxford, 1964.

1090 *Oxford Advanced Learner's Dictionary of Current English.* Ed. A. S. HORNBY *et al.* 3rd ed. Oxford, 1974.

1091 *Longman's English Larousse.* London, 1968.

American dictionaries:

1091a *Webster's New World Dictionary of the American Language.* Second College Edition. Ed. David B. Guralnik. Cleveland and N.Y., 1970. Rptd. and updated 1974.

1092 *Webster's New Collegiate Dictionary.* Springfield, Mass., 1973. [8th ed. of *Webster's Collegiate Dictionary*].

1093 *Funk and Wagnalls Standard College Dictionary.* N. Y., 1973.

1094 *The American Heritage Dictionary of the English Language.* N. Y., 1969.

D. Dialect Dictionaries

1095 WRIGHT, JOSEPH. *The English Dialect Dictionary: Being the Complete Vocabulary of All Dialect Words Still in Use, or Known to Have Been in Use During the Last Two Hundred Years.* 6 vols. London, 1898–1905. Rptd., 1961.

A comprehensive dictionary of more than 100,000 dialect words and phrases current in England, Ireland, Scotland, and Wales, mostly during the period 1700–1900. Main entries indicate part of speech, region used, pronunciation, meaning, and etymology. Illustrative quotations are provided. Vol. 6 includes a bibliography and an English dialect grammar.

1096 WENTWORTH, HAROLD. *American Dialect Dictionary.* N. Y., 1944.

A dictionary of some 13,000 American dialect words, including localisms, regionalisms, provincialisms, folk speech, urban speech, and New England and Southern dialect words which deviate "from General Northern, or Western." Entries give definitions, indicate the dialect area, and provide illustrative quotations.

E. Dictionaries of Slang and Unconventional Language

1097 PARTRIDGE, ERIC. *A Dictionary of Slang and Unconventional English: Colloquialisms and Catch-Phrases, Solecisms and Catachreses, Nicknames, Vulgarisms, and Such Americanisms as Have Been Naturalized.* 7th ed. 2 vols. London, 1970. Rptd. 2 vols in 1, N. Y., 1974.

A comprehensive dictionary of British slang and unconventional language. Its over 60,000 entries provide definitions and can also include references to the source of information, the area of use (geographical, occupational, etc.), the etymology, illustrative quotation, date, and cross-references. The 2nd volume is a supplement arranged on the same pattern as the basic list and includes words of more recent origin. Partridge has also published dictionaries of schoolboy slang, British and American underworld slang, and armed forces slang.

1098 WENTWORTH, HAROLD and STUART B. FLEXNER, eds. *Dictionary of American Slang.* N. Y., 1960. 2nd ed. with supplement, 1967.

A dictionary of slang terms used in the United States, including also colloquialisms, cant, jargon, argot, and idioms found in popular novels and movies. Where possible, the term is quoted in context and the source and date of the quotation are given, sometimes with additional explanation as to the circumstances in which the word is used. Includes some etymologies. Select bibliography.

1099 BERRY, LESTER V. and MELVIN VAN DEN BARK. *The American Thesaurus of Slang.* 2nd ed. N. Y., 1952.

A thesaurus of slang and unconventional speech in America. Arranged in two main parts – general slang and special slang – and within these parts organized in subject-category groups of words. Includes an extensive single-alphabet index of both the slang words and the category words used to classify them.

F. Period Dictionaries

100 BOSWORTH, JOSEPH. *An Anglo-Saxon Dictionary.* Ed. and enl. by T. NORTHCOTE TOLLER. London, 1882–98. Rptd., 1929, 1954. *Supplement* by T. NORTHCOTE TOLLER, 1908–21. Rptd., 1955. *Enlarged Addenda and Corrigenda by* ALISTAIR CAMPBELL, 1972.

The most extensive dictionary of English for the period before 1100; the original volume and supplements contain about 70,000 entries. Main entries provide inflected forms, part of speech designation, definition, and identified illustrative quotations. The supplements provide very important corrections to the main volume, as well as additions.

101 HALL, JOHN R. CLARK. *A Concise Anglo-Saxon Dictionary.* 4th ed. with supplement by HERBERT D. MERITT. London, 1960.

A brief dictionary (about 40,000 entries) but covering the English language up to 1200: "A considerable number of words from twelfth-century texts, which have not been recorded in Bosworth-Toller, has been included . . ."

102 KURATH, HANS and SHERMAN M. KUHN. *Middle English Dictionary.* Ann Arbor, Mich., 1954–   .

When completed this will be the most comprehensive dictionary of Middle English; it is projected to be about 10,000 pages long. It is appearing in fascicles: sections covering *E-F* were published first, followed by *D, C, B, A, G, K, L,* and *M*. Entries provide the etymology, definition, and examples quoted in context with the sources identified. The quotations are given in chronological order by date of MS.; the presumed date of composition is given in parentheses.

103 STRATMAN, FRANCIS H. *A Middle-English Dictionary Containing Words Used by English Writers from the Twelfth to the Fifteenth Century.* 4th ed. rev. by H. BRADLEY. Oxford, 1891. Rptd. London.

A one-volume dictionary of about 17,000 entries providing brief definitions, some abbreviated sources, and some illustrations of the word in context.

104 SKEAT, WALTER W. *A Glossary of Tudor and Stuart Words Especially from the Dramatists.* Ed. with additions by A. L. MAYHEW. Oxford, 1914. Rptd., N. Y., 1968.

A glossary of some 7,000 words appearing in Tudor and Stuart writings. Entries give definition and reference to where the word appears in the literature. Bibliography of references.

1105 NARES, ROBERT. *A Glossary; Or Collection of Words, Phrases, Names, and Allusions to Customs, Proverbs, etc.*, *Which Have Been Thought to Require Illustration in the Works of English Authors, Particularly Shakespeare and His Contemporaries.* Rev. and enl. ed. by JAMES O. HALLIWELL and THOMAS WRIGHT. 2 vols. London, 1876. Rptd.

Particularly good in words drawn from Shakespeare and other Elizabethan dramatists.

1106 HALLIWELL-PHILLIPS, JAMES. *A Dictionary of Archaic and Provincal Words, Obsolete Phrases, and Ancient Customs, from the 14th Century. Supplement* by T. L. O. DAVIES. 17th ed. 2 vols. in 1. London 1924. Orig. pub. 1847.

A dictionary of about 35,000 entries covering archaic and provincial words. Entries give definitions and identified illustrative quotations.

G. Foreign and Bilingual Dictionaries

1107 WALFORD, A. J., ed. *A Guide to Foreign Language Grammars and Dictionaries.* 2nd ed. rev. and enl. London, 1967. Rptd.

Critical review of grammars, dictionaries (general and special) and audio-visual aids covering, among other languages, French, Italian, Spanish and German. Annotated list of selected polyglot dictionaries. Index.

1108 COLLISON, R. L. W. *Dictionaries of Foreign Languages: A Bibliographical Guide to the General and Technical Dictionaries of the Chief Foreign Languages, With Historical and Explanatory Notes and References,* London, 1955. [For 2nd ed. see **1075**]

A general guide to the features (and sometimes the history) of about 1000 foreign language dictionaries. Arrangement is by language, from the more to the less familiar, and within each language by kinds of dictionaries – e. g., general, period, bilingual, slang, etc. Includes an appendix on technical dictionaries, a brief bibliography, and an author-subject-language-dialect index.

1109 ZAUNMÜLLER, WOLFRAM. *Bibliographisches Handbuch der Sprachwörterbücher. Ein internationales Verzeichnis von 5600 Wörterbüchern der Jahre 1460–1958 für mehr als 500 Sprachen und Dialekte. An Annotated Bibliography of Language Dictionaries. Bibliographie critique des dictionnaires linguistiques.* Stuttgart and N. Y., 1958.

A briefly annotated bibliography of 5,603 dictionaries of 387 languages, including some little known languages, but with major emphasis on the languages of Europe. Arranged alphabetically by language, with the larger sections devoted to major languages sub-divided by types of dictionaries. Recent dictionaries are listed first, then older. Includes author and language indexes.

1110 LIDDELL, HENRY GEORGE and ROBERT SCOTT. *A Greek-English Lexicon.* New ed. rev. and augmented, 2 vols. Oxford, 1925–40. *Greek-English Lexicon: A Supplement.* Ed. E. A. BARBER *et al.* Designed for use in conjunction with LIDDELL and SCOTT. Oxford, 1968.

Has about 10,000 entries. Based on F. L. C. F. Passow's *Handwörterbuch der griechischen Sprache,* but leaves out many of Passow's etymologies, proper names, place names etc.

1111 LEWIS, CHARLTON T. and CHARLES SHORT. *A Latin Dictionary.* Oxford, 1879. Often rptd.

Has about 60,000 entries, including proper and geographical names. Contains many citations from classical authors and gives source references. List of authors and works quoted.

1112 *Oxford Latin Dictionary.* Oxford, 1968–   .

Its purpose is to be "a dictionary independent alike of Lewis and Short on the one hand and the *Thesaurus linguae latinae* on the other ... aims to be one-third longer than Lewis and Short." Based on OED principles. Many quotations with source references. Different meanings are numbered. Fascicle V was published in 1975. Three more fascicles to come at intervals of about two years. The *OLD* will give a fuller account of the meaning and use of Latin words up to the end of the 2nd cent. A. D. than has previously been available in English.

1112a LATHAM, R. E. *Revised Medieval Latin Word-List from British and Irish Sources.* London, 1965.

Some 40,000 entry-words and references, with English equivalents and dated quotations.

1113 *The English Duden. A Pictorial Dictionary with English and German Indexes.* Ed. Bibliographisches Institut, Mannheim, and the modern Language Department of GEORGE G. HARRAP, London. 2nd rev. ed. Mannheim, 1960.

An adaptation of the German *Duden Bildwörterbuch,* Mannheim, 1958. Many American terms have been included in the complete revision (first edition published in 1936). Is now a more or less up-to-date dictionary in which all words that lend themselves to pictorial representation can be found in their proper context. The user can refer directly to the pictures, covering some 25,000 English words, or he can turn to English or German indexes. Each of the 368 topics has a vocabulary of 50 to 70 words. The illustrations are identical with the German volume and *Duden français: Dictionnaire en images,* édité par la rédaction du Bibliographisches Institut, Mannheim et la librairie M. Didier, Paris, 2. éd. corr. Mannheim, 1962.

1114 *Langenscheidts Enzyklopädisches Wörterbuch der Englischen und Deutschen Sprache. Langenscheidts Encyclopedic Dictionary of the English* *and German Languages.* Hrsg. OTTO SPRINGER. 4 vols. Berlin, 1962–75.

Teil I: *Englisch-Deutsch;* Part I: *English-German.* 2 vols. Berlin, 1962–63.

Teil II: *Deutsch-Englisch;* Part II: *German-English.* 2 vols. Berlin, 1974–75.

A comprehensive bilingual dictionary: Part I has 180,000 entries; Part II 200,000 entries. Main entries provide (1) spelling, (2) pronunciation, using a modification of the IPA, (3) indication of origin, (4) part of speech and, where appropriate, gender, (5) labels indicating, where appropriate, levels of usage, subject, and/or geographical area, (6) definition, including indication of grammatical context, illustrative phrases, idiomatic expressions, and synonyms, and (7) cross references. Appendixes provide additional proper names, guides to abbreviations, weights and measures, etc. Other Langenscheidt dictionaries offer various degrees of comprehensiveness: *Langenscheidts Groß-wörterbuch Englisch,* 120,000 entries; *Langenscheidts Handwörterbuch Englisch,* 75,000 entries; *Langenscheidts Deutsch-Englisches/Englisch-Deutsches Taschenwörterbuch,* 40,000 entries.

1115 *Harrap's Standard German and English Dictionary.* London, 1963– .
Part I: *German-English.* Vols. 1–2 (1963–67): *A–K.*

A comprehensive bilingual dictionary now in progress. Each of its two main parts will contain about 100,000 entries. Entries provide (1) spelling, (2) pronunciation, using a modification of the IPA, (3) part of speech, (4) labels indicating levels of usage, including some archaic words, slang, etc., and many indications of technical terms, (5) definitions, including U.S. and Canadian terms, Austrian and Swiss terms, etc. Does not include proper names. American words are supplied only when the English word would be misleading or unintelligible in America.

1116 *Harrap's New Standard French and English Dictionary.* Ed. J. E. MANSION. Rev. by R. P. L. and MARGARET LEDÉSERT. 2 vols. London, 1972.

A comprehensive French-English dictionary of more than 42,000 words. Entries give spelling, pronunciation (IPA is used), part of speech, gender, grammatical notes (forms of irregular verbs are given in the entry), definition(s), examples of usage and idiomatic expressions, indication of technical senses, etc.

1117 *Cassell's New French-English, English-French Dictionary.* 5th ed. Completely rev. by Denis Girard *et al.* London, 1964.

A compact French-English, English-French dictionary comprising more than 35,000 entries in each part. Entries give spelling, pronunciation (IPA is used), part of speech, grammatical notes, gender, definition(s), technical senses, usage examples and idiomatic expressions. Cassell and Co. also publish bilin-

gual dictionaries for Spanish, Italian, German, Dutch, etc. in this compact
desk dictionary size.

For special foreign language dictionaries of literary terms see entries
435 and **436**.

H. Special Dictionaries: Quotations, Pronunciation, Synonyms, etc.

1118 *The Oxford Dictionary of Quotations.* 2nd ed. London, 1953.

An anthology of some 40,000 familiar quotations arranged alphabetically by
author. Foreign language quotations are given both in the original language
and in translation; there is a separate keyword index for Greek quotations.
The main index, a very full keyword index comprising about ¹/₃ the bulk of
the dictionary, is arranged alphabetically. Does not include proverbs.

1119 BARTLETT, JOHN. *Familiar Quotations: A Collection of Passages,
Phrases, and Proverbs Traced to Their Sources in Ancient and Modern
Literature.* 14th ed. rev. and enl. Boston, 1968. Rptd., London, 1969.

An anthology of more than 100,000 quotations from all sources and times.
Arrangement is by authors chronologically, with quoted selections from each
author arranged in chronological order. Birth and death dates and pseudonyms of authors are given. Includes an alphabetical index of authors and a
very extensive alphabetically arranged keyword index comprising about ¹/₃
the bulk of the volume.

1120 *Webster's New Dictionary of Synonyms: A Dictionary of Discrimina-
ted Synonyms with Antonyms and Analogous and Contrasted Words.*
Springfield, Mass., 1968.

It is the purpose of the book to enable users to compare words of common
denotation and to distinguish differences in implications, connotations and
applications in word groups of similar meaning. Articles provide lists of
antonyms, analogous words (near synonyms) and contrasted words (near
antonyms), supported by quotations from outstanding writers. Introductory
matter: Survey of the History of English Synonymy; 'Synonym': Analysis
and Definition; etc.

1121 JONES, DANIEL. *Everyman's English Pronouncing Dictionary Containing over 58,000 Words in International Phonetic Transcription.*
13th ed. Ed. by A Gimson. London, 1967. Rptd. (with corr.) 1972.

Records the "Received Pronunciation" of nearly 44,000 ordinary words and
nearly 15,000 proper names and abbreviations (excluding the inflected forms).
Includes a "Glossary of Phonetic Terms" (a new feature) and a bibliography
"Some Useful Books for the Study of English Pronunciation." See also *BBC
Pronouncing Dictionary of British Names,* ed G. M. Miller, London, 1971.

1122 KENYON, JOHN SAMUEL and THOMAS ALBERT KNOTT. *A Pronouncing Dictionary of American English.* 2nd ed. Springfield, Mass., 1949.

Gives the pronunciation of the colloquial speech of educated Americans, recording variant pronunciations in different parts of the country. Besides ordinary words, it includes proper names, with an emphasis on America. A fair number of British personal and place-names, foreign names of general interest, and the more important names in literature, history, etc. are recorded.

1123 *The Oxford Dictionary of English Etymology.* Ed. C.T. Onions *et al.* Oxford, 1966.

A comprehensive etymological dictionary of about 24,000 words. Entries give information about the origins of the word, the date it entered the English language, and the history of its subsequent development and changes in meaning. Pronunciations are supplied with a modified IPA system.

1124 *Brewer's Dictionary of Phrase and Fable.* Centenary Edition. Rev. by IVOR H. EVANS. London, 1970. Rptd.

A dictionary of over 20,000 entries for phrases and fables touching such areas as romance, archeology, history, religion, literature, the arts, science, etc. Topics include names, both real and fictitious. Coverage of proverbial sayings and adages is exceptionally full. Entries range from such things as the principal versions of the English Bible in chronological order to national anthems, and to dogs. Many new phrases in use since the second world war have been included in the revised edition, and other older materials deleted; hence earlier editions may still contain useful materials.

1125 WHITING, B. J. and H. W. WHITING. *Proverbs, Sentences and Proverbial Phrases, from English Writings Mainly Before 1500.* Cambridge, Mass., 1968.

Contains about 10,000 proverbs, sentences, and proverbial phrases arranged under key words in alphabetical order. Entries give references to published sources and the date of the saying. There are indexes of important words and of proper nouns.

1126 TILLEY, MORRIS P. *A Dictionary of the Proverbs in England in the Sixteenth and Seventeenth Centuries: A Collection of the Proverbs Found in English Literature and the Dictionaries of the Period.* Ann Arbor, 1950.

A collection of 11,780 proverbs, with quotations chronologically given under each subject entry in the manner of the OED. Includes a bibliography of works quoted and proverb collections, indexes of significant words in proverbs, and a separate index of proverbs in Shakespeare.

1127 *The Oxford Dictionary of English Proverbs.* 3rd ed. rev. by F. P. WILSON. Oxford, 1970.

ABOUT 14,000 entries are listed in alphabetical order under the first significant word. Many cross-references from other key words make it possible to find any proverb without an index. Sources are given chronologically, with dates. There are many new entries owing to the compiler's own collections of proverbs and to the permitted use of Tilley's *Dictionary*, 1126.

1128 CIRLOT, JUAN E. *A Dictionary of Symbols*. Trans. from Spanish by JACK SAGE. London and N. Y., 1962.

A dictionary list arranged by names of symbols, with many illustrations. Entries range from two lines for *phallus* to several pages for *numbers*. Includes an introduction on symbolism, a bibliography, and a subject index.

For other special dictionaries see entries 393, 430–434, 630, 810, 811, 920, 987, 988, 990, 991, 1001, 1014, and 1015.

XXIII. Encyclopedias and Fact Books Supplementary to Encyclopedias

A. General Encyclopedias

1135 WALSH, S. PADRAIG. *Anglo-American General Encyclopedias: A Historical Bibliography 1703–1967.* N. Y., 1968.

An annotated bibliography of 419 English language encyclopedias published between 1703 and 1967. The basic list, titled "Historical Bibliography," is arranged alphabetically by title. Entries give full bibliographic citation, often including detailed information on publishing history, followed by comment on the size, arrangement, scope, and special features of each encyclopedia. Includes three indexes: (1) originators, compilers, and editors, (2) publishers and principal distributors, and (3) chronology of encyclopedias, 1703–1967. There is also a brief bibliographic appendix.

1136 COLLISON, ROBERT L. *Encyclopaedias: Their History throughout the Ages: A Bibliographical Guide with Extensive Historical Notes to the General Encyclopaedias Issued throughout the World from 350 B. C. to the Present Day.* N. Y. & London, 1964; 2nd ed. 1966.

A general guide to encyclopedias, with emphasis on historical development. Arranged as a series of chapters, each including a brief bibliography. Index.

1137 ZISCHKA, GERT A. *Index lexicorum: Bibliographie der lexikalischen Nachschlagewerke.* Wien, 1959.

A briefly annotated guide to about 7,000 encyclopedias and related reference works – encyclopedic dictionaries, biographical dictionaries, yearbooks, etc. – from the renaissance to the present. Arranged under subject headings; includes an author-subject index.

*

1138 *Chambers's Encyclopaedia.* 15 vols. 4th ed. rev. Oxford, 1967

A comprehensive general encyclopedia (some 12,500 pages and over 14 million words prepared by about 3,000 contributors) with special British emphasis. Its articles (about 25,000) tend to be on relatively narrow topics and range from a few lines to five or more pages, and some few (e.g., that on World War II) can extend to 50 pages. Many articles are initialed and include bibliographies. Vol. 15 provides an alphabetical subject index of some 225,000 entries; a classified index in which references and cross-references to articles are given under subject headings; an atlas with map index and gazetteer; a list of geographical terms; and a list of abbreviations.

1139 *The New Encyclopaedia Britannica.* 15th ed. 30 vols. Chicago, 1974.

History of the Britannica.

First published in Edinburgh in 1768–71; since 1910 published in the United States. Earliest editions are historically valuable but show distinct Scottish bias. The most important of the later editions are the 9th and the 11th (the 10th and the 12th and 13th editions were reissues of the 9th and 11th respectively with supplementary volumes); the 9th edition (24 vols., 1875–89) is particularly notable for the excellence of its articles on history and literature, and the 11th (26 vols., 1910–11) is often described as the best encyclopedia ever produced. The 14th edition (1929) was entirely revised and tended toward shorter and more popularly treated articles. In 1936 the *Britannica* began a process of "continuous revision" intended to be a program for systematically updating the entire encyclopedia every ten years, not by setting a completely new edition but by periodically altering individual plates of the 14th edition. For an analysis of the weaknesses which resulted from this procedure see Harvey Einbinder, *The Myth of the Britannica,* N.Y., 1964.

The 15th edition: scope and arrangement.

This latest edition of the Britannica consists of more than 42 million words and was compiled by a staff assisted by over 4,200 specialist advisors and contributors. Arrangement:

(1) *Propaedia: Outline of Knowledge and Guide to the Britannica.* 1 vol. An outline of the world of knowledge in 10 major divisions such as "Matter and Energy," "Human Life," etc.; each of these main divisions includes an introductory essay written by a specialist, followed by an elaborately detailed subject outline of the particular area of knowledge, each division of which includes references to articles and article sections in the other volumes of the encyclopedia.

(2) *Micropaedia: Ready Reference and Index.* 10 vols. A combination of index and short article reference encyclopedia. Entries are arranged alphabetically and range from a single line to about 750 words. Most entries cover relatively narrow topics – e.g., individual persons, places, etc. However, those *Micropaedia* entries which correspond to articles in the *Macropaedia* provide analyses of the contents of the *Macropaedia* articles, and give cross-references to other entries in the *Micropaedia.*

(3) *Macropaedia.* 19 vols. A broad topic encyclopedia of some 4,200 entries ranging from about 750 words to 1/4 million on topics such as "Visual Arts," "Education," etc. These articles are initialed by the specialists who wrote them and include often extensive bibliographies. The *Micropaedia* serves as the index to the *Macropaedia.*

For comment on the weaknesses of the 15th edition see Samuel McCracken, "The Scandal of 'Britannica 3'," *Commentary,* 61 (Feb., 1976), 63–67.

1140 *Encyclopedia Americana.* 30 vols. N.Y., 1918–20, with "continuous revision" thereafter.

A comprehensive general encyclopedia (over 26,000 pages and 30 million words compiled by more than 6000 contributors and advisory editors) with special American emphasis and special strength in science and the arts. Its articles (about 56,000) tend to be on relatively narrow topics and range from a few lines to more than 150 pages. Vol. 30 includes an alphabetical index of more than 350,000 entries. Since 1927 updating has been accomplished by "continuous revision"; articles are revised, added, or deleted either by altering the material on individual pages while leaving the pagination intact, or, in some cases, by excising or adding whole new pages, in which case page numbers are adjusted by adding sub-letters or by assigning one page more than one number. The most recently revised edition of the *Americana* was published in 1975.

1141 *The Columbia Encyclopedia.* 4th ed. Philadelphia, Pa., 1975.

A one volume general encyclopedia with American emphasis. Its articles (more than 50,000 entries and 6,600,000 words) are arranged alphabetically, letter-by-letter; article topics tend to be very narrow. Longer articles include bibliographies. Provides some 66,000 cross references. A complete revision of the 3rd edition, with about 7000 new articles and 75 % of existing articles revised.

1142 *Brockhaus Enzyklopädie in zwanzig Bänden, 17. völlig neubearb. Aufl. des Großen Brockhaus.* Wiesbaden, 1966–74.

A comprehensive international encyclopedia (over 16,000 pages, with about 225,000 entries prepared by some 1000 contributors). Its articles tend to be short and on relatively narrow topics, but some longer articles can run to thirty or more pages. Articles are unsigned; they include bibliographies, often extensive. Includes many illustrations, plates, and maps.

1143 *Meyers Enzyklopädisches Lexikon in 25 Bänden. 9., völlig neu bearb. Aufl. zum 150jährigen Bestehen des Verlages.* Bd. 1–   Mannheim, 1971–   .

A most comprehensive international encyclopedia which places particular emphasis on German-speaking countries. Up to 1975, 15 volumes had been published; when completed it is intended to comprise about 250,000 entries in some 22,000 pages. Articles are generally of medium length and unsigned; however each volume includes 4 or so long signed articles on broad topics of special importance. A special feature of this encyclopedia is the inclusion in every 3rd or 4th volume of *an addenda* section which updates the previously published volumes; the later *addenda* sections cumulate earlier ones.

1144 *La Grande Encyclopédie: inventaire raisonné des sciences, des lettres et des arts, par une societé de savants et de gens de lettres.* 31 volumes, Paris, 1886–1902.

A nineteenth-century French encyclopedia paralleling in scholarly accomplishment the 9th and 11th editions of the *Britannica*. Articles tend to be on relatively narrow topics, are signed, and contain bibliographies. Of great historical importance and still useful for biographical and historical subjects.

1145 *Grand Larousse encyclopédique en dix volumes.* Paris, 1960–64. *Supplément.* 1968.

An encyclopedia of over 10,000 pages which includes in its entries an extensive dictionary of French. Articles are unsigned and tend to be on relatively narrow topics, but some can be very lengthy. Very well illustrated and includes excellent maps; bibliographies are given at the end of each volume. The supplement adds another 1,000 pages comprising some 11,000 new articles, updating, in many cases, entries in the main work.

1146 *Encyclopaedia universalis.* Vol. 1– Paris, 1968– .

A new encyclopedia projected to be in 20 volumes. Its three-part arrangement parallels that of the 15th ed. of the *Encyclopedia Britannica:* (1) a 16 volume encyclopedia, with long signed articles which include bibliographies and cross-references, (2) a 3 volume "Thesaurus" which serves as an index to the main work, and (3) a one volume survey of general knowledge keyed to the enclyclopedia.

1147 *Enciclopedia Italiana di Scienze, Lettere ed Arti.* 36 vols. Roma, 1929–39. *Appendice I–III,* 5 vols, 1938–61.

A comprehensive international encyclopedia of over 42,000 pages. Its signed articles vary from less than a page to over 50 pages. Bibliographies are included. Some articles show a Fascist taint, but surprisingly few. This encyclopedia is notable particularly for its exceptionally full treatment of the arts and for its fine illustrations.

1148 *Grande Dizionario Enciclopedico.* Fondato da Pietro Fedele. 3rd ed. rev. and enl. 19 vols. Torino, 1967–1973.

A comprehensive international encyclopedia of some 15,000 pages. Articles are signed and include bibliographies. Exceptionally full illustrations, many in color. This edition is the result of a complete revision of the *Grande Dizionario Enciclopedico* published in 1954–61.

1149 *Grote Winkler Prins Encyclopedie in twintig delen.* 7. geheel nieuwe druk. 20 vols. Amsterdam, 1966–75.

A comprehensive international encyclopedia having both signed and unsigned articles. Includes bibliographies. Of particular value for its treatment of those areas involving the relations between England or America and the Netherlands.

B. Denominational Encyclopedias

1150 *Encyclopaedia Judaica.* 16 vols. Jerusalem, 1972.

A comprehensive international encyclopedia (over 12,000 pages and 14 million words) designed to provide information on all aspects of Jewish life and thought. Its more than 25,000 articles range from "capsule" biographies of about 150 words to articles of over 100,000 words. Articles are arranged alphabetically letter-by-letter under relatively broad subject headings; all articles include a bibliography and all are initialed by the author. Supplementary entries are given at the end of vol. 16. Vol. 1 is the index (about 250,000 entries including sub-entries and cross-references). *The Jewish Encyclopedia,* 12 vols., N.Y. and London, 1901–1906, is of historical value.

1151 *New Catholic Encyclopedia.* 15 vols. N.Y., 1967.

A comprehensive international encyclopedia (over 16,000 pages and 15 million words) covering "the teachings, history, organization, and activities of the Catholic Church, and all institutions, religions, philosophies and scientific and cultural developments affecting the Catholic Church from its beginnings to the present." Its more than 17,000 signed articles written by some 4,800 scholars range from entries of a few lines to extensive articles of many pages. Vol. 15 provides an analytical index of 350,000 entries with extensive cross-referencing. *The Catholic Encyclopedia,* 17 vols. N.Y., 1907–1922, is of historical value.

C. Special Encyclopedias

1152 *Encyclopedia of Philosophy.* 8 vols. N.Y., 1967.

A comprehensive encyclopedia of philosophy: coverage includes all historical periods and extends to the ideas in non-philosophical disciplines (e.g., physics, mathematics, biology, sociology) which have had an important impact on philosophical thought. Arrangement is alphabetical. The some 1,500 signed articles range from half a page to more than 50 pages and include extensive bibliographies. Many (over 800) are treatments of individual philosophers; the remaining articles cover relatively broad topics such as "being," "logic," "humanism," etc., as well as various kinds of arguments on specific philosophical problems. Vol. 8 provides an unusually elaborate subject index.

1153 WIENER, PHILIP P. ed. *Dictionary of the History of Ideas: Studies in Selected Pivotal Ideas.* 5 vols. N.Y., 1973.

An encyclopedic treatment of topics in the history of ideas. Arrangement is alphabetical. Articles cover subjects such as "Allegory in Literary History," "Theories of Beauty to the Mid-Nineteenth Century," "Literature and Its Cognates," etc. Articles are signed and contain bibliographies. Vol. 1 includes an "Analytical Table of Contents" in the front matter; vol. 5 is a 479 page single-alphabet subject index.

1154 *Encyclopedia of Religion and Ethics.* Ed. by JOHN HASTINGS. 12 vols. plus *Index.* Edinburgh, 1908–26.

A comprehensive encyclopedia covering all aspects of religion and ethics. Alphabetical articles range from very short to quite long; they contain bibliographies and many are extensively documented. The *Index* vol. provides a very full subject index and separate indexes to foreign words, scripture passages, and authors of the articles.

1155 *Encyclopedia of World Art.* 15 vols. N.Y., 1959–68. An English translation and enlargement of the *Encyclopedia universale dell'arte,* Rome, 1958–67.

A comprehensive international encyclopedia covering all aspects of architecture, sculpture, painting, and decorative art. Arrangement is alphabetical. The relatively long articles (about 1000 articles ranging from half a page to 60 pages) are signed, include extensive bibliographies, and treat the historical, conceptual, and geographical aspects of the arts they cover.

1156 THIEME, ULRICH and FELIX BECKER. *Allgemeines Lexikon der bildenden Künstler von der Antike bis zur Gegenwart, unter Mitwirkung von etwa 400 Fachgelehrten des In- und Auslands.* 37 Bde. Leipzig, 1907–50.

The most comprehensive encyclopedia of artists – painters, sculptors, etchers, architects, etc. – both living and dead, of all times and countries. Includes about 45,000 articles covering some 150,000 artists. Articles include bibliographies, and longer articles are signed. Supplemented by Hans Vollmer, *Allgemeines Lexikon der bildenden Künstler des XX. Jahrhunderts.* 6 Bde. Leipzig, 1953–62, which follows the same detailed pattern as its predecessor.

1157 *Grove's Dictionary of Music and Musicians.* 5th ed. 9 vols. N.Y., 1954. *Supplement,* 1961.

An encyclopedic compilation of about 40,000 entries covering all aspects of music – theory, history, terms, composers, musicians, and compositions – from about 1450 on. Puts special emphasis on English music. Articles are signed and frequently include bibliographies.

1158 *International Encyclopedia of the Social Sciences.* 17 vols. N.Y., 1968.

A comprehensive encyclopedia, international in scope, covering all the important topics in politics, economics, law, sociology, anthropology, penology, social work, and the like. Articles are arranged alphabetically, with extensive cross-referencing, and tend to be on rather broad topics (often several sub-articles go to make up the total treatment of a topic). Each article or sub-article is signed and includes a bibliography. Vol. 17 provides a directory of contributors, an alphabetical list of articles, a classified list of articles, and an elaborate subject index. The *International Encyclopedia of the Social*

Sciences is intended to be in some ways supplementary to the older (1930–35) *Encyclopedia of the Social Sciences,* 15 vols., N. Y.

1159 HOOPS, JOHANNES, hrsg. *Reallexikon der germanischen Altertums-kunde.* 4 Bde. Berlin, 1911–19. 2. neu bearb. u. erw. Aufl. hrsg. v. H. BECK *et al.* Berlin, 1968– .

An encyclopedia dealing with the life and culture of Germanic tribes from the beginnings to the end of the Old High German, Old Low German, and Old English periods. For the northern countries the 12th century was included in order to deal with the oldest literary documents. Longer articles are divided into sub-sections, each with extensive bibliography. Important for the background it supplies for the study of Old English literature and for its exceptionally full bibliographies.

For other special encyclopedias see entries **437–442, 630, 631, 809, 986, 989,** and **1000.**

D. Almanacs and Other Fact Books Supplementary to Encyclopedias

1160 WHITAKER, JOSEPH. *An Almanack For the Year of Our Lord [year].* London, 1869– .

An annual book of facts and statistical data about the United Kingdom, with some brief information on other parts of the world. Provides information on such diverse matters as the calendar, tides, astronomy, economics, holidays, famous personages, the peerage, the armed forces, population statistics, parliament, public officials, postal regulations, income tax, civil servants' salaries, etc. Includes reviews of the year for literature, science, films, and sports. Each volume has an extensive subject index.

1161 *Keesing's Contemporary Archives.* London, 1931– .

A weekly account of world events issued with an index that is revised and cumulated bi-weekly, quarterly, and annually. Arrangement of the weekly issues is classified, usually by broad geographical categories such as "United Kingdom," "Canada," etc. Separate subject and name indexes.

1162 *The [year] World Almanac and Book of Facts.* N.Y., 1868– .

A comprehensive annual statistical and factual survey with particular emphasis on the United States. Provides data on a host of subjects such as actors, art, books, cities, colleges, education, law, legislators, personalities, population, sports, world facts, etc. Elaborate subject index.

1163 *Information Please Almanac, Atlas, and Yearbook [year].* N.Y., 1947– .

An annual survey of facts and statistics, with particular emphasis on the United States. Coverage includes such topics as motion pictures, cabinet members, cities, colleges, copyright law, economics, historical events, education, world history, etc. Subject index.

1164 *Facts on File Yearbook [year].* N. Y., 1940–   .

A weekly account of world events, comprising some 8 to 16 pages of news articles grouped under such headings as "World Affairs," "National Affairs," "Space," "Arts," etc. An index is issued semi-monthly and cumulates monthly, quarterly, and yearly. The indexes are exceptionally full.

XXIV. Catalogues of and Guides to Libraries, Archives, and other Repositories

A. General Guides

1170 BRUMMEL, LEENDERT and E. EGGER. *Guide to Union Catalogues and International Loan Centers.* The Hague, 1961.

A general guide to printed union catalogues. Covers about 250 catalogues in 25 countries including America, England, and Europe. For further information on union catalogues and international loan services see "Select Bibliography of Union Catalogues and International Loans," UNESCO, *Bulletin for Libraries,* 22 (1968), 33–35.

1171 COLLISON, ROBERT. *Published Library Catalogues: An Introduction to Their Contents and Use.* London, 1973.

Arranged in two main parts. *Part One* is a descriptive analysis of published library catalogues arranged under various subject fields such as "Auction Sale Catalogues," "The Book Industry," "Literature," "History and Biography," etc. *Part Two* is a key to the abbreviations. Includes also a brief bibliography and a subject index.

1172 LEWANSKI, RICHARD C. *Subject Collections in European Libraries: A Directory and Bibliographical Guide.* N. Y. and London, 1965.

A guide to subject collections in about 6,000 libraries. Arranged in Dewey Decimal classes and geographically within each class. Entries describe the scope of the collection, photocopying facilities, restrictions on use, etc., and give library addresses and librarians' names. Appendixes provide information on the subject specializations of London metropolitan libraries, British regional libraries, East and West German libraries, etc. An outline of the Dewey Decimal subject classification categories is provided on pp. xxxiii–xxxvi. See also R. C. Lewanski, *European Library Directory: A Geographical and Bibliographical Guide. Führer durch die Bibliotheken Europas.* Florence, 1968.

1173 KRISTELLER, P. O. *Latin Manuscript Books Before 1600.* 3rd ed. N. Y., 1965.

A list of printed catalogues and unpublished inventories of manuscript collections in America and Europe. Arranged in three lists with extensive cross-referencing: (1) bibliography and statistics of libraries and collections, (2) works describing manuscripts of more than one city, and (3) printed catalogues and handwritten inventories of individual libraries. Because most catalogues and inventories do not distinguish between Latin and vernacular manuscripts, this work is in some respects a guide to manuscripts containing Old English, Middle English, and Early Modern English as well.

B. British Libraries and Collections

1174 *ASLIB Directory.* 3rd. ed. by BRIAN J. WILSON. 2 vols. London, 1968–70.

A guide to special information sources in Great Britain prepared for the Association of Special Libraries and Information Bureaus. Entries give information on the scope and character of the collection(s) and provide addresses, telephone numbers, etc. Vol. 2 includes the humanities. Extensive subject index.

1175 DOWNS, ROBERT B. *British Library Resources: A Bibliographical Guide.* Chicago, 1973.

A bibliography of 5039 catalogues, checklists, union lists, calendars, and other guides to British library holdings; intends to record all published accounts of British library resources. Arranged as a classified list by Dewey Decimal categories. Author and subject indexes.

1176 MORGAN, PAUL. *Oxford Libraries Outside the Bodleian.* Oxford, 1972. Rptd.

1177 MUNBY, A. N. L. *Cambridge College Libraries: Aids for Research Students.* 2nd ed. Cambridge, 1962.

1178 British Museum. *General Catalogue of Printed Books.* 263 vols. London, 1960–66. *Ten-Year Supplement 1956–1965.* 50 vols., 1968. Reissued in a compact edition providing the *General Catalogue* in 26 vols. and the *Supplement* in 5 vols., London, 1967–68. Other 10-yr. supplements to follow. Supercedes all these earlier editions: *Catalogue of the Printed Books,* 95 vols., 1881–1900; *Supplement,* 15 vols., 1900–1905; *General Catalogue* . . . 51 vols., 1931–54.

An author list with anonymous works by title or collective name (e.g., *bible*). Author entries often include biographical and critical works. The main catalogue has about 4 million entries and records all books held in the British Museum to 1955; supplements record acquisitions for the periods given in their titles. Entries provide author's full name (pseudonyms are often identified), full title, imprint, format, and sometimes notes on illustrations and other matters. Periodical publications are listed under that heading but are not complete; for periodicals and newspapers see also *Periodical Publications,* 2nd ed. (London, 1899–1900), rptd. as vol. 41 of the compact ed., and, also,

Catalogue of Printed Books. Supplement: Newspapers . . . 1801–1900 (London, 1905). Further references may be found in the unpublished catalogue of the British Museum Newspaper Library at Colindale.

1179 *Subject Index of the Modern Works Added to the Library of the British Museum in the Years 1881–1901.* 3 vols. London, 1902. Supplementary volumes (titles vary) for 1901–1950, 1956–1960 have been published during the period 1906–1966; the vol. for 1951–1955 has not yet been published.

A catalogue arranged alphabetically by subject and giving under each subject titles of books published or reissued from January 1881. The first volume includes works originally recorded in subject indexes published in 1886, 1891, and 1897, as well as additional works. The volume for 1916–1920 omits works dealing with World War I; these are included in a separate volume titled *Subject Index of Works Relating to the European War . . . 1914–1920.* For a subject index to books published before 1881, see Robert A. Peddie, 900.

1180 ESDAILE, A. *The British Museum Library: A Short History and a Survey.* London, 1946.

1181 The Trustees of the British Museum. *The British Museum: A Guide to Its Public Services.* London, 1962.

1182 London Library. *Catalogue of the London Library, St. James Square, London.* Original ed. London, 1847. Ist. ed., rev. and enl., 1903. 2nd ed., 2 vols., 1913–14. *Supplements, 1913–1950,* 3 vols., 1920–53.

Printed catalogues of holdings of the London Library arranged alphabetically by author. The library has especially strong holdings in literature and allied areas. Entries give short title, format, and date of publication; works about the author are given under his name. Further supplements are projected.

1183 London Library. *Subject Index of the London Library, St. James Square, London.* 4 vols. London, 1909–1955. Rptd., Nedeln, Liechtenstein, 1968.

A subject index of books in the London Library. Arranged alphabetically, with extensive cross-referencing. The library has particularly strong holdings in literature and related areas.

1184 ROTHSCHILD, NATHANIEL M. *The Rothschild Library: A Catalogue of the Collection of Eighteenth-Century Printed Books and Manuscripts.* 2 vols. Cambridge, 1954. Rptd., London, 1969.

1185 London University Library. *The Sterling Library: A Catalogue of the Printed Books and Literary Manuscripts Collected by Sir Louis Sterling and Presented by Him to the University of London.* Cambridge, 1954.

1185a *A Shakespeare Bibliography: The Catalogue of the Birmingham Shakespeare Library.* 7 vols. London, 1971.

A reprinting by photo-offset of the more than 40,000 entries in the Birmingham Shakespeare Library catalogue. Arranged in two main parts: volumes 1–3 reproduce the original guard book catalogue complete to 1932; volumes 4–7 reproduce entries from the card catalogue in use since 1932. The form and content of entries varies widely; details of arrangement and method of use are provided on pp. xv-xvii of volume 1. Volume 3 has an index of editors, translators, illustrators, and series in the guard book catalogue; volume 7 has a similar index for the card catalogue.

1186 HEPWORTH, PHILIP. *Archives and Manuscripts in Libraries.* 2nd ed. London, 1964.

A geographically arranged guide to archives and manuscript collections in Great Britain. Includes a list of printed catalogues and other guides to collections.

1187 *Guide to the Contents of the Public Record Office.* 3 vols. London, 1963–68.

An annotated guide to the state papers, legal records, and other documents held by the Public Record Office in London. Arranged as a classified guide by the departments to which records pertain. Each volume has indexes for personal names, places, and subjects. For valuable guidance in the use of the Public Record Office materials see also V. H. Galbraith's *An Introduction to the Use of Public Records*, London, 1934, and rptd. 1952 and 1963.

1188 Great Britain. Historical Manuscripts Commission. *A Guide to the Reports on Collections of Manuscripts of Private Families, Corporations, and Institutions in Great Britain and Ireland. Part 1, Topographical Guide.* London, 1914. *Part 2, Guide to the Reports of the Royal Commission on Historical Manuscripts [1870–1957].* London, 1935–38, 1966.

Indexes to the many volumes of the reports of the Royal Commission on Historical Manuscripts; these reports give very full accounts of the contents of manuscript collections in Great Britain and Ireland, usually reproducing in full or in part the contents of significant letters, and other documents. *Part I* is a place name index (e.g., *Penshurst*) and *Part 2* is an index to the names of persons (e.g., *Sidney, Sir Philip*) mentioned in the manuscripts. Individual volumes of the *Reports* also contain detailed subject indexes and glossaries.

For other catalogues and guides to collections of printed material and manuscripts see entries 112, 306, 361a, 397, 398, 398a, and 1010.

1189 KER, NEIL R. *Catalogue of Manuscripts Containing Anglo-Saxon.* London, 1957.

A descriptive catalogue of manuscripts containing writing in Anglo-Saxon, arranged alphabetically by the names of over 400 libraries or collections. Contains important prefatory material on Anglo-Saxon manuscripts, an appendix of Anglo-Saxon manuscripts written by foreign scribes, and indexes to collections of manuscripts, to paleographical and historical matters, including persons, and to owners. Extensive bibliography.

1189a GUDDAT-FIGGE, GISELA. *Catalogue of Manuscripts Containing Middle English Romances.* München, 1976.

Describes 99 MSS.

1190 KER, NEIL R. *Medieval Manuscripts in British Libraries.* 1– . Oxford, 1969– .

Intended, when completed, to be a descriptive catalogue of medieval manuscripts in English libraries alphabetically from Aberdeen to York. Vol. 1 covers the holdings of 48 collections of medieval manuscripts in London. Arrangement is alphabetical by name of collection. Entries give very full descriptions of the manuscripts including comments on contents.

1191 British Museum. *Catalogue of Additions to the Manuscripts in the British Museum in the Years [1783–1935].* 20 vols. London, 1850-- . A catalogue for the period 1936–1945 is in preparation.

Descriptive catalogues of manuscripts added to the British Museum collection from 1783 on. Arrangement is chronological by year of acquisition. Entries provide extensive descriptive comment on the manuscript or collection, including brief summaries of contents. Each volume has an extensive index of names. Should be supplemented by the following special manuscript catalogues:

British Museum. *Catalogue of Romances in the Department of Manuscripts* . . . 3 vols. London, 1883–1910. Rptd., 1961–63.
British Museum. *Catalogue of Additions to the Manuscripts: Plays Submitted to the Lord Chamberlain 1824–1851.* London, 1964.

1192 British Museum. *The Catalogues of the Manuscript Collection.* Rev. ed. by THEODORE C. SKEAT. London, 1962.

A guide to the catalogues of the various manuscript collections (e.g., Cottonian, Harleian, Arundel, etc.) of the British Museum.

An *Index of English Literary Manuscript Sources* is now in preparation; it is intended to serve as an index to the manuscripts of literary works by major British and Irish authors of the period 1450–1900. and will cover, also, contemporary transcripts, notebook and commonplace-book versions, printed books with authors' marginal notes, and corrected proofsheets and typescripts. Letters and business documents will not be included. For information write Dr. JOHN HORDEN, Institute of Bibliography and Textual Criticism, School of English, University of Leeds, Leeds LS2 9JT.

1193 COLLISON, R. L. *Fine Arts Libraries and Collections in Britain.* London, 1950. Rptd. from *Journal of Documentation,* 6 (1950), 57–69.

A survey of British libraries which are particularly devoted to one or more of the fine arts. The footnotes provide references to more detailed descriptions of individual libraries. See also M. W. Chamberlin's "Special Collections and Resources: Art Research Libraries in the U.S. and Western Europe," in *Guide to Art Reference,* Chicago, 1959, pp. 345–60.

C. American Libraries and Collections

1200 *Directory of Special Libraries and Information Centers.* 3rd ed. Ed. by MARGARET L. YOUNG, *et al.* 3 vols. Detroit, Mich., 1974.

Vol. 1 is a directory of about 14,000 special libraries and information centers in the United States and (in a separate list) Canada. Entries are arranged alphabetically by name of library or center; each entry gives information such as full address, telephone number, names of staff, special subjects and nature of special collections, a description of the scope of the holdings, information on access and reproduction facilities, and the availability of any special catalogues or indexes. Includes more than 5000 cross-references and an extensive repository and subject index with many references to language, literature, and to individual authors. Vols. 2 and 3 provide geographic, personnel, and other indexes and appendixes.

1201 ASH, LEE. *Subject Collections: A Guide to Special Book Collections and Subject Emphases as Reported by University, College, Public and Special Libraries and Museums in the United States and Canada.* 4th ed., rev. and enl. N.Y., 1974.

Arranged as a single-alphabet list of subject headings following the Library of Congress system; beneath each subject heading the arrangement is alphabetical by state, then by city. Entries (more than 70,000) give the library name, the division or department if any, available catalogues, available loan and reproduction facilities, restrictions on use of collection, name of librarian, address, etc.

1202 DOWNS, ROBERT B. *American Library Resources: A Bibliographical Guide.* Chicago, 1951. *Supplement, 1950–1961,* Chicago, 1962, *Second Supplement, 1961–1970,* 1972.

A list of printed catalogues, union lists, special collection descriptions, surveys of library holdings and the like arranged by Dewey Decimal classes. Lists about 6,000 titles, mostly published surveys of special holdings in American libraries. Both the main volume and the supplement have author-subject-library indexes.

1203 *The National Union Catalog, Pre-1956 Imprints: A Cumulative Author List Representing Library of Congress Printed Cards and Titles Reported by Other American Libraries.* London, 1968– .

An author list (anonymous works by title) of books and serials held in about 700 major libraries in the United States and Canada. When completed (about 1978) it will comprise some 610 vols. and over 13 million entries. Entries are photographic reproductions of LC cards or cards prepared by other participating libraries. Form of entries varies but can include author's name (pseudonyms are often identified), birth and death dates, title, imprint, height of volume in centimeters, notes on contents (e.g., whether the book contains a bibliography or illustrations), subject tracings, and code letters signifying what libraries hold copies of the book. When completed this edition will supersede the following earlier catalogues:

(1) *A Catalog of Books Represented by Library of Congress Printed Cards . . . to July 1942.* 167 vols. Ann Arbor, 1942–46. Rptd. 1949–50. Rptd., N. Y., 1958, 1963, and 1967.

(2) *Supplement: August 1, 1942 to December 31, 1947.* 42 vols. Ann Arbor, 1948. Rptd., 1960, 1963, and 1967.

(3) *Library of Congress Author Catalog: A Cumulative List . . . 1948–1952.* 24 vols. Ann Arbor, 1953. Rptd., N. Y., 1960, 1963, and 1967.

(4) *The National Union Catalog, 1952–1955 Imprints.* 30 vols. Ann Arbor, 1961.

1204 *The National Union Catalog: 1956–1967.* 125 vols. Totowa, N. J., 1970–72.

An author list (anonymous works by title) of books and serials acquired by about 1000 major libraries in the United States and Canada between 1956 and 1967. Entries are photographic reproductions of LC cards or cards prepared by other libraries. Form of entries varies but can include the same kinds of information found in the *National Union Catalog, Pre-1956 Imprints,* including symbols for locations of copies. This edition supersedes the following earlier catalogues:

(1) *The National Union Catalog: A Cumulative Author List Representing Library of Congress Printed Cards and Titles Reported by Other American Libraries. Cumulation for 1953–57.* 28 vols. Ann Arbor, 1958. Rptd. N. Y., 1961 and 1966. [Union coverage only for 1956–57.]

(2) *The National Union Catalog . . . 1958–1962.* 54 vols. N. Y., 1963.

(3) *The National Union Catalog: Cumulation for 1963–67.* 72 vols. Ann Arbor, 1969.

1205 *The National Union Catalog.* Washington, D. C., 1968– .

Continues the *National Union Catalog: 1956–1967,* **1024,** providing the same extensive library locations for books and serials and the same kinds of entries for materials from 1968 on. Appears monthly, with quarterly, annual, and quinquennial cumulations.

1206 *Library of Congress and National Union Catalog Author Lists, 1942–1962. A Master Cumulation.* 152 vols. Detroit, 1969–71.

Includes Library of Congress cards for 1942–55 and National Union Catalog cards for 1956–62. This catalog will be superseded by the *National Union Catalog Pre-1956 Imprints,* 1023, when it is completed, for the period 1942–55; it has already been superseded for the period 1956–62 by the *National Union Catalog: 1956–1967.*

1207 *Library of Congress Catalog: Books: Subjects.* [1950–1954]. Ann Arbor, Mich., 1955. Now published quarterly with annual cumulations, Washington, D. C., 1956–.

Lists of newly published Library of Congress printed cards arranged under subject headings given in the Library of Congress *Subject Headings Used in the Dictionary Catalogs of the Library of Congress.*

1209 Folger Shakespeare Library. Washington, D. C. *Catalog of Printed Books.* 28 vols. Boston, 1970.

An author list photo-offset from the cards of the Folger Shakespeare Library. Entries provide relatively full bibliographic information, and often, in the case of important editions, the entry will indicate to whom the individual book previously belonged, what its present condition is, etc. Because the Folger library includes not only works on Shakespeare but on the Renaissance generally, it is an important research tool for general Renaissance studies. See also the Folger's *Catalog of the Shakespeare Collection,* 2 vols., Boston, Mass., 1972, which is limited to the primary and secondary materials exclusively on Shakespeare.

1210 New York Public Library. *Dictionary Catalogue of the Henry W. and Albert A. Berg Collection of English and American Literature.* 5 vols. Boston, 1969.

1211 New York University. *Fales Library Checklist.* 2 vols. N. Y., 1970.

1212 HAMER, PHILIP M. *A Guide to Archives and Manuscripts in the United States. Compiled for the National Historical Publications Commission.* New Haven, Conn., 1961.

A general guide to collections of archives and manuscripts in the United States. Arranged alphabetically by state and within each state alphabetically by location. Entries describe the character and extent of holdings. Extensive subject index, including authors as subjects.

1213 *The National Union Catalog of Manuscript Collections.* Ann Arbor, Mich., 1962. Hamden, Conn., 1963. Washington, D. C., 1964– .

Now published annually by the Library of Congress. Each volume contains reproductions of cards representing manuscript collections in American repositories. Entries describe the contents of the collection, indicate whether the repository has a descriptive inventory of its contents, and give information on the subject of the collection, the number of items in it, and other pertinent information. Each volume is arranged by the number sequence of the Library of Congress cards it contains; cumulative subject, name, and repository indexes are published at intervals. At present 11 volumes have been published providing information on the contents of about 202,300 collections reported since 1959.

1214   *American Literary Manuscripts.* Austin, Texas, 1960. Rptd., 1971. Published under the auspices of the American Literature Group of the Modern Language Association of America.

A checklist of the holdings of about 2,350 manuscripts of American writers in about 270 American repositories. Arranged alphabetically by author's name with code symbols identifying collections of his manuscripts given beneath. A new and much more elaborate index of literary manuscripts is now in preparation.

1215   RICCI, SEYMOUR DE and W. J. WILSON. *Census of Medieval and Renaissance Manuscripts in the United States and Canada.* 3 vols. N.Y., 1935–40. Rptd., 1961. *Supplement.* Ed. CHRISTOPHER FAYE and WILLIAM H. BOND. N.Y., 1962.

A union list of about 12,000 medieval and Renaissance manuscripts in the United States (including Hawaii) and Canada. Arranged alphabetically by state, then by city, then by collection. Entries give a brief description of each manuscript and provide references to other existing printed descriptions and comments. Vol. 3 is an index volume including indexes to names, titles and headings, scribes and illuminators, *Incipits*, present owners, etc.

1216   YOUNG, WILLIAM C. *American Theatrical Arts: A Guide to Manuscript and Special Collections in the United States and Canada.* Chicago, 1971.

A guide to 138 manuscript and primary material collections on drama, drama criticism, and theatre, including vaudeville and the circus. Arranged in 2 parts: (1) a description of the manuscripts and special collections arranged first alphabetically by states and then by order of institution symbols used in the Library of Congress *National Union Catalogue* (a key to these symbols is provided) and (2) an index to persons and subjects.

D. Continental Libraries and Collections

1217   Bibliothèque Nationale, Paris. *Catalogue général des livres imprimés de la Bibliothèque Nationale: Auteurs.* 1–   (1897–   ).

An alphabetical author catalogue listing the holdings of the library only up to the date of publication of particular volumes (vol. 188 through 1959). Hence, there is a great difference in the scope of titles covered. Does not include title entries for anonymous books, corporate authors, or periodicals. Vol. 222 (Weule – Wiehr) was published in 1975.

The supplementary volumes include anonymous works and books published by joint authors:

Catalogue général des livres imprimés: auteurs, collectivités-auteurs, anonymes, 1960–1969. 1–   (1972–   ).

For information on libraries in other European countries, see **663** (pp. 10–16) and **1170–1172**.

Subject Index

(Numbers are entry numbers, not page numbers)

ABSTRACTS: American literature studies, 16–17, 256; dissertations, 820–823; English literature studies, 16–17; modern literature studies, 131–132; Renaissance studies, 55

ADDRESSES: black literary magazines, 843; contemporary authors, 176–182, 313–315; film distributors, 782; little magazine publishers, 841–843; newspaper publishers, 873–875; periodical publishers, 831–837; prominent persons, 955–956, 960–961, 964; publishers, 684, 723–726, 746–750; rare and used book dealers, 915–919; scholarly journals, 846–848; scholars, 974–979; small press publishers, 842

AESTHETICS: see *literary theory and criticism*

AFRO-AMERICANS: autobiographies, 938; index to periodical articles by and about, 865; folklore of, 1021; literary magazines, 843; literature of, 301a–309a

ALLUSIONS, HANDBOOKS OF: see *handbooks and chronologies*

ALMANACS: 1160, 1162–1163

ALTERNATIVE PRESS INDEX: 864

AMERICAN AUTHORS, BIO-BIBLIOGRAPHIES: see *bio-bibliographies*

AMERICAN ENGLISH DICTIONARIES: see *dictionaries*

AMERICAN HISTORY: see *history*

AMERICAN IMPRINTS, GUIDE TO: 727

AMERICAN INDIAN LITERATURE: 310

AMERICAN LITERATURE, ANTHOLOGIES: 327–332

AMERICAN LITERATURE, BIBLIOGRAPHIES, REVIEWS OF RESEARCH, AND INDEXES: general, 240–262; early period (1585–1830), 263–271; (1830–1875), 272, 273; rise of realism (1875–1900), 274–277; modern period (1900-present), 278–286; poetry, see 286a and cross-references following; drama, 287–292a; fiction 293–296; prose, see cross-references following 296; regional literature, 297–300; historical fiction, 301; Afro-American literature, 301a–309a; American Indian literature, 310; American literature, bio-bibliographies, 311–315

AMERICAN LITERATURE, HISTORIES: general, 315a–319; period and genre, 320–323

AMERICAN NATIONAL BIBLIOGRAPHY: 727–750

AMERICAN STUDIES: 257, 262

ANALYTIC BIBLIOGRAPHY: 570–579, 590–616

ANGLO-SAXON: see *Old English* and *Medieval*

ANGLO-SAXON MANUSCRIPTS: 1189

ANNALS: American literature, 324; English literature, 211; English, French, and German literature, 453

ANONYMOUS AND PSEUDONYMOUS WRITINGS: 966–968; the catalogues of the British Museum and the Library of Congress (see 1178 and 1203–1206) are often useful for the identification of anonymous and pseudonymous writing

ANTHOLOGIES: American literature, 327–332; English literature, 217–228; literary criticism, 490–492, 495–503, 505–529

ANTIQUARIAN BOOKS: see *rare and used books*

ARCHIVES AND MANUSCRIPT COLLECTIONS: British, 1186–1193, American, 1212–1216

ART: encyclopedias of, 1155–1156

ARTS, LITERATURE AND: see *literature and the other arts*

AUCTION RECORDS: 908–913, 1171

AUDIENCE: 550–556, 598, 647

AUGUSTAN: see *restoration and eighteenth century*

AUTHOR-AUDIENCE RELATIONSHIP: 550–556, 598, 647

AUTHORS' ADDRESSES: 176–182, 313–315

AUTHORS' BIOGRAPHIES: see *biography* and *bio-bibliographies*

AUTHORSHIP, EVIDENCES FOR: 503

AUTOBIOGRAPHY: 935–938; see also under *biography*

BALLAD: 1010, 1018, 1022, and 1007–1021 *passim*

BIBLE: catalogue of printed editions, 1002; concordances, 1003–1005

BIBLIOGRAPHICAL SERVICES: 681–683

BIBLIOGRAPHIES OF BIBLIOGRAPHY: literary, 1–3, 243–244; general, 669–675

BIBLIOGRAPHY, NATIONAL AND BOOK TRADE: American national bibliography, 727–750; bibliography of national bibliography, 671–672, 680–683; English national bibliography, 685–726; general national bibliography, 680–684

BIBLIOGRAPHY, TECHNICAL AND HISTORICAL: analytic, 570–579; descriptive, 605–616; editing, 617–629; encyclopedias of the book and printing industry, 630–631; general works, 570–579; history of printing and the book trade, 590–604; incunabula, 580–589

BILINGUAL DICTIONARIES: see *dictionaries, foreign and bilingual* and *dictionaries, guides to*

BIO-BIBLIOGRAPHIES: American authors,

174, 176–182, 311–315; British authors, 170–182

BIOGRAPHY, AUTOBIOGRAPHY, AND DIARY: 925–979; bibliographies of autobiographies, 935–938; bibliographies of biographies, 932–934; bibliographies of diaries, 939–943; bibliography of British and American genealogy and heraldry, 944; biographies and directories of scholars, 974–979; collections of American biography, 962–965; collections of British biographies, 957–961; collections of international biography, 952–956; histories of biography, 925–931; identification of anonymous and pseudonymous writings, 966–968; indexes to biographies, 945–951; other sources of biographical information, 92, 151, 170–182, 205–210, 214, 304, 311–315, 324–326, 390–392a, 437–442, 446–450a; portraits and photographs, 969–971

BIRMINGHAM SHAKESPEARE LIBRARY: 1185a

BLACK LITERATURE: see *Afro-American literature*

BOOK: encyclopedia of the printing industry, 631; glossary of booktrade terms, 920; glossary of printing terms, 630

BOOK AUCTION RECORDS: 908–913

BOOK PRICES: current, 721–726, 746–750; auction prices, 908–913; rare and used book prices, 908–920

BOOK REVIEWS: see *reviews*

BOOK TRADE: bibliographies, 590–595; glossary of terms, 920; historical studies, 596–604

BOOKS IN PRINT: British, 725–726; American, 747–750; see also under *reprints* and *microforms*

BOOKS, SUBJECT INDEXES: 900–903, 905; current publications, 721–724, 746, 749; in print, 725–726, 748–750; subject catalogues of major library collections, 1179, 1183, 1207; subject guides

lish, 74–76, 93–99, 121–123a, 136–138b, 145–147, 161, 169, 179, 203, 204; filmed fiction, 784; general bibliographies, indexes, and handbooks, 397–420; short story, 411–412, 418–420
FILM: bibliographies, indexes, and research guides, 796–808a; dictionaries and encyclopedias of terms and technical matters, 809–811; encyclopedia of, 809; general reference works, 786–795; primary materials, 361, 389, 776–785; reviews, 803; secondary materials, 257, 372a, 376, 379, 383, 383a, 396, 786–811
FINE ARTS LIBRARIES IN BRITAIN: 1193
FOLGER SHAKESPEARE LIBRARY: 1209
FOLKLORE AND POPULAR CUSTOM: abstracts, 1013; Afro-American folklore, 1021; ballads and songs, 1010, 1018, 1022; bibliographies, 248, 257, 1007–1013; dictionaries, 1014–1016; folk plays, 64; motif indexes, 38, 1018, 1020; popular antiquities, 1017; type classifications, 1019–1020
FOREIGN AND BILINGUAL DICTIONARIES, GUIDES: 1075, 1107–1109
FOREIGN LANGUAGE GRAMMARS: 1107
FRENCH DICTIONARIES: 1107–1109, 1116–1117
FRENCH LITERATURE: 450, 648
FURNITURE: 648

GENEALOGY AND HERALDRY: 944
GENERAL AND COMPARATIVE LITERATURE: 430–470
GENERAL LITERATURE: 430–457; general dictionaries of literary terms, 430–436; general literary handbooks and encyclopedias, and indexes, 437–457
GENRES: see *literary forms, poetry, drama, fiction, prose,* and the same headings under *English literature* and *American literature.*
GERMAN AND AUSTRIAN LITERATURES: 450a, 458–459, 648
GERMAN DICTIONARIES: 1107–1109, 1113–1115

GERMANIC ANTIQUITY: encyclopedia of, 1159
GLOSSARIES: see *dictionaries*
GOTHIC LITERATURE: 99, 404
GRAMOPHONE RECORDINGS: 767–775
GREEK AND ROMAN LITERATURE AND MYTHOLOGY: see *classic* and *classics*
GREEK DICTIONARIES: 1107–1110

HANDBOOKS AND CHRONOLOGIES: American literature, 209–211, 324–326, 358–360, 447–448; English, 205–216, 358–360, 447–448, 453; general, 437–449, 453; French, 450; German, 450a
HANDWRITING: 647
HERALDRY: 944
HISTORICAL DICTIONARIES: see *dictionaries*
HISTORICAL FICTION: 301, 402–402a
HISTORICAL MANUSCRIPTS COMMISSION: 1188
HISTORY: 1030–1069; sources of information, 1030, 1030a; world history, 1031–1033; British history, general, 1034–1043; British social history, 1044–1045; British medieval history, 1034, 1037a, 1041, 1045a, 1046; British renaissance, 1035, 1038–1039, 1047; British restoration and eighteenth century, 1036, 1040, 1049–1051; British nineteenth century, 1037, 1052–1053, 1056; British twentieth century, 1055–1056; dictionary of British history, 1042; American history, general, 1057–1069; American history, guides, dictionaries, and companions, 1057–1061; American social history, 1062–1063; American intellectual history, 1064–1069; history of ideas, 1153

IDEAS, HISTORY OF: encyclopedia, 1153
IMAGINARY VOYAGES: 406
INCUNABULA: 580–589, 685
INDEXES: consult appropriate subject headings
INDIAN LITERATURE: see *American Indian*

Names

Aarne, Antti 1019
Abrams, M. H. 217, 432, 488
Adams, Charles J. 998
Adams, James Trunslow 1058, 1059
Adelman, Irving 381, 414
Albérès, R.-M. 463a
Alden, John E. 702
Aldington, R. 986
Aldridge, John W. 495
Allibone, S. A. 213
Allison, Alexander W. 217a
Allott, Miriam 490
Altholz, Josef L. 1037
Altick, Richard D. 114, 189, 555, 642, 643, 649, 654, 925, 1054
Altschul, Michael 1034
Ames, D. 986
Amory, Hugh 913
Anderson, George K. 190
Anderson, Michael 392a
Andresen, Carl 989
Andrews, Wayne 1059
Angotti, Vincent L. 377
Arber, Edward 694, 709
Arnott, James F. 143
Ash, Lee 1201
Atkins, John H. 531
Avicenne, Paul 682

Bacon, Jean C. 852
Baer, D. Richard 794
Bailey, Richard W. 480
Baird, Donald 145
Baird, John D. 627
Baker, Blanch M. 373
Baker, Ernest A. 203, 402
Baker, Jeffrey A. 353
Baldensperger, F. 463
Ball, Robert H. 393
Ballinger, John 158

Barber, E. A. 1110
Barker, D. A. 1052
Barnes, Warner 575
Barnhart, Clarence L. 208, 1078a
Barrow, John G. 997
Bartlett, John 1119
Barzun, Jacques 409
Bateson, Frederick W. 4, 7
Batho, Edith C. 187
Batts, John Stuart 939a
Baugh, Albert C. 189
Baughman, Ernest W. 1020
Bawden, Liz-Anne 786b
Baxandall, Lee 477
Beach, Joseph W. 190
Beale, Walter H. 140a
Beasley, Jerry C. 95
Beaurline, Lester A. 644
Beaver, Harold 514a
Beck, H. 1159
Becker, Carl L. 1050
Becker, Felix 1156
Beckerman, Bernard 385
Beckson, Karl 432a
Bell, Inglis F. 145, 650
Bell, Marion V. 852
Benet, William Rose 442
Benham, Allen R. 29
Bennett, H. S. 183, 598
Bennet, Scott 623
Bentley, Gerald Eades 200
Bergeron, David M. 64
Bergonzi, Bernard 186
Bergquist, George W. 362
Bernard, Harry 298
Bernbaum, Ernest 105
Berry, Lester V. 1099
Berry, Lloyd E. 59
Bessy, Maurice 786
Besterman, Theodore 589, 670

248

Biddle, Martin 23b
Bishop, Caroly J. 848
Bishop, William W. 691
Black, Frank G. 97
Blair, Peter Hunter 1045a
Blake, R. E. 435
Blanck, Jacob N. 240, 241
Block, Andrew 96
Boase, Frederick 959
Bodgett, Harold W. 327
Bohn, H. G. 687
Bolton, W. F. 186
Bond, Donald F. 78, 79, 189, 648
Bond, Richmond P. 880
Bond, William H. 1215
Bonheim, Helmut W. 100
Bonser, Wilfried 1008, 1041
Booth, Wayne C. 493
Bordman, Gerald 38
Boswell, Eleanore 696
Bosworth, Joseph 1100
Bowers, Fredson 88, 605, 618, 621, 640
Bowman, Walter P. 393
Boys, Richard C. 57
Brack, O. M. Jr. 575
Bradley, H. 1103
Brand, John 1017
Bredvold, Louis L. 190, 223
Breed, Paul F. 382
Brett-James, Antony 453
Brewer, J. Mason 1021
Brigano, Russell C. 938
Briggs, Katherine M. 1016
Brigham, Clarence S. 886
Bristol, Roger P. 730, 731, 732
Bronson, B. H. 1022
Brooke, Tucker 189
Brooks, Cleanth 530
Brown, Carleton 36
Brown, Clarence 499
Brown, Stephen J. 149, 150
Browne, Nina E. 970
Browning, David Clayton 210
Bruce, James D. 41
Brummel, Leendert 1170
Bryer, Jackson 279
Bryer, Jackson R. 840a

Buchanan-Brown, J. 437
Buckley, Jerome H. 111, 227
Bühler, Curt F. 606a
Bufkin, Ernest C. 136
Bukalski, Peter J. 801
Burger, Konrad 581
Burke, W. J. 326
Burton, Dolores M. 480
Bush, Douglas 183, 994, 995, 996
Butt, John 187

Cady, Erwin Harrison 331
Caldwell, Harry B. 30, 64
Cameron, Kenneth W. 856
Campbell, Alistair 1100
Campbell, Oscar James 215
Cargill, Oscar 327, 1066
Case, Arthur E. 57
Cawelti, John G. 559
Cazamian, Louis 193
Chalmers, Alexander 220
Chambers, E. K. 183, 195, 198, 199
Chandler, G. 656
Chandler, Sue P. 315
Chapman, Dorothy 302
Chapman, Robert W. 211
Chardans, Jean-Louis 786
Chew, Samuel C. 189
Chicorel, Marietta 351, 352, 370, 374, 412, 770, 771, 772, 850, 947
Child, Francis James 1022
Chisholm, Margaret E. 765
Cirlot, Juan E. 1128
Clair, Colin 597
Clark, G. N. 1043
Clark, Harry Hayden 246
Clarke, I. F. 405
Clason, W. E. 810
Clavel, Robert 708
Clemen, W. 216
Cline, Gloria S. 353
Coan, Otis W. 297
Cohane, Christopher 85a
Colburn, William E. 647
Colby, Vineta 174
Cole, Maud D. 733
Coleman, Arthur 357, 380
Coleman, Edward 168

Halliwell-Philips, James 1106
Halpenny, Frances G. 629
Halperin, John 491
Hamer, Philip M. 1212
Hammond, N. G. L. 987
Handley-Taylor, Geoffrey 156, 160
Harari, Josué V. 476
Harbage, Alfred 141
Harbert, Earl N. 249
Hardwick, Michael 212
Harmon, Maurice 150a
Hart, James D. 324
Harte, Barbara 181
Hartnoll, Phyllis 390
Hartung, Albert E. 28
Harvey, Sir Paul 205, 450
Hastings, John 1154
Hatch, James V. 307
Havens, R. D. 101
Haviland, Virginia 164
Havlice, Patricia P. 244
Haycraft, Howard 172, 173, 174, 311
Haywood, Charles 1009
Hazlitt, W. Carew 1017
Hebel, William J. 221, 222
Hefling, Helen 948
Hendrick, George 295, 847
Heninger, S. K. Jr. 40a
Henkel, Arthur 542
Hepworth, Philip 1030, 1186
Herbert, A. S. 1002
Hermand, Jost 545
Herzberg, Max J. 325
Heseltine, J. E. 450
Hibbard, Addison 431
Highet, Gilbert 992
Highfill, Philip Jr. 92
Hill, Frank P. 268
Hill, Maureen 969
Hinman, Charleton 599
Hirschfelder, Arlene B. 310
Hiscock, Walter G. 701
Hoffmann, Frederick J. 840
Hollander, John 218
Holman, Hugh C. 293, 328, 431
Hoops, Johannes 1159
Horden, John 1192

Hornby, A. S. 1090
Horner, George F. 328
Houghton, Walter E. 855, 1053
Houle, Peter J. 39a
Houtchens, Carolyn W. 104
Houtchens, Lawrence H. 104
Howard, Patsy C. 21, 261
Howard-Hill, Trevor H. 1
Howe, George Frederick 1030a
Howe, W. D. 326
Hubbell, Jay B. 329
Hudson, Derek 514
Hudson, Hoyt H. 220
Hunger, Herbert 991
Hunter, George K. 183
Hurley, Paul 284b
Hyamson, Albert M. 945
Hyman, Stanley Edgar 485

Ireland, Norma O. 367, 664
Irish, Wynot R. 281

Jack, Ian R. 183
Jackson, William A. 698
Jaggard, William 67
Jahn, Janheinz 301a
Jantz, Harold S. 263
Jenkins, Frances B. 669
Jinks, William 797
Jobes, Gertrude 1015
Johnson, Allen 962
Johnson, Edgar 926
Johnson, Merle D. 241
Johnson, Thomas H. 1060
Jolliffe, P. S. 40
Jones, Brynmor 159
Jones, Daniel 1121
Jones, Edmund D. 508, 512
Jones, Howard Mumford 278, 315a
Jones, James Ifano 158
Jones, John Bush 616
Jones, Phyllis M. 513
Jordan, Frank Jr. 103
Juchoff, Rudolf 112

Kahrmann, Bernd 138
Kaiser, Frances E. 454
Kaplan, Louis 936
Katz, Joseph 608

Tennyson, G. B. 228
Thieme, Ulrich 1156
Thompson, James 655
Thompson, Lawrence S. 729
Thompson, Stith 645, 1018, 1019
Thomson, Ruth G. 364, 365
Thorne, J. O. 952
Thorpe, James E. 540, 617, 640, 641
Thrall, William Flint 431
Thurston, Jarvis A. 418
Tilley, Morris P. 1126
Tilton, Eva Maude 754
Titus, Edna B. 869
Tobias, Richard C. 118, 120
Tobin, James E. 80
Toller, T. Nonthcote 1100
Totok, Wilhelm 663
Traill, H. D. 1045
Trent, William P. 318
Trevelyan, George Macaulay 1044, 1045
Tuck, Donald H. 408
Tucker, Lena L. 29
Tucker, Martin 129, 130, 496, 497
Turberville, A. S. 1049
Turner, Darwin T. 303
Tuve, Rosemund 49a
Tye, J. R. 857
Tyler, Gary R. 380
Tyler, Moses Coit. 320

Ulrich, C. F. 840
Urdang, Laurence 1088

Vail, R. W. G. 728
Van Den Bark, Melvin 1099
Van Doren, Mark 58
Van Patten, Nathan 3
Vesenyi, Paul E. 830
Vinson, James 176, 178, 179
Vollmer, Hans 1156

Walcutt, Charles C. 355
Walford, Albert J. 660, 1107
Walker, Warren S. 419
Wall, Edward C. 852, 901, 1083
Waller, Alfred R. 184
Walsh, S. Padraig 1135
Walzel, Oskar 443

Wann, Louis 327
Ward, A. C. 447
Ward, Adolphus W. 184
Ward, William S. 110, 883, 884
Warren, Austin 482
Watkin, E. I. 1052
Watson, George 4, 5, 6, 534
Watt, Ian 122
Watt, Robert 686
Wearing, Peter 120a
Weber, Brom 332
Weed, Katherin K. 880
Wegelin, Oscar 265, 267, 269
Wehrli, Max 483
Weimann, Robert 537
Weinberg, Bernard 532
Weiser, Irwin H. 282
Weiss, Anne 326
Weiss, Irving 326
Weisstein, Ulrich 466
Wellek, René 482, 533
Wells, John E. 27
Wells, Stanley 70, 141a
Wentworth, Harold 1096, 1098
Wertheim, Stanley 273
Whitaker, Joseph 1160
White, Beatrice 198, 199
White, S. H. 402a
White, William 284a
Whitesell, Edwin J. 355
Whiting, B. J. 1125
Whiting, H. W. 1125
Whitlow, Roger 308
Wiener, Philip P. 1153
Wiles, Roy 882
Wiley, Paul L. 137
Wilford, John 713
Williams, Franklin B. Jr. 56
Williams, Neville 1032
Williams, Raymond 1056
Wilpert, Gero von 436, 440
Wilson, Brian J. 1174
Wilson, E. G. 107
Wilson, F. P. 183, 1127
Wilson, Harris W. 124a
Wilson, W. J. 1215
Wimsatt, William 530

WITHDRAWAL